FRAMING LANGUAGES AND LITERACIES

In this seminal volume, leading language and literacy scholars clearly articulate and explicate major social perspectives and approaches in the fields of language and literacy studies. Each approach draws on distinct bodies of literature and traditions and uses distinct identifiers, labels, and constellations of concepts; each has been taken up across diverse global contexts and is used as rationale and guide for the design of research and of educational policies and practices. Authors discuss the genesis and historical trajectory of the approach with which they are associated; offer their unique perspectives, rationales, and engagements; and investigate implications for understanding language and literacy use in and out of schools.

The premise of the book is that understanding concepts, perspectives, and approaches requires knowing the context in which they were created, the rationale or purpose in creating them, and how they have been taken up and applied in communities of practice. In some cases the chapter author is the creator of the perspective, and in others a person who is strongly identified with the approach. Accessible yet theoretically rich, this volume is indispensable for researchers, students, and professionals across the fields of language and literacy studies who want to know what theories to use, how to develop theoretical frameworks that have explanatory power, what the difference is between various theoretical constructs, and how they might inform research design and educational initiatives.

Margaret R. Hawkins is a Professor in the Department of Curriculum & Instruction and in the Doctoral Program in Second Language Acquisition at the University of Wisconsin-Madison, USA.

FRAMING LANGUAGES AND LITERACIES

Socially Situated Views and Perspectives

Edited by Margaret R. Hawkins

Routledge
Taylor & Francis Group

NEW YORK AND LONDON

First published 2013
by Routledge
711 Third Avenue, New York, NY 10017

Simultaneously published in the UK
by Routledge
2 Park Square, Milton Park, Abingdon, Oxon OX14 4RN

Routledge is an imprint of the Taylor & Francis Group, an informa business

Library of Congress Cataloging in Publication Data
Framing languages and literacies : socially situated views and perspectives / edited by Margaret R. Hawkins.
   pages cm
Includes bibliographical references and index.
1. Literacy—Social aspects.   2. English language—Study and teaching—Social aspects.   I. Hawkins, Margaret R., 1953- editor of compilation.
LC149.F69 2013
302.2'244—dc23   2012039719

ISBN: 978-0-415-81055-5 (hbk)
ISBN: 978-0-415-81056-2 (pbk)
ISBN: 978-0-203-07089-5 (ebk)

Typeset in Bembo and Stone Sans
by RefineCatch Limited, Bungay, Suffolk, UK

Dedication

To Millicent, and others around the world in like circumstances. You are why this work matters.

CONTENTS

PREFACE

The fields of language and literacy studies, like many of their disciplinary counterparts, have long been more fully in the domain of scholars and researchers than of practitioners. Academia and scholarship have not, by and large, driven educational practice, nor been highly visible in educational policy decisions. Yet it is clear that our conceptualizations of language and literacy (or math, or science) do indeed shape how we go about the business of teaching and learning within and outside of educational institutions. They shape our notions of what is to be learned, through what means and methods, and with the use of which materials and tools. Historically, language and literacy (in the singular) have been viewed as monolithic entities, comprised of discrete sets of knowledge and skills to be internalized by the individual. The trajectories of the fields of language and literacy—ways of understanding what language and literacy are, and what language and literacy work entails—have expanded and changed rapidly in the past few decades, and hold significant implications for policy and practice.

There is now a solid corpus of literature that approaches languages and literacies (in the plural) from socially situated perspectives. These approaches often spring from diverse disciplinary foundations, and represent differing views (to greater and lesser extents) of what languages and literacies are and mean. All stress a *practice*-oriented perspective, and look to how people engage and what they do with languages and literacies in communication and interaction, as opposed to a more historical view of what discrete sets of information and skills reside within their heads. One clear point that emerges is the inter-relationships between, and inseparability of, the constructs of languages and literacies; they are mutually constitutive, although not mutually defining.

This book, in addition to an introductory chapter intended to situate readers in social approaches to language and literacy studies, includes nine chapters in which authors articulate key socially oriented perspectives in language and literacy studies, situating each in its unique context, and tracing its development, uptake and influence. Scholars who authored the concepts, or those most closely associated with them, were invited to participate, and asked to define their perspective, and to discuss its genesis, the way in which its been taken up and utilized, and its implications for research and for practice. They were invited to write themselves into their texts—to include an autobiographical component if they chose to do so. Each approach offers situated understandings of languages and literacies in use; however, each highlights and foregrounds different issues and concerns, and holds different implications for practice.

There has not, to date, been a work that looks among and across major social perspectives as this volume does. The result is a must-read for scholars in the fields of language and literacy studies, graduate students in fields related to language (including applied linguistics and second language acquisition), literacy and education more generally, educational professionals and policy-makers, and those who create and produce educational materials. It illuminates not only the approaches represented, but the historical trajectories and discussions from which they have emerged, as well as the relationships, inter-relationships and distinctions among them. These understandings are critical not only as an intellectual exercise, but also to designing (and critically consuming) literacy, language and educational research, and to the design of educational environments, programs, policies and practices.

Acknowledgements

My thanks, first and foremost, go the authors of these chapters for your significant contributions to research, scholarship and practice, and for working so closely with me on this project. I do appreciate the willingness, responsiveness and enthusiasm that have been the hallmark of this volume. Thanks also to all of the graduate students—mine and others'—whose many questions and tireless quests as emerging scholars provided the impetus for this work. To Angela Creese— thanks for serving as reviewer extraordinaire; to my close colleagues whose conversations have shaped my thinking (at the great risk of leaving some folks out, a shout-out to Suresh Canagarajah, Cathy Compton-Lilly, Glynda Hull, Gillian Kasirye, Stacey Lee, Constant Leung, Bonny Norton, Kelly Toohey, Guadalupe Valdes, Ken Zeichner). And to the folks at Routledge and RefineCatch who have given support to make this happen: in particular to Andrew Weckenman, Emma Håkonsen, Heather Cushing, Libby Eves, and Mark Fisher, and especially, with gratitude, to Naomi Silverman. Last, but not least, to my children, Becky, Annie and Sam, for your constant and continual support.

Margaret R. Hawkins

1

INTRODUCTION

Margaret R. Hawkins

Introduction

Communication is central to the human endeavor. Language and literacy are primary tools for, and modes of, communication; they constitute, represent and disseminate thought and knowledge. It's easy to see why language and literacy have become central constructs in many disciplines and discourses, and in educational initiatives focused on learning (in homes, schools and communities). What may be less transparent, however, are the debates and contestations over what 'language' and 'literacy' are and mean, and what implications might be for differing definitions and understandings.

In earlier work, I have mapped parallel trajectories in the fields of literacy, education/teacher education, and language studies (e.g., Hawkins, 2004, 2011, 2012). In essence, I claim that early work in each area was rooted in structural and psychological approaches: the ability to use literacy and language, and to learn, were attributed to sets of individual features, skills and dispositions residing within and belonging to an individual. Literacy has historically been viewed as the encoding and decoding of print and text; learning as internalizing codified forms of knowledge; and language as a set of vocabulary, forms/structures, and functions which learners must master.

However, beginning in the late 1970s and early 1980s, and gaining momentum throughout the 1990s, these fields, as well as others in the social sciences, have undergone what has been referred to as a 'social turn,' focusing attention on human interaction, activities and practices. This trajectory can be traced in anthropology (e.g., Gompers, 1982; Holland & Quinn, 1987; Hymes, 1974), psychology (e.g., Cole, 1985; Cole & Griffin, 1986; Rogoff, 1990; Wertsch, 1985), cognition and learning sciences (e.g., Lave & Wenger, 1991), composition theory (e.g., Bazerman, 1989; Trimbur, 1994), linguistics (e.g., Halliday & Hassan, 1985; Lakoff, 1987) and other disciplinary areas.

Although the theoretical geneses and trajectories of thought differ by discipline, all move away from individual, in-the-head views of knowing and learning, toward learning and knowing as processes that occur through human engagement in specific situated tasks and interactions, and as mediated through the tools and activities used in carrying them out. People are seen as members of communities of practice (Lave & Wenger, 1991), and their ways of thinking and being—their identities—are shaped by their participation and membership. The languages and literacies they come to use are artifacts of this engagement; they acquire the distinctive forms of languages and literacies used in the (multiple) communities in which they are participants. Further, the larger cultural, institutional, and political contexts in which human activities and interactions take place contribute to the shaping of what occurs within them, as do the historical trajectories in which they are situated that are laden with beliefs, patterns and values. No longer can learning, or language and literacy use, be considered aseptic, impartial, or value-neutral.

As one example of taking up the 'social turn,' in a 1994 article entitled "Taking the social turn: Teaching writing post-process," composition theorist John Trimbur reflects on the then-current status of composition studies as:

> . . . what has come to be called the 'social turn' of the 1980s, a post-process, post-cognitivist theory and pedagogy that represents literacy as an ideological arena and composing as a cultural activity by which writers position and reposition themselves in relation to their own and others' subjectivities, discourses, practices, and institutions.
>
> *(Trimbur, 1994, p. 109)*

This, then, reflects the social turn as a revisioning of human activity (as situated and social), and also leads us to begin to imagine the significant implications for learning and teaching. While there are still a plethora of policies, institutions and people that promulgate skill-based literacy (reading and writing) and language learning, and policies and institutions worldwide promoting teaching and learning as drill-and-rote exercises for mastery of information, discourses around language, literacy and learning have been recast, and debates rage around them.

Situated Languages and Literacies

This volume focuses on social conceptions and perspectives regarding languages and literacies, illuminating issues that are not only central to human interaction but also to education worldwide. The languages and literacies that people command are artifacts of their positioning within specific communities, and enable them to claim (or cause them to be denied) membership within them. They are shaped by where individuals come from and their trajectories through life—who they are and have been—and they shape who people are able to be, and how they perceive themselves and others. Languages and literacies are pluralized; we each have repertoires that include multiple varieties/genres/forms of languages and literacies upon which we draw to communicate appropriately in specific situated interactions. Dating from the early 1980s, when Shirley Brice Heath brought to our attention the differences in engagement with language and literacy practices of children and families in three very different communities in the Piedmont region of the Carolinas (Heath, 1982, 1983), scholars have turned attention to the ways in which children are socialized into particular understandings and usages of languages and literacies from their homes and communities, and the impact of these 'ways with words' on their schooling. And, as has now been repeatedly demonstrated, success—whether in school or more generally in life—depends on which forms of languages and literacies we have command of, and if we have the fluency to shift seamlessly between various registers, styles and genres to use those which are situationally appropriate. In the singular, 'language' and 'literacy' cannot connote this complexity—they can only reference singular, monolithic (usually officially sanctioned) notions, which fail to recognize the complexity of languages and literacies in use across the domains of people's lives.

In the trajectory of language and literacy studies, for reasons perhaps made clear by the above discussion, the focus has increasingly crystallized on issues of positioning, power, equity and justice. From the 1990s through the present, theorists and practitioners alike have acknowledged power differentials in forms of languages and literacies. Put simply, there are forms of languages and literacies that are gateways to success in schools and elsewhere, and others that hold lower societal and educational status. People who are apprenticed to, and acquire, forms that don't hold sway in schools—those that don't align with mainstream language and literacy practices valued in schools—do not have the same educational access or opportunities as those who have command of school-based forms. Scholars and educators who engage with social perspectives on languages, literacies and learning in current times (times in which children who differ from the mainstream in language use, ethnicity, cultural background, socioeconomic status and dis/ability status increasingly experience school failure) thus concern themselves with illuminating issues of and implications for social justice.

The Social Turn in Language and Literacy Studies

While there are disciplinary boundaries in language and literacy studies, such that one might identify one's primary disciplinary home as, say, applied linguistics, or second language acquisition, or composition studies, etc., the fields and subfields are (perhaps arguably) irrevocably intertwined, and mutually dependent. We couldn't engage in literacy practices without language (although there are literacy representations that rely on other modalities), nor are there any longer many language practices that do not call for shared forms of literacies. The oracy/literacy divide (Ong, 1982) has now long been complexified, and language and literacy are no longer viewed as a simple binary (e.g., Bigelow & Tarone, 1994), nor are relationships between input/output and writing/speaking and listening/reading (e.g., Chafe, 1985; Swain & Lapkin, 2002; for a fuller discussion see Gee, 2012). The social turn, through acknowledging languages and literacies as constructed and utilized between people in situated communicative activities, enables us to identify, theorize and investigate these interconnections.

A view of languages, literacies and learning as situated social practices places primacy on the situation, or context. In our 21st century world, as scholars from virtually all disciplines recognize, the rapid flow of people, ideas, knowledge and resources across national and international borders results in ever-shifting and expanding 'contact zones,' where languages, literacies, communities, and identities are continuously and fluidly created, defined and redefined. If learning is defined as meaning-making through negotiation of new concepts and ideas within communities of practices; if languages are defined as the forms through which people communicate; and if literacies are defined as the ability to convey, construct, and take meaning through representational forms; then the rapidity with which new local, national and transnational communities are formed, the rapidly proliferating repertoires of resources being created and utilized, and the flow of human and material resources across traditional boundaries in new economic and global configurations provides a clear mandate for theoretical perspectives and research in languages and literacies that support understandings of and implications for education in changing times.

Language and literacy scholars are, indeed, responding to this mandate, and simultaneously raising awareness that such a mandate exists and that perspectives and practices must change. There is now a robust corpus of social approaches and perspectives designed to shed light on definitions and understandings of languages and literacies. Consistent with disciplinary historical trajectories described above, each perspective draws on distinct bodies of literature and traditions to articulate an understanding of social languages and/or literacies, and uses distinct identifiers, labels, and constellations of concepts. Each major perspective has been taken up by communities of practice globally, and is used as rationale and guide for the design of educational policies and practices across a variety of contexts. However, there has not, to date, been a work that looks among and across major perspectives.

The Book

As a scholar, a mentor of graduate students, a teacher educator, and a consultant to educators and education programs internationally, I am frequently asked questions about what theories to use, how to develop theoretical frameworks that have explanatory power, what the difference is between the various theoretical constructs, and how they might inform research designs and educational initiatives.

I believe that an understanding of the concepts, perspectives and approaches entails an understanding of the context in which they were created (the flows of discourses that contributed to shaping them), the rationale or purpose in creating them (what issues they spoke to), and what they have come to mean (how they have been taken up and applied in communities of practice). Thus this volume includes a variety of approaches and perspectives and articulates these points. This volume seeks to 1) clearly articulate and explicate major social perspectives and approaches in language and literacy studies; 2) provide the genesis and historical trajectory of each approach; 3) offer the author's perspective, rationale and engagement; 4) demonstrate how the approach has been taken up and utilized in research and scholarship; and 5) investigate implications for educational policies and practices.

In order to do this, major perspectives in language and literacy studies were identified, and key scholars associated with the perspectives were asked to contribute chapters. In some cases, the chapter author is the creator of the perspective. In others, the chapter author is someone currently strongly identified with the approach within the fields of language and literacy studies. While there is no claim that *all* social approaches and perspectives are represented, many key contributions have been included. Chapter authors were asked to define their particular perspective, discuss its genesis, and address why it matters to language and literacy teaching and learning and to research. It was suggested that they include a biographical component and personal perspective, although that wasn't mandatory. The format was not proscribed; rather it was left to the individual author to determine what they'd like to say and how. The results, as you will see, are compelling chapters; each has a unique format and style. While they are not uniform, they present rich accounts of the ideas, beliefs and views that shape social fields of language and literacy studies.

The book, subsequent to this introductory chapter, is comprised of nine chapters. In Chapter 2, *BICS and CALP: Empirical Support, Theoretical Status, and Policy Implications of a Controversial Distinction*, Jim Cummins articulates the empirical and theoretical origins of his now-classic BICS/CALP distinction. He traces the theoretical trajectory, then illustrates through examples how the distinction can help interpret and critique educational policy and practice. A particularly interesting aspect of this chapter is his overview of the critiques that scholars have leveled against this perspective, with his responses to each.

The third chapter, *Systemic Functional Linguistics*, authored by J. R. Martin, is replete with an articulation of the perspective (proposed as a 'model') supported by diagrammatic illustrations. He defines and explains systemic functional linguistics (SFL) as an "appliable linguistics," traces its trajectory from Halliday through contributions from other scholars, closely articulates the ways in which the model has been used in literacy education, and draws connections to current theories and approaches in social literacies, thus making clear how the model informs connections between language and literacy. He reviews the literature on how SFL has been used in literacy research and taken up in various literacy movements, and how it has impacted literacy curricula.

In the fourth chapter, *Discourses In and Out of School: Looking Back*, James Paul Gee offers a personal narrative of intellectual discovery leading to the creation of his conceptualization of "Big-D Discourses." Integrating the theoretical constructs that shaped his thinking into his professional trajectory, he defines the perspective, traces its development, and illustrates through analyses of language-in-use why it matters to people's lives and futures. He illuminates connections to school language and literacy practices, including particularly the teaching of reading. In this chapter Gee explicates the inseparability of languages, literacies, people's practices in the world, social contexts, identities and learning, and shows how this perspective helps us to understand students' learning trajectories in schools. He concludes with new applications of the perspective and new directions for his work.

Vaidehi Ramanathan offers the fifth chapter, *A Postcolonial Perspective in Applied Linguistics: Situating English and the Vernaculars.* Offering a postcolonial perspective on English as a world language, Ramanathan proffers a personalized account of her work in educational sites in Gujarat, India, and shows how a postcolonial perspective enables understandings of societal and educational inequities. She defines and describes a postcolonial framework, situating it within the Indian context. With a particular focus on the divide between English-medium (EM) and Vernacular-medium (VM) education, illustrating with data she collected from three Gujarati sites, she portrays the ways in which language policy, instructional language, literacy initiatives and practices, and education are interwoven, and are tied to societal stratifications. Attending to the educational context, she traces Gandhian influences on both formal and informal educational environments, and ultimately situates language and literacy studies, and education, squarely within the realm of ethics, showing that postcolonial perspectives have the power to offer voice and visibility to those who have been historically oppressed.

Chapter 6, *"Multiliteracies": New Literacies, New Learning* is authored by Bill Cope and Mary Kalantzis. In this reprint from *Pedagogies: An International Journal*, Cope and Kalantzis revisit the history of the New London Group and the creation of the concept of multiliteracies. They situate the genesis of the work within discourses operant in the particular historical context, provide a rationale for its appropriateness and applicability in changing economic, social and educational times, and discuss its trajectory and influence since its 1996 inception. They address at length pedagogical implications ('a pedagogy of multiliteracies'), consonant with pedagogy as a central design tenet of the perspective. They then briefly describe some of the many ways internationally that multiliteracies has been taken up pedagogically, heuristically and conceptually since its inception.

In Chapter 7, *Regrounding Critical Literacy: Representation, Facts and Reality*, Allan Luke brings to the forefront the "relationship between cultural systems of representation ... and social and economic reality" (this volume, p. 137).

He connects critical literacy—including forms of literacy, flows of literacy, representational means and modes of literacy—to the shaping of people's everyday lives and experience, and their educational opportunities. Luke outlines what he views as the two major approaches to critical literacy: critical pedagogy and critical text analysis, seating them within multidisciplinary theoretical foundations. He addresses each, discussing critical text analysis through discourse analytic approaches, retaining a focus on what he sees as the central issue: critical literacy's potential, through cultural, linguistic and pedagogic practices, to promote analysis and critique of all texts with the goal of transforming social worlds to be more just and equitable.

Nancy H. Hornberger, in Chapter 8, discusses *Biliteracy Continua*. She defines the concept, tracing its genesis in her earlier work. She also describes how it has been taken up and applied by others as a research lens. Situating it within the field of sociolinguistics, she details how major shifts in the field have impacted the development of the model, connecting it to various current conceptualizations of language, language use, literacy, and schooling. In an extensive discussion of the development of biliteracy, Hornberger draws on work addressing translanguaging in classrooms and translanguaging pedagogies, thus highlighting pedagogic approaches and implications. She calls for more attention to, and inclusion of, 'minoritized' texts and literacies in the school curriculum in order to reposition minority students in their school and community contexts, and reviews literature that highlights work and scholarship being done in this area.

Chapter 9, *Indigenous Literacies: Continuum or Divide?*, is authored by Teresa L. McCarty. McCarty begins with an overview of the current (endangered) statuses of indigenous languages. She examines what counts as literacy in geographically diverse Native American communities, providing a sociocultural and sociohistorical context. She then turns her discussion to the role of literacy (particularly multimodal literacies) in language planning and revitalization; illustrating, through her extensive knowledge of the history and practices of the Navajo/Diné in the American Southwest, educational initiatives undertaken to draw on, incorporate and maintain Diné language and culture in the pursuit of educational achievement. She reviews parallel cases of the Maori and of Hawaiians, showing how these "success stories . . . have empowered learners while reuniting older and younger generations. . . " (this volume, p. 181). McCarty then moves to a discussion of the effects of technology on indigenous language trajectories. She concludes by addressing the affordances and constraints of school-based pedagogies, and pointing to the importance of literacy engagement in both community and school. This chapter ultimately highlights the fluid and ever-changing nature of language and literacy practices as they are embedded in historical, cultural and material contexts.

The final chapter, *Digital Literacies*, by Steven L. Thorne (Chapter 10), begins with an in-depth overview of the culturally and socially situated nature of literacy, showing how literacy has "evolved in ecological relation with distinctive social and community purposes" (this volume, p. 194). He then turns to digital literacies and texts, showing the range of types of communicative activities, chronicling the historical shift and theorizing engagement, highlighting the ways in which identity and community become mutually constituted. Thorne discusses the significance of the 'new media studies,' and reviews the historical trajectory of work on digital literacy and education, directly addressing practices and effects that have been reported in research on instruction in second and foreign language contexts. Through an examination of research on and examples from specific digital literacy practices (e.g., participation in fan fiction and various types of gaming), Thorne shows implications of digital literacies for recasting understandings of literacy, for possibilities of hybridized and 'remixed' literacy engagements, and for new ways of languaging and problem-solving, and ultimately calls for new pedagogical approaches and designs, contexts and curricula.

Authors of chapters in this collection, as requested, have each defined their respective areas, discussed geneses and historical trajectories, documented engagement, and addressed applications for research, policy and practice, including schooling and pedagogical issues. There are remarkable patterns throughout of common themes, interests and concerns. Most compelling to me, perhaps, is the common focus on how forms of languages and literacies connect to and play out in human lives, and are not solely discussed as explanatory of, but also as contributing to and even shaping human and societal initiatives and development. They are deeply and inextricably intertwined with who we are (individually and collectively) and who we can be. And this is why these perspectives are fundamental to our fields and to our world.

References

Bazerman, C. (1989). *Shaping written knowledge.* Madison: University of Wisconsin Press.

Bigelow, M., & Tarone, E. (1994). The role of literacy level in second language acquisition: Doesn't who we study determine what we know? *TESOL Quarterly 38*(4), 689–700.

Chafe, W. (1985). Linguistic differences produced by differences between speaking and writing. In D. R. Olson, N. Torrance, & A. Hildyard (Eds.), *Literacy, language, and learning: The nature and consequences of reading and writing* (pp. 105–123). Cambridge, UK: Cambridge University Press.

Cole, M. (1985). Society, mind and development. In F. Kessel & A. W. Siegel (Eds.), *Houston Symposium IV* (pp. 89–114). New York, NY: Praeger Publishers.

Cole, M., & Griffin, P. (1986). A sociohistorical approach to remediation. In S. deCastell, K. Egan, & A. Luke (Eds.), *Literacy, society, and schooling: A reader* (pp. 110–131). Cambridge, UK: Cambridge University Press.

Gee, J. P. (2012). *Social linguistics and literacies: Ideology in discourses* (4th ed.). New York, NY: Routledge Press.

Gompers, J. J. (Ed.). (1982). *Language and social identity.* Cambridge, UK: Cambridge University Press.

Halliday, M. A. K., & Hassan, R. (1985). *Language, context & text: Aspects of language in a social-semiotic perspective.* Oxford, UK: Oxford University Press.

Hawkins, M. R. (2004). Researching English language and literacy development in schools. *Educational Researcher, 33*(3), 14–25.

Hawkins, M. R. (Ed.). (2011). *Social justice language teacher education.* Clevedon UK: Multilingual Matters.

Hawkins, M. R. (2012). English as a second language: Domestic and international issues. In J. A. Banks (Ed.), *Encyclopedia of diversity in education.* Thousand Oaks, CA: Sage.

Heath, S. B. (1982). What no bedtime story means: Narrative skills at home and school. *Language in Society, 11*(1), 49–76.

Heath, S. B. (1983). *Ways with words: Language, life and work in communities and classrooms.* Cambridge, UK: Cambridge University Press.

Holland, D., & Quinn, N. (Eds.). (1987). *Cultural models in language and thought.* Cambridge, UK: Cambridge University Press.

Hymes, D. (1974). *Foundations of sociolinguistics.* Philadelphia: University of Pennsylvania Press.

Lakoff, G. (1987). *Women, fire and dangerous things.* Chicago, IL: University of Chicago Press.

Lave, J., & Wenger, E. (1991). *Situated learning: Legitimate peripheral participation.* Cambridge, UK: Cambridge University Press.

Ong, W. J. (1982). *Orality and literacy: The technologizing of the word.* London, UK: Methuen.

Rogoff, B. (1990). *Apprenticeship in thinking: Cognitive development in social context.* Oxford, UK: Oxford University Press.

Swain, M., & Lapkin, S. (2002). Talking it through: Two French immersion learners' response to reformulation. *International Journal of Educational Research, 37*(3–4), 285–304.

Trimbur, J. (1994). Taking the social turn: Teaching writing post-process. *College Composition and Communication, 45*(1), 108–118.

Wertsch, J. V. (1985). *Vygotsky and the social formation of mind.* Cambridge, MA: Harvard University Press.

2

BICS AND CALP

Empirical Support, Theoretical Status, and Policy Implications of a Controversial Distinction

Jim Cummins

Origins of the Distinction

The distinction between *basic interpersonal communicative skills* (BICS) and *cognitive academic language proficiency* (CALP) was introduced by Cummins (1979) in order to draw attention to the very different time periods typically required by immigrant students to acquire conversational fluency in their second language (L2) as compared to grade-appropriate academic proficiency in that language. Among immigrant students who are exposed to the L2 in school and the wider environment, conversational fluency in everyday social situations is usually acquired to a functional or peer-appropriate level within about two years of initial exposure to the L2. However, immigrant students typically require at least five years to catch up to native speakers in academic aspects of the second language (Cummins, 1981a).

The terms 'conversational fluency' and 'academic language proficiency' are used interchangeably with BICS and CALP in the remainder of this chapter. Conversational fluency is defined as the ability to carry on a conversation in familiar everyday situations. By contrast, academic language proficiency reflects an individual's access to and command of the specialized vocabulary, functions, and registers of language that are characteristic of the social institution of schooling. The BICS/CALP distinction emerged from several empirical and theoretical sources and these are briefly reviewed in the following sections.

Empirical Origins

Skutnabb-Kangas and Toukomaa (1976) initially brought attention to the fact that Finnish immigrant children in Sweden often appeared to educators to be fluent in both Finnish and Swedish but still showed levels of verbal academic performance in both languages considerably below grade/age expectations. The BICS/CALP distinction highlighted a similar reality and formalized the difference between conversational fluency and academic language proficiency as conceptually distinct components of the construct of "language proficiency." The distinction initially emerged from an analysis of more than 400 psychological assessments administered to English language learners (ELL) in a large Canadian school system (Cummins, 1980, 1984). The teacher referral forms and psychological and/or speech/language assessment reports showed that teachers and psychologists often assumed that students had overcome all difficulties with English when they could converse easily in the language and appeared to understand instructions and questions. Yet these students frequently performed poorly on English academic tasks within the classroom (hence the referral for psychological assessment) as well as on the verbal scales of the cognitive ability test administered as part of the assessment. Many students were designated as having learning or communication disabilities despite the fact that they had been in Canada for a relatively short period of time (e.g., 1–3 years). Thus, the conflation of L2 conversational fluency with L2 academic proficiency contributed directly to a problematic diagnosis of cognitive deficits and inappropriate placement of bilingual students in special education programs.

The need to distinguish between conversational fluency and academic aspects of L2 performance was further highlighted by a reanalysis of language performance data involving 25 percent of the grades 5, 7 and 9 students in the Toronto Board of Education (Cummins, 1981a). These data showed that there was a gap of several years, on average, between the attainment of peer-appropriate fluency in English and the attainment of grade norms in academic aspects of English. Conversational aspects of proficiency reached peer-appropriate levels usually within about two years of exposure to English but a period of 5–7 years was required, on average, for immigrant students to approach grade norms in academic aspects of English (e.g., vocabulary knowledge). The differential time periods required to attain peer-appropriate L2 conversational fluency as compared to meeting grade expectations in academic language proficiency have been corroborated in many research studies carried out during the past 30 years in Canada (Klesmer, 1994), Europe (Snow and Hoefnagel-Hohle, 1978), Israel (Shohamy et al., 2002), and the United States (Collier, 1987; Hakuta, Butler, & Witt, 2000; Thomas & Collier, 2002).

Subsequent empirical research has highlighted the classroom realities underlying the BICS/CALP distinction. For example, Vincent's (1996) ethnographic study of second generation Salvadorean students in Washington, DC, reported that students began school in an English-speaking environment and "within their first two or three years attained conversational ability in English that teachers would regard as native-like" (p. 195). Vincent suggested, however, that this fluency is largely deceptive:

> The children seem to have much greater English proficiency than they actually do because their spoken English has no accent and they are able to

converse on a few everyday, frequently discussed subjects. Academic language is frequently lacking. Teachers actually spend very little time talking with individual children and tend to interpret a small sample of speech as evidence of full English proficiency.

(Vincent, 1996, p. 195)

Theoretical Origins and Evolution

At a theoretical level, the BICS/CALP distinction was used to critique Oller's (1979) claim that all individual differences in language proficiency (both L1 and L2) could be accounted for by just one underlying factor, which he termed *global language proficiency*. Oller synthesized a considerable amount of data showing strong correlations between performance on cloze tests of reading, standardized reading tests, and measures of oral verbal ability (e.g., vocabulary measures). Cummins (1979), however, pointed out that it is problematic to incorporate all aspects of language use or performance into just one dimension of general or global language proficiency because different components of L1 and L2 proficiency follow very different developmental trajectories. For example, if we take two monolingual English-speaking siblings, a 12-year-old child and a 6-year-old, there are enormous differences in these children's ability to read and write English and in the depth and breadth of their vocabulary knowledge, but minimal differences in their phonology or basic fluency. The 6-year-old can understand virtually everything that is likely to be said to her in everyday social contexts and she can use language very effectively in these contexts, just as the 12-year-old can. In other words, some aspects of children's L1 development (e.g., phonology) reach a plateau relatively early whereas other aspects (e.g. vocabulary knowledge) continue to develop throughout our lifetimes. Similarly, as pointed out above, very different trajectories characterize L2 development among immigrant children with L2 phonology and fluency developing to peer-appropriate levels much more rapidly than is typically the case for academic aspects of language. The very different developmental trajectories in L1 and L2 refute the claim that all aspects of language proficiency reflect a single unitary proficiency dimension.

The initial BICS/CALP distinction was elaborated into two intersecting continua (Cummins, 1981b) that highlighted the range of contextual support and cognitive demands involved in particular language tasks or activities. The horizontal continuum ranged from context-embedded to context-reduced, while the vertical continuum ranged from cognitively undemanding to cognitively demanding, resulting in four quadrants that varied in the degree of contextual support and cognitive demand associated with language activities. Internal and external dimensions of context were distinguished to reflect the fact that "context" is constituted both by what we bring to a task (e.g., our prior knowledge, interests, and motivation) and the range of supports that may be incorporated in the task itself (e.g., visual supports such as graphic organizers). This quadrants framework extended the BICS/CALP distinction into the realm of pedagogy. Specifically, it was argued that effective instruction for ELL students should focus primarily on context-embedded and cognitively demanding tasks. It was also recognized, however, that these dimensions cannot be specified in absolute terms because what is "context-embedded" or "cognitively demanding" for one learner may not be so for another as a result of differences in internal attributes such as prior knowledge or interest.

The BICS/CALP distinction was also related to the theoretical distinctions of several other theorists, among them Bruner's (1975) *communicative and analytic competence*, Donaldson's (1978) *embedded and disembedded language*, and Olson's (1977) *utterance and text*. The essential distinction reflects the extent to which the communication of meaning is strongly supported by the immediate social context and face-to-face interpersonal cues (e.g., gestures, facial expressions, intonation, etc.) or supported primarily by linguistic cues of the kind found in text and in more formal communicative situations. The term "context-reduced" was used rather than "decontextualized" in recognition of the fact that all language and literacy practices are contextualized; however, the range of supports to meaning in many academic contexts (e.g., textbook reading) is reduced in comparison to the contextual support available in face-to-face contexts.

In later accounts of the framework (Cummins, 2000, 2001), the distinction between conversational fluency and academic language proficiency was related to the work of several other theorists. For example, Gibbons' (1991) distinction between *playground language* and *classroom language* highlighted the fact that classroom language is very different from playground language:

> The playground situation does not normally offer children the opportunity to use such language as: *if we increase the angle by 5 degrees, we could cut the circumference into equal parts.* Nor does it normally require the language associated with the higher order thinking skills, such as hypothesizing, evaluating, inferring, generalizing, predicting or classifying. Yet these are the language functions which are related to learning and the development of cognition; they occur in all areas of the curriculum, and without them a child's potential in academic areas cannot be realized.
>
> *(Gibbons, 1991, p. 3)*

Additional theoretical connections were made to the work of Biber (1986) and Corson (1995, 1997). For example, Biber's (1986) factor analysis of more than one million words of English spoken and written text from a wide variety of genres revealed underlying dimensions very consistent with the distinction between conversational and academic aspects of language proficiency. For example, telephone and face-to-face conversation were at opposite extremes from official documents and academic prose on Textual Dimensions 1 and 2 (Interactive vs. Edited Text, and Situated vs. Abstract Content).

Similarly, Corson (1995, 1997) highlighted the enormous lexical differences between typical conversational interactions in English as compared to academic or literacy-related uses of English. The high-frequency everyday lexicon of English conversation derives predominantly from Anglo-Saxon sources while the relatively lower frequency academic vocabulary is primarily Graeco-Latin in origin (see also Coxhead, 2000).

Conversational and academic language registers were also related to Gee's (1990) distinction between *primary* and *secondary* discourses (Cummins, 2001). Primary discourses are acquired through face-to-face interactions in the home and represent the language of initial socialization. Secondary discourses are acquired in social institutions beyond the family (e.g., school, business, religious, and cultural contexts) and involve acquisition of specialized vocabulary and functions of language appropriate to those settings. Secondary discourses can be oral or written and are equally central to the social life of non-literate and literate cultures. Examples of secondary discourse common in many non-literate cultures are the conventions of story-telling or the language of marriage or burial rituals which are passed down through oral tradition from one generation to the next. Within this conception, academic language proficiency reflects an individual's access to and command of the secondary discourses required to function effectively within the social sphere of schooling. In principle, the secondary discourses of schooling are no different than secondary discourses in other spheres of human endeavour—for example, avid amateur gardeners and professional horticulturalists have acquired vocabulary related to plants and flowers far beyond the knowledge of those not involved in this sphere of activity.

Other ways in which the original BICS/CALP distinction has evolved include:

• The addition of *discrete language skills* as a component of language proficiency that is distinct from both conversational fluency and academic language proficiency (Cummins, 2001). Discrete language skills involve the learning of rule-governed aspects of language (including phonology, phonics, grammar, spelling, punctuation, etc.) where acquisition of the general case permits generalization to other instances governed by that particular rule. Discrete language skills can sometimes be learned in virtual isolation from the development of academic language proficiency as illustrated in the fact that some students who can "read" English fluently may have only a very limited understanding of the words they can decode. Discrete language skills was incorporated into the distinction between conversational fluency and academic language proficiency in order to account for the fact that systematic phonics instruction shows no relationship to the development of reading comprehension after grade 1 among normally achieving and low achieving students (Cummins, 2007; National Reading Panel, 2000). Thus, while the teaching of discrete language skills is certainly an important dimension of literacy instruction, it does not directly promote the development of academic language proficiency.

- The embedding of the BICS/CALP distinction within a broader framework of academic development in culturally and linguistically diverse contexts that specifies the role of societal power relations in framing teacher–student interactions and determining the social organization of schooling (Cummins, 1986, 2001). Teacher–student interactions are seen as a process of negotiating identities, reflecting to varying degrees coercive or collaborative relations of power in the wider society. This socialization process within the school determines the extent to which students will engage academically and gain access to the academic registers of schooling.

From Research and Theory to Policy and Practice

Evaluating Theoretical Constructs

Theories and theoretical constructs, such as BICS/CALP, must be consistent with the empirical data to have any claim to validity. However, any set of theoretical constructs represents only one of potentially many ways of organizing or viewing the data. For example, different disciplines (e.g., neurology versus cognitive science) may describe and explain the same phenomenon quite differently but in equally valid ways. Also, within a particular discipline, the phenomena may be synthesized legitimately into very different theoretical frameworks depending on the purpose of the framework, the audience envisaged, and the outcomes desired. The process is analogous to observing any object (e.g., a house); when we move and shift our perspective (e.g., look from the side as compared to the front of the house) we see a different image although the object of our observation has not changed in any way. Similarly, the perspective we bring to any observation influences what we see; thus, a prospective home buyer will "see" the house differently than a building inspector. Thus, theoretical frameworks provide alternative perspectives on particular phenomena in specific contexts and for particular purposes.

Theoretical claims, or frameworks that integrate these claims, are not valid or invalid, true or false in any absolute sense; rather, they should be judged by criteria of *adequacy* and *usefulness*. "Adequacy" refers to the extent to which the claims or categories embedded in the framework are consistent with the empirical data and provide a coherent and comprehensive account of the data. "Usefulness" refers to the extent to which the framework can be used effectively by its intended audience to generate greater understanding of empirical phenomena and to implement educational policies and practices that derive from this understanding.

Ideally, theoretical constructs and frameworks are in constant dialogue with practice. The relationship between theory and practice is two-way and ongoing: practice generates theory, which, in turn, acts as a catalyst for new directions in practice, which then inform theory, and so on. Theory and practice are infused within each other. Adequacy and usefulness are never absolutes. Certainly, in the case of BICS/CALP, more detailed theoretical accounts and frameworks may be more "adequate" in capturing specific details of L2 language and literacy development. However, gains in specificity and/or complexity may be made at the expense of usefulness. Too much detail may lead educators and policy-makers to lose sight of the "big picture" while excessive theoretical complexity or language that is alien to educators and policy-makers will reduce the likelihood of implementation. Thus, the BICS/CALP construct and subsequent elaborations outlined above all extend in two ways: they link with the empirical and theoretical literature on L2 language and literacy development on the one hand, but they are also grounded in concrete educational policies and classroom practice, and their purpose is to stimulate sustained dialogue with these policies and practice.

The sections above have provided evidence that the BICS/CALP distinction is consistent with the empirical data and therefore adequate to account for the data. The usefulness of the constructs for elucidating educational policies and practices is considered in the next section.

Viewing Educational Policies and Practice Through the Lens of BICS/CALP

The BICS/CALP distinction has influenced both policy and practice related to the instruction and assessment of second language learners in a range of educational contexts. For example, it has been invoked in policy discussions related to:

- The amount and duration of funding necessary to support immigrant students who are learning the school language as an L2;
- The kinds of instructional support that immigrant students need at different stages of their acquisition of conversational and academic language;
- The extent to which ELL students should be included in nationally mandated high-stakes testing; for example, in the United States under the No Child Left Behind (2001) legislation, ELL students were exempted from standardized testing only in their first year of learning English. After that period, their scores were interpreted, along with the scores of other students, as reflective of the quality of instruction in a particular school. Clearly, this policy is absurd and self-defeating in light of the typical timelines involved in the development of academic language proficiency among immigrant students.
- The extent to which psychological testing of immigrant students for diagnostic purposes through their L2 is valid and ethically defensible in their early years of schooling in the host country.

Two concrete examples will illustrate the extent to which the distinctions between conversational fluency, discrete language skills, and academic language proficiency can help interpret and critique specific educational policies and practices. The first comes from a debate about bilingual education on the CNN program *TalkBack Live* (October 11, 2000) that pitted conservative social activist Ron Unz, who initiated Proposition 227 that severely curtailed bilingual education in California in 1997, against Executive Director of the National Association for Bilingual Education, Delia Pompa. Part of the transcript of this debate, moderated by Bobbie Battista, is outlined below:

> BATTISTA: Well, let me ask you this. Let me ask you this to help us understand. What is the average length of time that it takes a child in Texas to learn English?
>
> POMPA: The average length of time it takes children in Texas and in the United States and worldwide is about three years.
>
> BATTISTA: And in Texas you're saying it's three years, not five?
>
> POMPA: I don't believe it's five years for most children. There's research that says it takes children up to five years, but on average children are in bilingual education programs for about three years.
>
> BATTISTA: What's the average length of time, Ron, if they're immersed in English? What's the average length?
>
> UNZ: Well under one year. Now here's the whole thing. What Delia Pompa just said is nonsense. All of the bilingual researchers, all of them, claim that it takes five to seven years for a child to learn English. The reason she's not quoting that five to seven year figure is it would make her a laughing stock because everybody knows that's nonsense.
>
> *(http://transcripts.cnn.com/TRANSCRIPTS/0010/11/tl.00.html)*

The debate on how long it takes children to "learn English" degenerates into an evidence-free verbal brawl because neither participant distinguishes between the time periods required to develop conversational fluency in English as compared to academic language proficiency. Unz's claim ("under one year") might have had some limited plausibility if he had specified that he was talking about conversational fluency. However, all of the research evidence supports the claim that, on average, at least five years (and frequently longer) is required for immigrant/ELL students to catch up academically in English. Unz's claim that "everybody knows that's nonsense" could have been instantly refuted by Pompa if she had made the distinction between conversational and academic English. Instead, however, she reverts to her belief that "I don't believe it's five years for most children" opening herself up to ridicule from Unz who (accurately) notes that "all of the bilingual researchers ... claim that it takes five to seven years for a child to learn English." Obviously, Unz omits to mention that this claim is specific to the time period required for students to meet grade expectations in *academic* English.

It is worth noting that Unz's optimistic expectations about the transformative effects of English-only instruction have not been borne out by the empirical evidence. An analysis of the effects of the implementation of Proposition 227 in California reported that English language learners had less than a 40 percent chance of being redesignated as English-proficient after 10 years of instruction in California schools (Parrish et al., 2006). After three years of instruction only 12 percent of English language learners met the redesignation criteria.

A second example of how the BICS/CALP distinction speaks to issues in educational policy and practice comes from the (Cummins, 1980, 1984) study of psychological assessments carried out on ELL students. The assessment illustrates how implicit assumptions on the part of school professionals about the nature of language proficiency can directly affect bilingual students' educational placement and instructional experiences. As reported in Cummins (1984), the psychological assessment for one student (PR) read as follows:

> PR was referred in first grade by the school principal who noted that "PR is experiencing considerable difficulty with grade one work. An intellectual assessment would help her teacher to set realistic learning expectations for her and might provide some clues as to remedial assistance that might be offered."
>
> *(Cummins, 1984, p. 38)*

No mention was made of the fact that the child was learning English as an additional language; this only emerged when the child was referred by the second grade teacher in the following year. Thus, the psychologist does not consider this as a possible factor in accounting for the discrepancy between a verbal IQ of 64 and a performance (nonverbal) IQ of 108. The assessment report read as follows:

> Although overall ability level appears to be within the low average range, note the significant difference between verbal and nonverbal scores.... It would appear that PR's development has not progressed at a normal rate and consequently she is, and will continue to experience much difficulty in school. Teacher's expectations at this time should be set accordingly.
>
> *(Cummins, 1984, p. 39)*

The relevance of the BICS/CALP distinction to interpretation of this assessment derives from the fact that the child's English communicative skills were presumably sufficiently well developed that the psychologist (and possibly the teacher) was not alerted to her linguistic background. This led the psychologist to infer from her low verbal IQ score that "her development has not progressed at a normal rate" and to advise the teacher to set low academic expectations for the child since she "will continue to experience much difficulty in school."

In summary, the two examples outlined above illustrate not only the adequacy of the BICS/CALP distinction to account for the data but also its usefulness as a means of communicating to educators the fallacies in the claims made by both

Unz and Pompa and the instructional recommendations made by the psychologist in relation to PR. The next section reviews and responds to some of the major critiques made of the BICS/CALP distinction.

Critique and Response

Since 1983, when Edelsky and colleagues published a detailed critique of the BICS/CALP distinction and other theoretical constructs advanced by Cummins (1981b), there have been numerous additional attempts to discredit the theoretical and educational legitimacy of the distinction. Many of these critiques have been summarized and responded to in Cummins (2000) and Cummins and Swain (1983) and thus this section will offer only an outline of the major points of contention.

Four major criticisms of BICS/CALP can be distinguished:

- The conversational/academic language distinction reflects an autonomous perspective on language that ignores its location in social practices and power relations (Edelsky et al., 1983; Romaine, 1989; Troike, 1984; Valdés, 2004; Wald, 1984; Wiley, 1996).
- CALP or academic language proficiency represents little more than "test-wiseness"—it is an artifact of the inappropriate way in which it has been measured (Edelsky 1990; 2006; Edelsky et al., 1983; MacSwan, 2000; Martin-Jones & Romaine, 1986).
- The notion of CALP promotes a "deficit theory" that attributes bilingual students' academic difficulties to their "low CALP" rather than to inappropriate schooling (Edelsky, 1990, 2006; Edelsky et al., 1983; Martin-Jones & Romaine, 1986; MacSwan, 2000; Rolstad & MacSwan, 2008).
- The BICS/CALP distinction is oversimplified and unhelpful in understanding the nature of academic language and the challenges it poses for ELL students (e.g., Scarcella, 2003; Valdés, 2004).

In response to these critiques, Cummins and Swain (1983) and Cummins (2000) pointed out that the construct of academic language proficiency does not in any way depend on test scores to support either its construct validity or relevance to education. This is illustrated in Vincent's (1996) ethnographic study and Biber's (1986) and Corson's (1995) research on the English lexicon discussed above. Furthermore, the BICS/CALP distinction has been integrated since 1986 with a detailed sociopolitical analysis of how schools construct academic failure among subordinated groups. The framework documents educational approaches that challenge this pattern of coercive power relations and promote the generation of power and the development of academic expertise in interactions between educators and students (Cummins, 1986, 2001). Thus, the claim that bilingual students' academic difficulties are attributed to "low CALP" is simply wrong. In fact, as noted above, the BICS/CALP distinction was used to identify prejudicial policies and practices that were denying bilingual/ELL students access to equitable and effective learning opportunities.

Scarcella's claim that the distinction is oversimplified derives from taking the constructs out of their original dialogical or discursive context and arguing that they are not useful or appropriate in a very different dialogical context. She argues that the dichotomous conceptualization of language incorporated in the BICS/CALP distinction "is not useful for understanding the complexities of academic English or the multiple variables affecting its development" (Scarcella, 2003, p. 5). She concludes that the distinction is "of limited practical value, since it fails to operationalize tasks and therefore does not generate tasks that teachers can use to help develop their students' academic English" (p. 6). Scarcella goes on to elaborate a useful framework for conceptualizing academic language and generating academic tasks. What she fails to acknowledge, however, is that the BICS/CALP distinction was not formulated as a tool to generate academic tasks. As noted above, it addresses a very different set of theoretical, policy, and classroom instructional issues and makes no claim to "usefulness" with respect to operationalizing academic tasks.

Valdés (2004) likewise addresses the extent to which a unitary notion of CALP is compatible with a New Literacies perspective on the multiple forms of literacy that are embedded in complex social and cultural practices. Again, the conversational fluency/academic language proficiency distinction is in no way incompatible with a view of literacies as multiple, contextually-specific, and constantly evolving. In some discursive contexts and for some purposes, it is more useful to articulate a simple distinction than to try to capture the enormous complexity of language use and multiple literacies development. To illustrate, the fact that the concept of "Asian" can be broken down into an almost infinite array of national, regional, and social identities does not invalidate the more general descriptor of "Asian." In some discursive contexts and for some purposes it is legitimate and useful to describe an individual or a group as "Asian" despite the fact that it greatly oversimplifies the complex reality of "Asian-ness." Similarly, in certain discursive contexts and for certain purposes it is legitimate and useful to talk about conversational fluency and academic language proficiency despite the fact that these constructs incorporate multiple levels of complexity. Thus, research studies on how long it typically takes immigrant students to catch up to grade norms in academic language proficiency have, within the context of the research, focused on literacy as an autonomous skill measured by standardized tests but have nevertheless contributed in substantial ways to promoting equity in schooling for these students.

Conclusion

The distinction between conversational fluency and academic language proficiency addresses a variety of policy, instructional, and assessment issues related to

ELL/bilingual students. For example, it helps account for the longer time periods typically required for ELL students to catch up academically in English as compared to acquiring fluent conversational skills in English. It also draws attention to the potential for discriminatory assessment of bilingual students when their L2 conversational fluency is conflated with the development of L2 academic skills. The distinction is compatible with detailed analyses of the linguistic dimensions underlying a wide variety of authentic oral and written texts in English (Biber, 1986) and is also consistent with the different lexical realities of everyday conversational English as compared to literate forms of English (Corson, 1995, 1997).

The critique that the BICS/CALP distinction represents an autonomous rather than an ideological orientation to language and literacy ignores the fact that the distinction is embedded within a framework that attributes the causes of subordinated students' school failure to the operation of coercive power relations in school and society. It also fails to acknowledge that in the context of some research questions and policy issues, it *is* legitimate to focus on language and literacy development outside of an explicitly ideological orientation. For example, highlighting the social and contextually specific dimensions of cognition does not invalidate a research focus on what may be happening inside the heads of individuals as they perform cognitive or linguistic tasks. Similarly, few would dismiss the entire field of corpus linguistics simply because it typically focuses on language patterns and behavior in relative isolation from the broader social context.

In summary, within the context of the criteria that have been articulated for evaluating any theoretical construct or framework, the BICS/CALP distinction is clearly *adequate* insofar as it is consistent with the empirical data and consonant with similar distinctions made by numerous other theorists. None of the critiques of the distinction have claimed that conversational and academic language are indistinguishable (although MacSwan, 2000, argues that academic language proficiency reflects *literacy* rather than language, which is totally acquired in the early years of life and therefore not subject to further development throughout schooling). With respect to *usefulness,* many of the critiques view the distinction as problematic and not at all useful in understanding patterns of language development among L1 and L2 learners. However, the fact that the distinction persists after more than 30 years and has entered the lexicon of ESL teachers and other educators concerned with the academic development of bilingual/ELL students suggests that its usefulness does resonate within the educational communities to which it was directed.

References

Biber, D. (1986). Spoken and written textual dimensions in English: Resolving the contradictory findings. *Language, 62*, 384–414.

Bruner, J. S. (1975). Language as an instrument of thought. In A. Davies (Ed.), *Problems of language and learning* (pp. 61–88). London, UK: Heinemann.

Collier, V. P. (1987). Age and rate of acquisition of second language for academic purposes. *TESOL Quarterly, 21*, 617–641.

Corson, D. (1995). *Using English words.* New York, NY: Kluwer.

Corson, D. (1997). The learning and use of academic English words. *Language Learning, 47*, 671–718.

Coxhead, A. (2000). A new academic word list. *TESOL Quarterly, 34*, 213–238.

Cummins, J. (1979). Cognitive/academic language proficiency, linguistic interdependence, the optimum age question and some other matters. *Working Papers on Bilingualism,* No. 19, 121–129.

Cummins, J. (1980). Psychological assessment of immigrant children: Logic or intuition? *Journal of Multilingual and Multicultural Development, 1*, 97–111.

Cummins, J. (1981a). Age on arrival and immigrant second language learning in Canada: A reassessment. *Applied Linguistics, 1*, 132–149.

Cummins, J. (1981b). The role of primary language development in promoting educational success for language minority students. In California State Department of Education (Ed.), *Schooling and language minority students: A theoretical framework.* Los Angeles: Evaluation, Dissemination and Assessment Center California State University.

Cummins, J. (1984). *Bilingualism and special education: Issues in assessment and pedagogy.* Clevedon, UK: Multilingual Matters.

Cummins, J. (1986). Empowering minority students: A framework for intervention. *Harvard Education Review, 15*, 18–36.

Cummins, J. (2000). *Language, power and pedagogy: Bilingual children in the crossfire.* Clevedon, UK: Multilingual Matters.

Cummins, J. (2001). *Negotiating identities: Education for empowerment in a diverse society* (2nd ed.). Los Angeles: California Association for Bilingual Education.

Cummins, J. (2007). Pedagogies for the poor? Re-aligning reading instruction for low-income students with scientifically based reading research. *Educational Researcher, 36*, 564–572.

Cummins, J., & Swain, M. (1983). Analysis-by-rhetoric: Reading the text or the reader's own projections? A reply to Edelsky et al. *Applied Linguistics, 4*, 23–41.

Donaldson, M. (1978). *Children's minds.* Glasgow, UK: Collins.

Edelsky, C. (1990). *With literacy and justice for all: Rethinking the social in language and education.* London, UK: The Falmer Press.

Edelsky, C. (2006). *With literacy and justice for all: Rethinking the social in language and education* (3rd ed.). Mahwah, NJ: Lawrence Erlbaum Associates.

Edelsky, C., Hudelson, S., Flores, B., Barkin, F., Altweger, B., & Jilbert, K. (1983). Semilingualism and language deficit. *Applied Linguistics, 4*, 1–22.

Gee, J. P. (1990). *Social linguistics and literacies: Ideologies in discourses.* New York, NY: Falmer Press.

Gibbons, P. (1991). *Learning to learn in a second language.* Newtown, Australia: Primary English Teaching Association.

Hakuta, K., Butler, Y. G., & Witt, D. (2000). *How long does it take English learners to attain proficiency?* Santa Barbara: University of California Linguistic Minority Research Institute.

Klesmer, H. (1994). Assessment and teacher perceptions of ESL student achievement. *English Quarterly, 26*(3), 8–11.

MacSwan, J. (2000). The threshold hypothesis, semilingualism, and other contributions to a deficit view of linguistic minorities. *Hispanic Journal of Behavioral Sciences, 22*, 3–45.

Martin-Jones, M., & Romaine, S. (1986). Semilingualism: A half-baked theory of communicative competence. *Applied Linguistics, 7,* 26–38.

National Reading Panel. (2000). *Teaching children to read: An evidence-based assessment of the scientific research literature on reading and its implications for reading instruction.* Washington, DC: National Institute of Child Health & Human Development.

No Child Left Behind Act of 2001, Pub. L. No. 107–110 (2001).

Oller, J. (1979). *Language tests at school: A pragmatic approach.* London, UK: Longman.

Olson, D. R. (1977). From utterance to text: The bias of language in speech and writing. *Harvard Educational Review, 47,* 257–281.

Parrish, T., Merickel, A., Pérez, M., Linquanti, R., Socias, M., Spain, A., & Brock, L. (2006). *Effects of the implementation of Proposition 227 on the education of English learners, K-12: Findings from a five-year evaluation (final report).* Palo Alto, CA, and San Francisco, CA: American Institutes for Research and WestEd.

Rolstad, K., & MacSwan, J. (2008). BICS/CALP: Theory and critique. In J. Gonzalez (Ed.), *Encyclopedia of bilingual education* (pp. 62–65). Thousand Oaks, CA: Sage.

Romaine, S. (1989). *Bilingualism.* Oxford, UK: Oxford University Press.

Scarcella, R. (2003). *Academic English: A conceptual framework* [Technical Report 2003–1]. Santa Barbara, CA: The University of California Linguistic Minority Research Institute.

Shohamy, E., Levine, T., Spolsky, B., Kere-Levy, M., Inbar, O., & Shemesh, M. (2002). *The academic achievements of immigrant children from the former USSR and Ethiopia.* Report (in Hebrew) submitted to the Ministry of Education, Israel.

Skutnabb-Kangas, T., & Toukomaa, P. (1976). *Teaching migrant children's mother tongue and learning the language of the host country in the context of the socio-cultural situation of the migrant family.* Helsinki, Finland: The Finnish National Commission for UNESCO.

Snow, C. E., & Hoefnagel-Hohle, M. (1978). The critical period for language acquisition: Evidence from second language learning. *Child Development, 49,* 1114–1128.

Thomas, W. P., & Collier, V. P. (2002). *A national study of school effectiveness for language minority students' long-term academic achievement.* Santa Cruz, CA: Center for Research on Education, Diversity and Excellence, University of California-Santa Cruz. Retrieved April 12, 2004, from http//www.crede.ucsc.edu.

Troike, R. (1984). SCALP: Social and cultural aspects of language proficiency. In C. Rivera (Ed.), *Language proficiency and academic achievement.* Clevedon, UK: Multilingual Matters.

Valdés, G. (2004). Between support and marginalization: The development of academic language in linguistic minority children. *International Journal of Bilingual Education and Bilingualism, 7,* 102–132.

Vincent, C. (1996). *Singing to a star: The school meanings of second generation Salvadorean students.* Unpublished doctoral dissertation, George Mason University, Fairfax, VA.

Wald, B. (1984). A sociolinguistic perspective on Cummins' current framework for relating language proficiency to academic achievement. In C. Rivera (Ed.), *Language proficiency and academic achievement* (pp. 55–70). Clevedon, UK: Multilingual Matters.

Wiley, T. G. (1996). *Literacy and language diversity in the United States.* Washington, DC: Center for Applied Linguistics and Delta Systems.

3

SYSTEMIC FUNCTIONAL LINGUISTICS

J. R. Martin

Systemic Functional Linguistics

Functionality

Systemic Functional Linguistics (hereafter SFL) is a functional model of language and social context, founded on and elaborating the insights of M. A. K. Halliday and his colleagues. Eggins (1994) and Halliday and Matthiessen (2009) provide introductions to the model as a whole. Halliday (2009) compiles key passages from his collected works; Hasan, Matthiessen, and Webster (2005a, 2005b) and Webster (2009) offer a comprehensive tour of current SFL research and practice.

SFL is a functional model in at least three senses of the term. First it uses function labels alongside class labels in its descriptions of linguistic phenomena. So alongside describing the kind of thing an item is (e.g., adjective, preposition, nominal group, verbal group, clause, clause complex) it also describes the role an item plays in larger units—e.g., adjective or verb as Epithet (**bright** *star*/**shining** *star*), numeral or noun as Classifier (**first** *prize*/**cash** *prize*), nominal group as Actor or Goal (**the champion lost**/**the champion** *was defeated*). Halliday & Matthiessen (2004) is the canonical reference text for this approach to grammatical description; Thompson (2004) provides an accessible introduction; Coffin, Donohue, and North (2009) compare this functional approach with traditional and formal perspectives. The function labels make it possible to focus more specifically on the meaning a given structure makes, which is critical for interpreting the functions of literacy in domestic and institutional life.

Second, SFL foregrounds a paradigmatic perspective on language, which it models as a reservoir of choices manifested through the function structures introduced above. Whether we realise 'the champion' in the exemplar above as

Actor or Goal for example is a question of VOICE and thus of choices we make about whether someone simply undergoes a process or is impacted upon by it (*the champion lost/the champion was defeated*), and if impacted upon, whether we want to explicitly target another participant as responsible (e.g., *the champion was defeated/ the champion was defeated **by the second seed***). As outlined in Halliday and Matthiessen (2004, 2009), choices tend to cluster in relation to the kinds of meaning being made and these clusters can be generalised as metafunctions—namely, the ideational choices construing our experience of the world, the interpersonal choices enacting our social relations, and the textual choices weaving these meanings together into coherent and relevant texture (see Figure 3.1).

Third, SFL is functional in the sense of having been designed as an appliable linguistics—by which is meant a model of language that can be used to address language problems as they arise in communities (Halliday, 2008a). The two types of functionality introduced above are crucial parts of this appliable design feature. Accordingly SFL has been widely used in educational, clinical, forensic and many other contexts; as far as literacy is concerned, work in education has been especially prominent. Halliday in Halliday and Hasan (2006) comments retrospectively on the SFL-informed literacy education research initiated in Britain in the 1960s (see also Pearce, Thornton, & Mackay, 1989). Christie (1992), Feez (1998, 2002), Gebhart and Martin (2011), Macken-Horarik (2002), Martin (1993a, 2001, 2006, 2009) and Martin and Rose (2005, 2007) survey Australian-inspired initiatives associated with the so-called 'Sydney School' of educational linguistics (Hyon, 1996; Johns, 2002).

FIGURE 3.1 Metafunctions (Kinds of Meaning): Ideational, Interpersonal, and Textual.

Stratification

In addition to the trinocular complementarity of ideational, interpersonal and textual metafunctions noted above, SFL models language along a cline of abstraction as a series of interdependent levels or strata. Language itself is typically interpreted from a tri-stratal perspective—i.e., phonology/graphology realising lexicogrammar realising (discourse) semantics (e.g., Martin & Rose, 2003/2007); these language strata are seen as realising social context, modelled as the strata of register and genre in Martin and Rose (2008), Martin and White (2005). As outlined in Figure 3.2, this kind of modelling involves privileging context from a social semiotic perspective as higher levels of meaning realised through language. Register, in models of this kind, is also interpreted from a metafunctional perspective, with ideational meaning construing field, interpersonal meaning enacting tenor and textual meaning composing texture with respect to mode.

Strata and metafunction thus cross-classify language as a reservoir of meaning, and provide the basic cartography of the model (cf. for example the front cover of Halliday & Matthiessen, 2004). Further dimensions relating to instantiation (the relation of the reservoir to instances of language use—i.e., texts) and individuation (the relation of the reservoir to repertoires of user identities) are discussed in Halliday and Matthiessen (2009), Bednarek and Martin (2010), and Martin and White (2005). For applications of the model to a variety of language families from a functional language typology perspective, see Caffarel, Martin, and Matthiessen (2004).

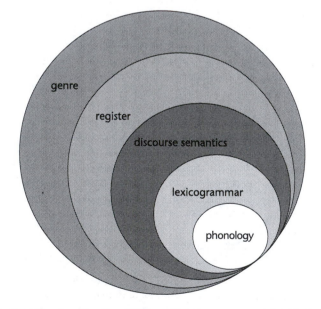

FIGURE 3.2 Stratification (Levels of Abstraction): Language and Social Context.

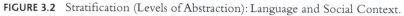

Multimodality

The social semiotic perspective on language and social context introduced above has encouraged work on multimodal discourse analysis in order to deal with texts composed of language and additional modes of meaning. Inspired by Kress and van Leeuwen's (1996/2006) work on images, SFL scholars have applied the notions of function, choice, and metafunction outlined above to the analysis of action (Martinec, 2000), paralanguage (Martinec, 2004), music and sound (van Leeuwen, 1999), 3-D space (Stenglin, 2008a, 2008b), new media design (Martinec & van Leeuwen, 2009) and mathematical symbolism and diagrams (O'Halloran, 2005). The revolutionary impact of this work on SFL-informed discourse analysis is reviewed in Martinec (2005); for a productive renovation of its foundations, see Bateman (2008, 2011). Exemplary collections of papers in this ever-expanding field of SFL-informed social semiotics include Dreyfus, Hood, and Stenglin (2011), O'Halloran (2004), Royce and Bowcher (2007), Unsworth (2008) and Ventola and Guijarro (2009). Painter, Martin, and Unsworth (2013) develop Kress and van Leeuwen's seminal work for the analysis of children's picture books.

Literacy

The work on language and image introduced above has enabled a multimodal perspective on literacy in relation to texts materialised as page or screen. Unsworth (2001) explores the implications of this perspective for education, van Leeuwen and Humphrey (1996) look at imaging in secondary school geography, and Coffin and Derewianka (2009) consider verbiage/image relations in school history. The problem of modelling the relation between verbiage and image is explored in Martinec and Salway (2005), Royce (2007), and Martin and Rose (2008).

Halliday (1985/1989) and (2008b) outline his views on the complementarity of spoken and written discourse as far as language is concerned. As a first step in his reasoning we can note the different kinds of complexity afforded by speaking and writing. As far as lexical density is concerned, speaking tends to have fewer lexical items (content words) per ranking[1] clause than writing; with grammatical intricacy on the other hand, speaking increases the possibility of deploying many more ranking clauses per clause complex (per sentence) than writing. Then as a second step we can consider the functional pressures from which these complementary forms of complexity arise. This brings us to Halliday's most important insight into the nature of literacy, his concept of grammatical metaphor, arising from his work on the evolution of science discourse in English and Chinese (several of the seminal papers are compiled in Halliday and Martin (1993), Halliday (2004); see also Simon-Vandenbergen, Taverniers, & Ravelli, 2003).

Basically what we are concerned with here is the relationship between lexico-grammar and discourse semantics as far as making meaning is concerned. When this relationship is congruent, the various elements of semantic figures[2] map naturally onto corresponding grammatical word groups and phrases. The people,

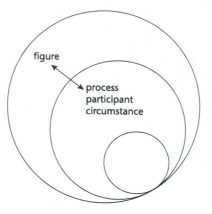

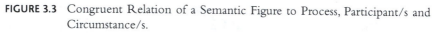

FIGURE 3.3 Congruent Relation of a Semantic Figure to Process, Participant/s and Circumstance/s.

places and things involved in figures are expressed as clause participants (nominal groups); the events in which they participate and the states they are in get expressed as processes (verbal groups); and their setting in time and place is expressed as circumstances (adverbial groups and prepositional phrases). The distribution of the congruent realisation of a semantic figure is outlined in Figure 3.3.

This is the normal pattern of realisation for spontaneous spoken discourse and informal writing in everyday story genres. Here's a slightly edited example from a recount by My Lai massacre whistle-blower Ron Ridenhour, who is relating an episode[3] from his tour of duty in Vietnam (it has a congruently expressed semantic figure):

1. Occasional lines of North Vietnamese soldiers were trudging along the trail below us.

Semantic figure	Congruent grammatical expression	
people	participant (nominal group)	*occasional lines of North Vietnamese soldiers*
event	process (verbal group)	*were trudging*
setting	circumstance (prepositional phrase)	*along the trail below us*

Less commonly in this written recount, typically in the context of evaluation, Ridenhour expresses his semantic figures as clause participants (nominal groups). Below for example he refers to the trail below his outpost as *a major route of gook infiltration.* . . . In this case the semantic figure of the North Vietnamese soldiers trudging along the trail is expressed grammatically as a participant in a relational process commenting on the significance of the trail under surveillance (*a **major** route*).

2. It was ... a major route of **gook infiltration west to the coast from the Ho Chi Minh trail.**

Semantic figure	Incongruent grammatical expression	
people, event & setting	participant (nominal group)	*gook infiltration west to the coast from the Ho Chi Minh trail*

Realised as a nominal group, the soldiers involved function as a Classifier, the event as a Thing and the setting as Qualifiers:

Classifier	Thing	Qualifiers
gook	infiltration	west to the coast from the Ho Chi Minh trail

We find the same kind of pattern later on. The semantic figure of Ridenhour's patrol landing in the rice paddy and hurrying to the relative safety of the jungle is evaluated as *a nearly perfect insertion.* Expressing himself congruently Ridenhour might have written that *the helicopters inserted the patrol almost perfectly.*

3. It had been a nearly perfect **insertion**—except for one thing.

Deictic	Epithet	Thing
a	nearly perfect	insertion

This step makes it possible to imagine an even more incongruent alternative, in which Ridenhour's evaluation of the landing is made Thing (and *the insertion* functions as Thing in a qualifying nominal group):

4. {The near **perfection** of the insertion} surprised almost everyone.

Deictic	Epithet	Thing	Qualifier
the	near	perfection	of the insertion

Here's another attitudinal example, with Ridenhour's evaluation of the jungle at the edge of the paddy expressed as a nominal group:

5. Six figures in camouflage, boonie hats, grenade-laden web-belts and full field packs, pounding heavily through thigh-high grass, lumbering toward **the relative safety of the jungle at the edge of the paddy.**

Deictic	Epithet	Thing	Qualifier
the	relative	safety	of the jungle ...

These alternative congruent and incongruent ways of expressing a semantic figure as a clause or a participant are outlined in Figure 3.4. The process

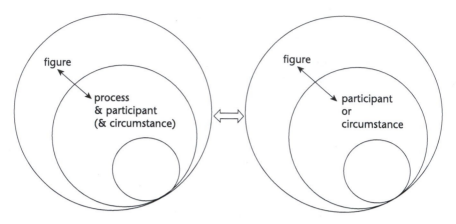

FIGURE 3.4   Alternative Congruent and Incongruent Expression of Figures.

of expressing figures as participants within clauses is referred to as grammatical **metaphor** because: (i) there are two layers of meaning involved (e.g., the grammatical expression of the landing as a participant, and underlying this the semantic configuration of an event along with the people, places and things involved); (ii) the two layers are in a figure/ground relationship with grammar in the foreground; and (iii) the semantics is symbolised by the grammar and so recoverable. With grammatical metaphor there is thus some tension between the discourse semantics and its grammatical expression. The meaning the grammar makes cannot be taken simply at face value.

In many texts, of course, events don't happen in isolation but form activity sequences reflecting the goings on in one or another field. Here's a sequence of events from Ridenhour's story, with temporal relations between most events and a causal explanation of why his patrol had to spend the night at the nearest firebase after evacuation from their observation post.

> 6.   We'd been in the air only a few minutes
> **when** the pilot changed direction
> **and** headed for the nearest firebase . . .
> **Now**, our pilots told us, we were going to be dumped there for the night
> **while** they headed off as makeshift medevacs.
> (implicit **because**) There were some wounded who had to be gotten
>   out now,
> **while** there was some light left.

In texts of this kind we observe a congruent relationship between semantic sequences of events and their realisation, clause by clause, in grammar—with conjunctions (or simple juxtaposition) marking relationships of addition, comparison, time and cause between clauses. This 'natural' expression of a semantic sequence as a series of clauses is outlined in Figure 3.5.

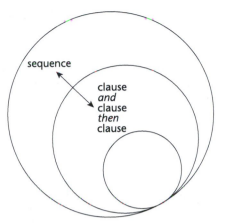

FIGURE 3.5 Congruent Realisation of Semantic Sequences to Clauses Linked by Conjunctions.

Alternatively a sequence of figures can be expressed in a single clause. There are several ways of doing this. The basic strategy is to realise the logical relation between figures as a circumstance, process or participant. With circumstances, a preposition codes the semantic link between figures, one of which is realised incongruently in the following nominal group:

after our evacuation *we were dumped at the nearest firebase.*

circumstance	participant	process	circumstance
after our evacuation	we	were dumped	at the nearest firebase

When the logical relation between figures is expressed as a process, then both figures are realised as participants:

This **was followed** *by our dumping at the nearest firebase.*

participant	process	participant
this	was *followed*	by our dumping at the nearest firebase

Logical relations can also be expressed as Things in nominal groups realising figures:

the **follow-up** *to this was our dumping at the nearest firebase.*

participant	process	participant
The *follow-up* to this	was	our dumping at the nearest firebase

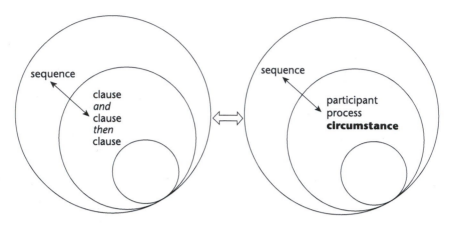

FIGURE 3.6 Incongruent Realisation of a Sequence as a Circumstance.

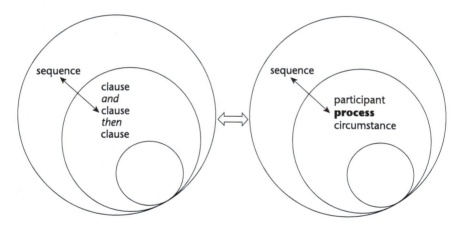

FIGURE 3.7 Incongruent Realisation of a Sequence as a Process.

Comparable patterns are found for causal connections. The following examples incongruently paraphrase the relation between the patrol's landing at the firebase and the need to evacuate wounded soldiers:

[circumstance] This was **because of** the need to evacuate some wounded soldiers.

[process] This **was caused** by the need to evacuate some wounded soldiers.

[participant] The **reason** for this was the need to evacuate some wounded soldiers.

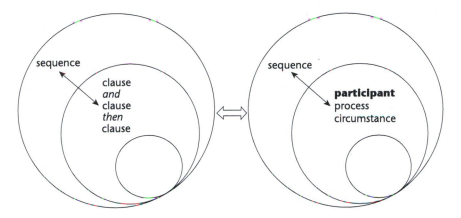

FIGURE 3.8 Incongruent Realisation of a Sequence as a Participant.

As we can see, expressing a sequence incongruently within a single clause depends on expressing one or both of the figures involved incongruently as nominal groups. In 7, to give one further example, Ridenhour explains that jungle rot is caused by a combination of incongruent qualities (of being filthy, damp and wet) plus some kind of bacteria.

7. Jungle rot, for those of you who don't know, is a kind of ulceration that appears on your skin and is caused by **a combination of filth and dampness, wetness** and some bug, I'm sure. It begins as just a little small open sore and it just spreads and spreads and spreads and gets bigger and bigger and bigger and Bernhardt had these open wounds all over his legs, could barely walk. Two days after he went into the brigade aid station he was at 2nd Surgical Hospital in Chu Lai, which is where I was then and we were all ready to come home.[4]

Realising cause as a process between participants opens up the possibility of introducing a wide range of finely nuanced consequential relations that cannot be realised by conjunctions alone. Ridenhour draws on two of these (*promote, bring about*) to explain why he is not writing to the press and electronic media in extract 8 below.

8. I feel that this action, while probably it **would promote** attention, **would not bring about** the constructive actions that the direct actions of the Congress of the United States **would (bring about).**

Note as well that realising figures as participants opens up the possibility of packaging up just the right information as causes and effects—e.g., *this action;*

attention; and *the constructive actions that the direct actions of the Congress of the United States would (bring about)* in 8 above.

Space precludes a more detailed presentation of grammatical metaphor here. Halliday's key insight is that grammatical metaphor is not a matter of style, but rather a semiotic resource that has evolved to expand the meaning potential of writing in literate cultures (by which I mean cultures that have either invented or borrowed writing and deployed it for institutional purposes of various kinds). Ideationally it enables the construal of abstract participants condensing flexible arrays of meaning as nominal groups (a crucial resource for the generation of technicality through definitions); these may in turn enter into relations of cause and effect affording explanations that cannot be realised through causally connected congruent clauses. Interpersonally, grammatical metaphor makes flexible arrays of meaning available for evaluation, since most lexical resources for attitude key on nominal groups—e.g., *it had been a **nearly perfect** insertion* above (Martin & White, 2005). Textually it facilitates the organisation of coherent information flow as flexible arrays of meaning are positioned appropriately as Theme or New and scaffold one or more higher levels of periodicity in edited writing (Martin & Rose, 2003/2007).

Halliday's work on the ways in which grammatical metaphor makes science discourse possible has inspired work on the construal of uncommon sense discourse in a range of disciplines (e.g., Martin & Wodak, 2003, Coffin, 2006, Oteiza, 2006, Achugar, 2008, on history; O'Halloran, 2005, on mathematics; Wignell, 2007a, 2007b, on social science). This research has re-invigorated the long standing dialogue between SFL and Bernstein's sociology of education, particularly in relation to his work on knowledge structure (Bernstein, 1996/2000; Christie & Martin, 2007; Christie & Maton, 2011; Muller, 2000). Analysis of grammatical metaphor has also played an important role in Critical Discourse Analysis, as part of the deconstruction of politically interested spin (Martin, 2008) and the investment of power in discourse across a range of sites (Martin, 2000).

What this research has shown is that literacy is not simply a question of the channel or medium of communication—i.e., spoken or written, and if written, page or screen. In SFL terms what is crucial here is the register variable mode, conceived, as noted above, as a recurrent higher order pattern of the meanings a particular channel affords. As corpus linguistics has long ago shown (e.g., Biber, 1986), features of 'written' modes in SFL terms are found in speaking, and features of 'spoken' modes in writing. As far as grammatical metaphor is concerned, some of us (university lecturers for example) do have to learn to talk like books; and as Ridenhour's examples above illustrate, in story genres we regularly write similarly to the way we speak. That said, Halliday is proposing that cultures without the medium of writing can neither evolve nor deploy grammatical metaphor for the ideational, interpersonal and textual effects outlined above. And this means they cannot construe the disciplinary discourses of science, social science and humanities and the technology and bureaucracy they afford (Martin, 1993c).

This in turn makes them vulnerable to colonisation by cultures wielding these semiotic tools, and where their population is small enough imperialising literacy regularly brings them to the point of extinction within one or two generations. Individuals not taking control of grammatical metaphor in a literate society are comparably disempowered. It is for reasons of this kind that SFL has been particularly concerned with the educational implications of literacy, as surveyed below.

Literacy Education

For more than three decades now, educators and functional linguists in Australia have been co-operatively engaged in action research projects designed to enhance literacy teaching and learning across all sectors of schooling. In these projects the notion of genre, defined for practical purposes as a staged goal-oriented social process, has played a central role. Hyon (1996) provides a canonical discussion of the role of genre in these initiatives in relation to the EAP and New Rhetoric traditions. Australian programs are reviewed in Christie (1992), Christie and Unsworth (2005), Feez (2002), Macken-Horarik (2002), Martin (1993a, 1998, 1999a, 1999b, 2001) and Martin and Rose (2005). Cope and Kalantzis (1993), Feez (1998), and Rose and Martin (2012) provide useful introductions; Schleppegrell (2004) develops the central themes for a North American reader-ship; and Christie and Derewianka (2008) provide a valuable development perspective. The Australian programs are often characterised as genre-based literacy initiatives because they interpret literacy teaching as an apprenticeship into written genres.

In the 1980s this research concentrated on writing in primary school, with a special focus on Indigenous and migrant Australian students who were learning English as a second language outside the home. At the time, Australia had em-braced process writing and whole language as hegemonic informing practices for its primary school literacy curriculum. This pedagogy had given rise to classrooms in which a very narrow range of writing was undertaken by students (Rothery, 1996), who were regularly invited to write on a topic of their own choice in any form they chose and where teachers played a facilitating rather than a modelling role. As a result, most students had to make use of one or two text types they were familiar with from spoken language outside the school—including short observa-tions and comments on past experience, and recounts of unproblematic sequences of events. This limited experience of writing as speaking-written-down did very little to prepare students for learning across the curriculum in primary school, for writing in the specialised subject areas of secondary school, or for dealing with various community genres they might encounter as the most fluent English speaking member of their family. Consequently, as an issue of social justice, inter-ventions were developed to broaden the range of writing undertaken, including the design of innovative pedagogy and curriculum to achieve this goal. These initiatives inspired important related work in adult migrant English teaching, reviewed by Feez (2002) and modelled in Feez (1998). In this adult sector, 'needs-based' programs were re-formulated in terms of genre, by way of establishing explicit goals that could be measured in relation to outcomes-based curricula.

In the 1990s the focus of this work was extended to writing in secondary school and the workplace, as reviewed by Veel (2006) and exemplified in Christie and Martin (1997). This involved mapping the literacy demands of disciplines and workplaces as families of genres (e.g., Coffin, 2006, on history; Macken-Horarik, 2002, and Veel, 1997, on school science; Korner, McInnes, & Rose, 2007, on science based industry) and mapping the relationships between school and workplace literacies. This disciplinary focus encouraged us to develop models of the role played by language and other modalities of communication in constructing knowledge (Christie & Martin, 2007), and the role played by evaluative language in giving value to this knowledge (Martin & White, 2005; Martin, Matruglio, & Maton, 2010).

By the noughts, this writing research had been complemented by a focus on reading, which is particularly foregrounded in Rose's *Reading to Learn* initiatives[5] (Rose, 2004, 2005, 2006, 2007, 2008, 2010; see also Martin, 2006; Martin & Rose, 2005, 2007; Rose & Martin, 2012). This work pays close attention to global micro-interactions between teachers and students around texts, including innovative work on the design of specialised cycles of localised interaction for reading instruction. This decade also featured Sydney School initiatives in relation to teaching English for Academic Purposes (EAP) in tertiary sectors of education, both face-to-face and online (e.g., Mahboob, Dreyfus, Humphrey, & Martin, 2010).

Fundamental to all of this action research was mapping the relevant literacy curriculum as a system of genres, taking into account the key genres through which the knowledge of a particular sector of schooling was construed. An exemplary typology for secondary school history genres is outlined in Figure 3.9 (after Coffin, 1997, 2000, 2006; Martin, 2002; Martin & Rose, 2008). In this diagram a taxonomy of secondary school history genres is presented. This outline has been scaled from top to bottom with respect to the distance between various written history genres and spoken genres with which students could reasonably be expected to be familiar; the scale takes into account factors such as temporal and causal organisation, external or internal conjunctive relations, generic and specific participants, and grammatical metaphor (Martin & Rose, 2003/2007). This diagram can be read as a network of choices, with arrows pointing to important distinctions in social function and semantic orientation, beginning for example with the distinction between texts that are chronologically organised according to the sequence of events they describe ('field time') and those that are rhetorically organised in terms of an unfolding argument.

The cline from genres that resemble familiar spoken genres in some respects to more specialised written academic genres was used as the basis for building learner

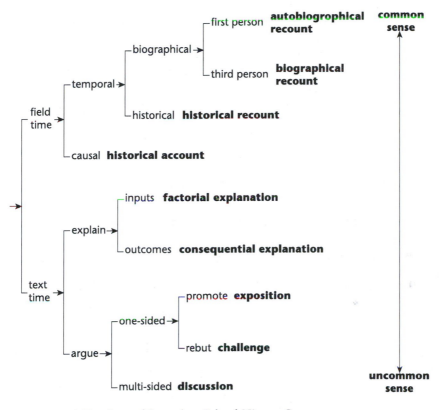

FIGURE 3.9 A Typology of Secondary School History Genres.

pathways, in order to manage an accumulating control of reading and writing in each discipline. A spiral curriculum of this nature is outlined in Figure 3.10 below for the history genres in Figure 3.9. Pathways of this kind make it possible for teachers to plan across phases and even across sectors of education for what can be assumed from previous learning, and for students to move from one genre to another without having to take too much on board. This means a 'zone of proximal development' can be established, with teachers providing the 'scaffolding' students need to develop their literacy repertoire; Gibbons' work on bridging discourses (e.g., 2002, 2006, 2009) underscores the affinity between Sydney School pedagogy and neo-Vygotskyan paradigms that sustain a mentoring relation between teachers and students. (For discussion of the relation of everyday discourse to the specialised discourse of disciplines in school and professional contexts see Christie & Martin, 2007; Christie & Maton, 2011.)

Alongside mapping curriculum, genre theory was also used to design pedagogy, drawing on insights into spoken language development in the home (Halliday, 2003; Painter, 1984, 1986, 1989, 1991, 1996, 1999, 2000, 2003a, 2003b, 2004, 2009). Inspired by Painter's concept of 'guidance through interaction in the context of

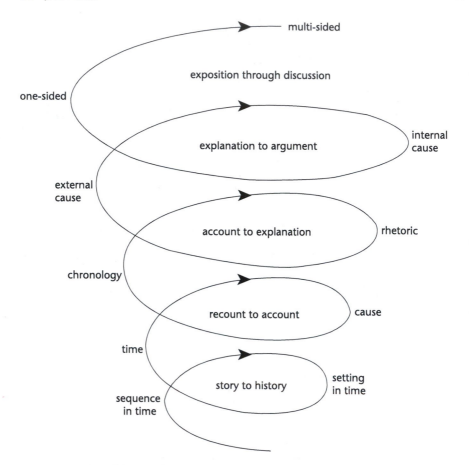

multi-sided

exposition through discussion

one-sided

explanation to argument

internal
cause

external
cause

account to explanation

rhetoric

chronology

recount to account

cause

time

story to history

setting
in time

sequence
in time

FIGURE 3.10 Spiral Curriculum (Learner Pathway) for History Genres.

shared experience', Rothery (1989, 1996) led a group of teachers and teacher/ linguists in the design of the teaching/learning cycle outlined in Figure 3.11 (Rothery, 1996). The cycle features a deconstruction stage, where models of the target genre are presented, a joint construction stage where teachers scribe another model text in the same genre based on suggestions from students, and an individual construction stage where students write in genre for the first time on their own. All stages involve setting context and building up field (i.e., shared knowledge about content) and a critical orientation to the genre (typically informed by CDA with respect to a written text's function in the culture). More recently this cycle has been further developed, as noted above, with an orientation to reading by Rose (Martin, 2006; Martin & Rose, 2005, 2007; Rose, 2004; Rose & Martin, 2012). Martin (1999b) discusses the development of this curriculum genre for teaching writing in relation to Bernstein's (1996) work on the strength of boundaries between topics and the range of interactions in which teachers and students engage.

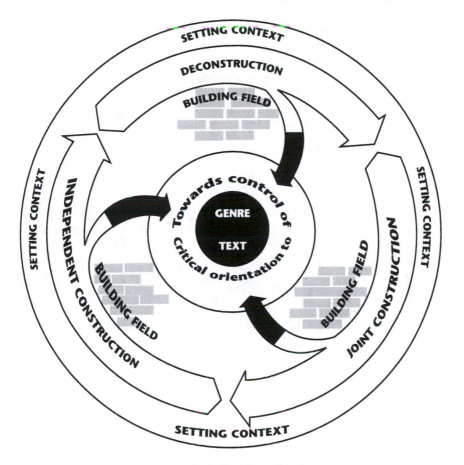

FIGURE 3.11 Teaching/Learning Cycle for Mentoring Genre.

Another distinctive feature of the pedagogy outlined here has been the explicit use of knowledge about language (hereafter KAL) as teachers apprentice students into literate modes (Rothery, 1989). It was clear from Halliday and Painter's work on language development in the home before school that talk about language was a natural part of scaffolding spoken modes (cf. Halliday, 1993; Painter, 1999). Unfortunately, in Australia, radical progressivist (now presenting themselves as constructivist) literacy paradigms such as process writing and whole language had removed all knowledge about language from school curricula, arguing that it was useless (as research had supposedly shown) and harmful (since it took time way from real language learning)—often pointing to claims made about how the mother tongue is learned at home by scholars who had never carefully considered the actual nature of caregiver/child interactions as Halliday and Painter had done. Accordingly we had to begin from scratch, starting at the level of genre, to reintroduce KAL. We had considerable success in primary school, as far as names for genres and their stages was concerned. Progress at the levels of register, discourse semantics, lexicogrammar and phonology/graphology has been much slower—especially with respect to functional grammar, where unfamiliar terminology (i.e., something more than the name of a few word classes such as noun, verb and adjective) has created opportunities for politicians, progressivist/constructivist curriculum designers, formal linguists with misgivings about SFL and the media to undermine implementations. How intriguing it is to have worked on literacy teaching in a culture where professionally informed talk about language is taboo!

The absence of knowledge about language in successive generations of curricula and teacher training not only has a crippling effect on the apprenticeship of students into literate modes but on the apprenticeship of teachers into re-designed literacy pedagogy as well. A common response to in-service programs emphasising the importance of scaffolding in relation to pedagogy such as that modelled in Figure 3.11 involves teachers claiming that they already interact with their students, in just the ways that are being promoted as a change in practice. In almost all cases what this means is that there is indeed dialogue in these teachers' classrooms—but since they have never audio/visually recorded their own teaching practice and analysed it for exchange structure and genre (as undertaken in Christie, 2002), they cannot actually bring to consciousness the kind of interaction through which they are engaging their students. This is an ongoing challenge for genre-based literacy programs where both what students are expected to read and write and the classroom practices through which it is taught are ideally subjected to informed systemic functional semiotic analysis across an appropriate range of strata and metafunctions.

By way of closing this discussion it may be useful to position the Sydney School literacy project in relation to alternative positions as far as pedagogic discourse is concerned (cf. Alexander, 2000, for an informative world tour of culture and pedagogy). Bernstein's (1990, pp. 213–214) topology of theories of instruction has been adapted as Figure 3.12. He outlines the key axes as follows:

> The vertical dimension would indicate whether the theory of instruction privileged relations internal to the individual, where the focus would be *intra-individual,* or ... relations *between* social groups (inter-group). In the first case ... the theory would be concerned to explain the conditions for changes within the individual, whereas in the second the theory would be concerned to explain the conditions for changes in the relation between social groups. The horizontal dimension would indicate whether the theory articulated a pedagogic practice emphasising a logic of acquisition or ... a logic of transmission. In the case of a logic of acquisition ... the acquirer is active in regulating an *implicit* facilitating practice. In the case of a logic of

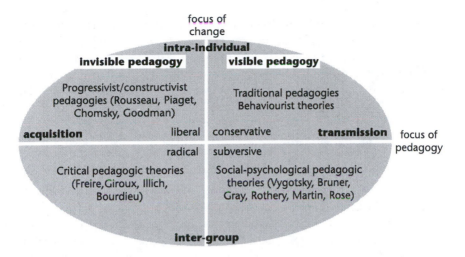

FIGURE 3.12   Types of Pedagogy (after Bernstein, 1990).

transmission the emphasis is upon *explicit* effective ordering of the discourse
to be acquired, by the transmitter.

(Bernstein, 1990, pp. 213–214)

Bernstein also comments (1990, p. 73): "It is a matter of interest that this top
right-hand quadrant is regarded as conservative but has **often produced very
innovative and radical acquirers**. The bottom right-hand quadrant shows a
radical realisation of an apparently conservative pedagogic practice . . . each theory
will carry its own conditions of contestation, 'resistance', subversion."[6] As the
matrix implies, our approach in the lower right-hand quadrant has always been a
visible and interventionist one (Painter & Martin, 1986; Hasan & Martin, 1989[7];
Cope & Kalantzis, 1993)—with a relatively strong focus on the transmission of
identified discourse competences and on the empowerment of otherwise
disenfranchised groups in relation to this transmission. As such it resonates with
the social constructivist position articulated by Mercer and his colleagues in
Britain (1994, 1995, 2000); at the same time it has to be said that American
implementations of neo-Vygotskyan ideals seem to slide in that culture rather
seamlessly into a co-opting upper left-hand progressivist quadrant (see for example
Wells' social constructivist manifesto[8] in Appendix I of Wells, 1999).

Disposition to Teach and Learn

As will be clear from the discussion above, Sydney School genre-based literacy
programs are distinctive in that they are informed by a conception of SFL as an
appliable linguistics—appliable in this case to literacy apprenticeship in education.

It has been driven by a concern for social justice, inspired by Halliday's conception of linguistics as an ideologically committed form of social action. Throughout, the project has involved what is generally referred to as action research, bringing together the work of educators, functional linguists and Bernsteinian sociologists of education in a transdisciplinary initiative undertaken to redistribute the discursive resources of post-Fordist capitalism by changing literacy pedagogy and curricula. Obviously, with a goal of this kind, work is ongoing, in an ever increasing range of sites around the world.

As a final word, let me invoke professorial privilege with a couple of anecdotes. In March 2010, I attended for the first time the annual TESOL (Teaching English to Speakers of Other Languages) convention, held in Boston, and faithfully attended all the plenary sessions and as many parallel sessions as I could fit in. Except for the SFL-informed colloquium in which I was involved and my own luminary lecture, the word teaching was never mentioned. Later that year, in June, I attended an e-learning conference held at City University Hong Kong. Once again, in the presentations I attended other than my own, the word teaching was never mentioned; everyone I complained to found it hard to imagine successfully promoting an e-teaching conference. Overwhelmingly, the focus was on learners interacting, face-to-face or online, with no attention paid to teachers' agentive role—as if that is all it takes to learn.

Let me close therefore by drawing on some words of wisdom from two of my most inspirational teachers. First Halliday, drawing on his own language development research in relation to work by Lemke:

> ... just as children are predisposed to learn, so parents, and "others", are pre-disposed to teach ... Lemke (1984) has shown that a theory of learning must take account of the human predisposition to teach—as well as of the teaching function, in a broader sense, that is a feature of the environment as a whole.
> *(Halliday, 2003, p. 338)*

And second Lemke, for the published version of parts of the sadly unpublished material Halliday is referring to:

> ... a back-up strategy has survived in the many species that are specifically *social*: the same lifelong chemistry-plus-environment strategy that results in children who are primed to learn also results in adults who are primed to teach. The selective sensitivity of the child gets tuned to a reliable source of information, reliable because that source—other people in its community— has similarly evolved to provide just that kind of information (e.g., about the local language in use in the community in that generation). The child sets off a teacher-response in adults just as adults set off a learner-response in children (this is stronger the younger the children are).
> *(Lemke, 1995, p. 160)*

Orienting along these lines, one of the main contributions of the Sydney School to literacy education has been to get teachers teaching again, taking advantage of their disposition to teach in tandem with students' disposition to learn. This, to be clear, is not a return to the traditional upper right-hand quadrant of the pedagogy topology in Figure 3.12. Rather it involves a radical change of practice as outlined above, for which teachers are not prepared in pre-service training and for which very scarce resources are available for in-service support. And to be successful such a change involves implementing the principle of 'guidance though interaction in the context for shared experience' for teachers as well as their students—and thus providing the degrees of scaffolding teachers need in order to become authoritative literacy mentors for every student in their class.

We do need to keep in mind however that practices can change; in Australia at least, teachers have made quite radical changes before. Progressivist educators were able, in the 1970s and 1980s, to persuade them that what Halliday has aptly called 'benevolent inertia' was a more suitable role for them to play than the direct teaching. They learned to bite their tongues, as one Australian process writing manual reports:

> One of the greatest temptations was to tell children what and how to write. I had to literally bite my tongue and remember that children can think for themselves.
>
> *(Scott, 1983, p. 1)*

They also learned to apologise for any slip-ups in their implementation of the process writing curriculum regimen. As one of the Year 2 teachers Cate Poynton and I were observing in the mid-1980s stated, immediately upon giving some advice to students about some writing they were about to undertake: "I know I'm not supposed to tell them anything, but after all, I **am** their teacher!"

The challenge of course is to get off the pendulum, which lurches back and forth in so many cultures between progressivist/constructivist and traditional approaches (the upper left and right quads of Bernstein's topology[9]). There are alternatives, if we are talking about social justice and democratic outcomes—and if we are serious. SFL-informed conceptions of literacy and of writing pedagogy/ curriculum are one alternative—a serious one.

Notes

1   Halliday's distinction of hypotaxis and embedding is crucial to the characterisations of complexity reviewed here. By ranking clauses he means clauses that are not embedded in or as nominal or in adverbial groups (*the champion* [[*who lost*]], [[*what he lost*]], *served faster* [[*than the second seed*]]); hypotactic clauses, whether expanding (*he lost because* **he** **served poorly**) or projected (*he thought* **he'd win**), are considered dependent but not embedded (and are therefore ranking clauses).

2 The terms figure and sequence are taken from Halliday and Matthiessen (1999); English grammar terms are from Halliday and Matthiessen (2004).

3 Ridenhour texts in this Chapter are taken from this website: http://www2.iath. virginia.edu/sixties/HTML_docs/Texts/Narrative/Ridenhour_Jesus_01.html

4 http://www.law.umkc.edu/faculty/projects/ftrials/mylai/ridenhour_ltr.html

5 For web access go to http://www.readingtolearn.com.au/

6 At the time of writing this, Bernstein was unaware of our pedagogic initiatives; developing acquaintance is documented in Christie (1999).

7 See especially the papers by Painter, Rothery, and Jones et al. therein.

8 To be fair, there are many places in Wells' book (and in Wells, 2002) where teacher-centred activities are acknowledged—but the teacher is completely elided from the manifesto. Brophy (2002) provides a balanced overview of social constructivist teaching initiatives. Muller (2000) critiques the very disturbing supposedly 'progressive' implementation of social constructivist principles in South Africa after apartheid (see also Taylor, Muller, & Vinjevold, 2003); Hattie's (2009) meta-analysis confirms the damage done by invisible pedagogy done around the world.

9 Bernstein's (1990) suggestion that what we are really looking at here is a struggle between the pedagogies of the old and new middle class should give every educator pause.

References

Achugar, M. (2008). *What we remember: The construction of memory in military discourse.* Amsterdam, The Netherlands: Benjamins.

Alexander, R. (2000). *Culture & pedagogy: International comparisons in primary education.* Oxford, UK: Blackwell.

Bateman, J. (2008). *Multimodality and genre: A foundation for the systematic analysis of multimodal documents.* London, UK: Palgrave Macmillan.

Bateman, J. (2011). The decomposability of semiotic modes. K. O'Halloran & B. Smith (Eds.), *Multimodal studies: Exploring issues and domains.* London, UK: Routledge.

Bednarek, M., & Martin, J. R. (Eds.). (2010). *New discourse on language: Functional perspectives on multimodality, identity and affiliation.* London, UK: Continuum.

Bernstein, B. (1990). *Class, codes and control: Vol. 4. The structuring of pedagogic discourse.* London, UK: Routledge.

Bernstein, B. (1996). *Pedagogy, symbolic control and identity: Theory, research, critique.* London, UK: Taylor & Francis. [Revised Edition, 2000]

Biber, D. (1986). Spoken and written textual dimensions in English: Resolving the contradictory findings. *Language, 62*(2), 384–414.

Brophy, J. (Ed.). (2002). *Social constructivist teaching: Affordances and constraints.* London, UK: Elsevier.

Caffarel, A., Martin, J. R., & Matthiessen, C. M. I. M. (Eds.). (2004). *Language typology: A functional perspective.* Amsterdam, The Netherlands: Benjamins.

Christie, F. (1992). Literacy in Australia. *Annual Review of Applied Linguistics, 12,* 142–155.

Christie, F. (Ed.). (1999). *Pedagogy and the shaping of consciousness: Linguistic and social processes.* London, UK: Cassell.

Christie, F. (2002). *Classroom discourse analysis.* London, UK: Continuum.

Christie, F., & Derewianka, B. (2008). *School discourse: Learning to write across the years of schooling.* London, UK: Continuum.

Christie, F., & Martin, J. R. (Eds.). (1997). *Genre and institutions: Social processes in the workplace and school.* London, UK: Cassell.

Christie, F., & Martin, J. R. (Eds.). (2007). *Language, knowledge and pedagogy: Functional linguistic and sociological perspectives.* London, UK: Cassell.

Christie, F., & Maton, K. (Eds.). (2011). *Disciplinarity: Functional linguistic and sociological perspectives.* London, UK: Continuum.

Christie, F., & Unsworth, L. (2005). Developing dimensions of an educational linguistics. R. Hasan, C. M. I. M. Matthiessen, & J. Webster (Eds.), *Continuing discourse on language: A functional perspective* (pp. 217–250). London, UK: Equinox.

Coffin, C. (1997). Constructing and giving value to the past: An investigation into secondary school history. In F. Christie & J. R. Martin (Eds.), *Genre and institutions: Social processes in the workplace and school* (pp. 196–230). London, UK: Cassell.

Coffin, C. (2000). Defending and challenging interpretations of the past. *Revista Canaria de Estudios Ingleses, 40,* 135–154.

Coffin, C. (2006). *Historical discourse: The language of time, cause and evaluation.* London, UK: Continuum.

Coffin, C., & Derewianka, B. (2009). Multimodal layout in school history books: The texturing of historical interpretation. In G. Thompson & G. Forey (Eds.), *Text-type and texture* (pp. 191–215). London, UK: Equinox.

Coffin, C., Donohue, J., & North, S. (2009). *Exploring English grammar: From formal to functional.* London, UK: Routledge.

Cope, W., & Kalantzis, M. (Eds.). (1993). *The powers of literacy: A genre approach to teaching literacy.* London, UK: Falmer Press, & Pittsburg, PA: University of Pittsburg Press.

Dreyfus, S., Hood, S., & Stenglin, M. (Eds.). (2011). *Semiotic margins: Meaning in multimodalities* (pp. 243–270). London, UK: Continuum.

Eggins, S. (1994). *An introduction to systemic functional linguistics.* London, UK: Pinter.

Feez, S. (1998). *Text-based syllabus design.* Sydney, Australia: National Centre for English Language Teaching and Research (NELTR), Macquarie University.

Feez, S. (2002). Heritage and innovation in second language education. In A. M. Johns (Ed.), *Genre in the classroom: Applying theory and research to practice* (pp. 43–69). Mahwah, NJ: Lawrence Erlbaum.

Gebhart, M., & Martin, J. R. (2011). Grammar and literacy learning. In D. Fisher & D. Lapp (Eds.), *Handbook of research on teaching the English language arts* (pp. 297–304). Mahwah, NJ: Erlbaum.

Gibbons, P. (2002). *Scaffolding language, scaffolding learning: Teaching second language learners in the mainstream classroom.* Portsmouth, NH: Heinemann.

Gibbons, P. (2006). *Bridging discourse in the ESL classroom: Students, teachers and researchers.* London, UK: Continuum.

Gibbons, P. (2009). *English learners academic literacy and thinking: Learning in the challenge zone.* Portsmouth, NH: Heinemann.

Halliday, M. A. K. (1985). *Spoken and written language.* Geelong, Australia: Deakin University Press [Republished by Oxford University Press, 1989].

Halliday, M. A. K. (1993). Towards a language-based theory of learning. *Linguistics and Education, 5*(2), 93–116.

Halliday, M. A. K. (2003). *The language of early childhood.* In J. J. Webster (Ed.), *Collected works of M. A. K. Halliday* (Vol. 4). London, UK: Continuum.

Halliday, M. A. K. (2004). *The language of science.* In J. J. Webster (Ed.), *Collected works of M. A. K. Halliday* (Vol. 5). London, UK: Continuum.

Halliday, M. A. K. (2008a). Working with meaning: Towards an appliable linguistics. In J. J. Webster (Ed.), *Meaning in context: Strategies for implementing intelligent applications of language studies* (pp. 7–23). London, UK: Continuum.

Halliday, M. A. K. (2008b). *Complementarities in language*. Beijing, China: Commercial Press.

Halliday, M. A. K. (2009). *The essential Halliday* (J. J. Webster, Ed.). London, UK Continuum.

Halliday, M. A. K., & Hasan, R. (2006). Retrospective on SFL and Literacy. In R. Whittaker, M. O'Donnell, & A. McCabe (Eds.), *Language and literacy: Functional approaches* (pp. 15–44). London, UK: Continuum.

Halliday, M. A. K., & Martin, J. R. (1993). *Writing science: Literacy and discursive power*. London, UK: Falmer.

Halliday, M. A. K., & Matthiessen, C. M. I. M. (1999). *Construing experience through language: A language-based approach to cognition*. London, UK: Cassell.

Halliday, M. A. K., & Matthiessen, C. M. I. M. (2004). *An introduction to functional grammar* (3rd ed.). London, UK: Edward Arnold.

Halliday, M. A. K., & Matthiessen, C. M. I. M. (2009). *Systemic functional grammar: A first step into theory*. Beijing, China: Higher Education Press.

Hasan, R., & Martin, J. R. (Eds.). (1989). *Language development: Learning language, learning culture* [Meaning and choice in language: Vol. 27]. Norwood, NJ: Ablex.

Hasan, R., Matthiessen, C. M. I. M. & Webster, J. J. (Eds.). (2005a). *Continuing discourse on language* (Vol. 1). London, UK: Equinox.

Hasan, R., Matthiessen, C. M. I. M. & Webster, J. J. (Eds.). (2005b). *Continuing discourse on language* (Vol. 2). London, UK: Equinox.

Hattie, J. A. C. (2009). *Visible learning: A synthesis of over 800 meta-analyses relating to achievement*. London, UK: Routledge.

Hyon, S. (1996). Genre in three traditions: Implications for ESL. *TESOL Quarterly, 30*(4), 693–722.

Johns, A. M. (Ed.). (2002). *Genre in the classroom: Applying theory and research to practice*. Mahwah, NJ: Lawrence Erlbaum.

Korner, H., McInnes, D., & Rose, D. (2007). *Science literacy*. Sydney, Australia: NSW Adult Migrant Education Service.

Kress, G., & van Leeuwen, T. (1996). *Reading images: The grammar of visual design*. London, UK: Routledge [Revised 2nd ed., 2006].

Lemke, J. L. (1995). *Textual politics: Discourse and social dynamics*. London, UK: Taylor & Francis.

Macken-Horarik, M. (2002). 'Something to shoot for': A systemic functional approach to teaching genre in secondary school science. A. M. Johns (Ed.), *Genres in the classroom: Applying theory and research to practice* (pp. 17–42). Mahwah, NJ: Lawrence Erlbaum.

Mahboob, A., Dreyfus, S., Humphrey, S., & Martin, J. R. (2010). Appliable linguistics and English language teaching: The Scaffolding Literacy in Adult and Tertiary Environments (SLATE) Project. In A. Mahboob & N. Knight (Eds.), *Appliable linguistics* (pp. 25–43). London, UK: Continuum.

Martin, J. R. (1993a). Genre and literacy: Modelling context in educational linguistics. *Annual Review of Applied Linguistics, 13*, 141–172.

Martin, J. R. (1993b). Life as a noun. In M. A. K. Halliday & J. R. Martin (Eds.), *Writing science: Literacy and discursive power* (pp. 221–267). London, UK: Falmer.

Martin, J. R. (1993c). Technology, bureaucracy and schooling: Discursive resources and control. *Cultural Dynamics, 6*(1), 84–130.

Martin, J. R. (1998). Practice into theory: Catalysing change. In S. Hunston (Ed.), *Language at work* (pp. 151–167). Clevedon, UK: Multilingual Matters.

Martin, J. R. (1999a). Linguistics and the consumer: Theory in practice. *Linguistics and Education, 9*(3), 409–446.

Martin, J. R. (1999b). Mentoring semogenesis: 'Genre-based' literacy pedagogy. In F. Christie (Ed.), *Pedagogy and the shaping of consciousness: Linguistic and social processes* (pp. 123–155). London, UK: Cassell.

Martin, J. R. (2000). Close reading: Functional linguistics as a tool for critical analysis. In L. Unsworth (Ed.), *Researching language in schools and communities: Functional linguistics approaches* (pp. 275–303). London, UK: Cassell.

Martin, J. R. (2001). Giving the game away: Explicitness, diversity and genre-based literacy in Australia. In R. de Cilla, H. Krumm, & R. Wodak (Eds.), *Loss of communication in the information age* (pp. 155–174). Vienna, Austria: Verlag der Osterreichischen Akadamie der Wissenschaften.

Martin, J. R. (2002). Writing history: Construing time and value in discourses of the past. In M. J. Schleppegrell & M. C. Colombi (Eds.), *Developing advanced literacy in first and second languages: Meaning with power* (pp. 87–118). Mahwah, NJ: Lawrence Erlbaum.

Martin, J. R. (2003). Making history: Grammar for explanation. In J. R. Martin & R. Wodak (Eds.), *Re/reading the past: Critical and functional perspectives on discourses of history* (pp. 19–57). Amsterdam, The Netherlands: Benjamins.

Martin, J. R. (2006). Metadiscourse: Designing interaction in genre-based literacy programs. In R. Whittaker, M. O'Donnell, & A. McCabe (Eds.), *Language and literacy: Functional approaches* (pp. 95–122). London, UK: Continuum.

Martin, J. R. (2008). Incongruent and proud: De/vilifying 'nominalisation'. *Discourse & Society, 19*(6), 801–810.

Martin, J. R. (2009). Genres and language learning: A social semiotic perspective [Special issue on 'Foreign/second language acquisition as meaning-making: A systemic-functional approach', edited by H. Byrnes]. *Linguistics and Education, 20*, 10–21.

Martin, J. R., Matruglio, E., & Maton, K. (2010). Historical cosmologies: Epistemology and axiology in Australian secondary school history. *Revista Signos, 43*(74), 433–463.

Martin, J. R., & Rose, D. (2003). *Working with discourse: Meaning beyond the clause*. London, UK: Continuum [2nd rev. ed., 2007].

Martin, J. R., & Rose, D. (2005). Designing literacy pedagogy: Scaffolding asymmetries. In R. Hasan, C. M. I. M. Matthiessen, & J. Webster (Eds.), *Continuing discourse on language* (pp. 251–280). London, UK: Equinox.

Martin, J. R., & Rose, D. (2007). Interacting with text: The role of dialogue in learning to read and write. *Foreign Languages in China, 4*(5), 66–80.

Martin, J. R. & Rose, D. (2008). *Genre relations: Mapping culture*. London, UK: Equinox.

Martin, J. R., & White, P. R. R. (2005). *The language of evaluation: Appraisal in English*. London, UK: Palgrave.

Martin, J. R., & Wodak, R. (Eds.). (2003). *Re/reading the past: Critical and functional perspectives on discourses of history*. Amsterdam, The Netherlands: Benjamins.

Martinec, R. (2000). Types of process in action. *Semiotica, 130*(3/4), 243–268.

Martinec, R. (2004). Gestures which co-occur with speech as a systematic resource: The realisation of experiential meaning in indexes. *Social Semiotics, 14*(2), 193–213.

Martinec, R. (2005). Topics in multimodality. In R. Hasan, C. M. I. M. Matthiessen & J. Webster (Eds.), *Continuing discourse on language* (Vol. 1, pp. 157–181). London, UK: Equinox.

Martinec, R., & Salway, A. (2005). Image-text relations in new (and old) media. *Visual Communication, 4*(3), 337–371.

Martinec, R., & van Leeuwen, T. (2009). *The language of new media design*. London, UK: Routledge.

Mercer, N. (1994). Neo-Vygotskyan theory and classroom education. In R. Stierer & J. Maybin (Eds.), *Language, literacy and learning in educational practice* (pp. 92–110). Clevedon, UK: Multilingual Matters.

Mercer, N. (1995). *The guided construction of knowledge: Talk amongst teachers and learners.* Clevedon, UK: Multilingual Matters.

Mercer, N. (2000). *Words and minds: How we use language to work together.* London, UK: Routledge.

Muller, J. (2000). *Reclaiming knowledge: Social theory, curriculum and education policy.* London, UK: Routledge.

O'Halloran, K. (Ed.). (2004). *Multimodal discourse analysis: Systemic functional perspectives.* London, UK: Continuum.

O'Halloran, K. (2005). *Mathematical discourse: Language, symbolism and visual images.* London, UK: Continuum.

Oteiza, T. (2006). *El Discurso Pedagogico de la historia: un analisis lingusitico sobre la construccion ideologica de la historia de Chile* (1970–2001). Santiago, Chile: Frasis.

Painter, C. (1984). *Into the mother tongue: A case study of early language development.* London, UK: Pinter.

Painter, C. (1986). The role of interaction in learning to speak and learning to write. In C. Painter & J. R. Martin (Eds.), *Writing to mean: Teaching genres across the curriculum* (pp. 62–97). Applied Linguistics Association of Australia.

Painter, C. (1989). Learning language: A functional view of language development. In R. Hasan & J. R. Martin (Eds.), *Language development: Learning language, learning culture* (Vol. 27, pp. 18–65). Norwood, NJ: Ablex.

Painter, C. (1991). *Learning the mother tongue* (2nd ed.). Geelong, Australia: Deakin University Press.

Painter, C. (1996). The development of language as a resource for thinking: A linguistic view of learning. In R. Hasan & G. Williams (Eds.), *Literacy in society* (pp. 50–85). London, UK: Longman.

Painter, C. (1999). *Learning through language in early childhood.* London, UK: Cassell.

Painter, C. (2000). Researching first language development in children. In L. Unsworth (Ed.), *Researching language in schools and communities: Functional linguistics approaches* (pp. 65–86). London, UK: Cassell.

Painter, C. (2003a). The use of a metaphorical mode of meaning in early language development. A. M. Simon-Vandenbergen, M. Taverniers, & L. Ravelli (Eds.), *Metaphor: Systemic-functional perspectives* (pp. 151–167). Amsterdam, The Netherlands: Benjamins.

Painter, C. (2003b). Developing attitude: An ontogenetic perspective on APPRAISAL [Special issue on 'Negotiating heteroglossia: Social perspectives on evaluation', edited by M. Macken-Horarik & J. R. Martin]. *Text, 23*(2), 183–210.

Painter, C. (2004). The 'interpersonal first' principle in child language development. In G. Williams & A. Lukin (Eds.), *Language development: Functional perspectives on species and individuals* (pp. 133–153). London, UK: Continuum.

Painter, C. (2009). Language development. In M. A. K. Halliday & J. J. Webster (Eds.), *Continuum companion to systemic functional linguistics* (pp. 87–103). London, UK: Continuum Press.

Painter, C., & Martin, J. R. (Eds.). (1986). *Writing to mean: Teaching genres across the curriculum.* Applied Linguistics Association of Australia.

Painter, C., Martin, J. R., & Unsworth, L. (2013). *Reading visual narratives.* London, UK: Equinox.

Pearce, J., Thornton, G., & Mackay, D. (1989). The programme in linguistics and language teaching, University College London, 1964–1971. In R. Hasan & J. R. Martin (Eds.), *Language development: Learning language, learning culture* (Vol. 27, pp. 329–368). Norwood, NJ: Ablex.

Rose, D. (2004). Sequencing and pacing of the hidden curriculum: How indigenous children are left out of the chain. In J. Muller, A. Morais, & B. Davies (Eds.), *Reading Bernstein, Researching Bernstein* (pp. 145–170). London, UK: Routledge Falmer.

Rose, D. (2005). Democratising the classroom: A literacy pedagogy for the new generation. *Journal of Education, 37*, 127–164.

Rose, D. (2006). Literacy and equality. In A. Simpson (Ed.), *Proceedings of the National Conference on Future Directions in Literacy* (pp. 188–203). Sydney, Australia: University of Sydney. Available from www.edsw.usyd.edu.au/schools_teachers/prof_dev/resources/Lit_proceedings.pdf

Rose, D. (2007). Towards a reading based theory of teaching. Plenary paper in *Proceedings 33rd International Systemic Functional Congress (2006)*. Available from http://www.pucsp.br/isfc/proceedings/

Rose, D. (2008). Writing as linguistic mastery: The development of genre-based literacy pedagogy. In R. Beard, D. Myhill, J. Riley, & M. Nystrand (Eds.), *Handbook of writing development* (pp. 151–166). London, UK: Sage.

Rose, D. (2010). Beating educational inequality with an integrated reading pedagogy. In F. Christie & A. Simpson (Eds.), *Literacy and social responsibility: Multiple perspectives*. London, UK: Equinox.

Rose, D., & Martin, J. R. (2012). *Learning to write, reading to learn: Genre, knowledge and pedagogy in the Sydney School*. London, UK: Equinox.

Rothery, J. (1989). Learning about language. In R. Hasan & J. R. Martin (Eds.), *Language development: Learning language, learning culture* (Vol. 27, pp. 199–256). Norwood, NJ: Ablex.

Rothery, J. (1996). Making changes: Developing an educational linguistics. In R. Hasan & G. Williams (Eds.), *Literacy in society* (pp. 86–123). London, UK: Longman.

Royce, T. (2007). Intersemiotic complementarity: A framework for multimodal analysis. In T. Royce & W. Bowcher (Eds.), *New directions in the analysis of multimodal discourse* (pp. 63–11). Mahwah, NJ: Lawrence Erlbaum.

Royce, T., & Bowcher, W. (2007). *New directions in the analysis of multimodal discourse*. Mahwah, NJ: Lawrence Erlbaum.

Schleppegrell, M. J. (2004). *The language of schooling: A functional linguistic perspective*. Mahwah, NJ: Erlbaum.

Scott, D. (1983). *A manual for the writing teacher*. Melbourne, Australia: Centre for Study of Urban Education, La Trobe University.

Simon-Vandenbergen, A. M., Taverniers, M., & Ravelli, L. (Eds.). (2003). Grammatical metaphor: Views from systemic functional linguistics. In E. F. Konrad Koerner (Series Ed.), *Amsterdam Studies in the theory and history of linguistic science*. Amsterdam, The Netherlands: Benjamins.

Stenglin, M. (2008a). Space Odyssey: Towards a social semiotic model of 3D space. *Visual Communication, 8*(1), 235–264.

Stenglin, M. (2008b). Olympism: How a Bonding icon gets its "charge". In L. Unsworth (Ed.), *Multimodal semiotics: Functional analysis in contexts of education*. London, UK: Continuum.

Taylor, N., Muller, J., & Vinjevold, P. (2003). *Getting school working: Research and systemic school reform in South Africa*. Cape Town, South Africa: Pearson Education.

Thompson, G. (2004). *Introducing functional grammar* (2nd ed.). London, UK: Arnold

Unsworth, L. (2001). *Teaching multiliteracies across the curriculum: Changing contexts of text and image in classroom practice*. Buckingham, UK: Open University Press.

Unsworth, L. (2008). *New literacies and the English curriculum: Multimodal perspectives*. London, UK: Continuum.

van Leeuwen, T. (1999). *Speech, music, sound*. London, UK: Macmillan.

van Leeuwen, T., & Humphrey, S. (1996). On learning to look through a geographer's eyes. In R. Hasan & G. Williams (Eds.), *Literacy in society* (pp. 29–49). London, UK: Longman.

Veel, R. (1997). Learning how to mean—scientifically speaking: Apprenticeship into scientific discourse in the secondary school. In F. Christie & J. R. Martin (Eds.), *Genre and institutions: Social processes in the workplace and school* (pp. 161–195). London, UK: Cassell.

Veel, R. (2006). The 'Write it Right' project. In R. Whittaker, M. O'Donnell, & A. McCabe (Eds.), *Language and literacy: Functional approaches* (pp. 66–92). London, UK: Continuum.

Ventola, E., & Guijarro, A. J. M. (Eds.). (2009). *The world told and the world shown: Multisemiotic issues*. London, UK: Palgrave Macmillan.

Webster, J. J. (Ed.). (2009). *A companion for systemic functional linguistics*. London, UK: Continuum.

Wells, G. (1999). *Dialogic inquiry: Toward a sociocultural practice and theory of education*. Cambridge, UK: Cambridge University Press.

Wells, G. (2002). Learning and teaching for understanding: The key role of collaborative knowledge building. In J. Brophy (Ed.), *Social constructivist teaching: Affordances and constraints*. London, UK: Elsevier.

Wignell, P. (2007a). Vertical and horizontal discourse and the social sciences. In F. Christie & J. R. Martin (Eds.), *Language, knowledge and pedagogy: Functional linguistic and sociological perspectives* (pp. 184–204). London, UK: Cassell.

Wignell, P. (2007b). *On the discourse of social science*. Darwin, Australia: Charles Darwin University Press.

4

DISCOURSES IN AND OUT OF SCHOOL

Looking Back

James Paul Gee

Background: Religion and Theoretical Linguistics

In the mid-1960s, in my early teens, I spent a number of years in a Catholic seminary near my hometown of San Jose, California. The school was isolated, sitting up on a mountain surrounded by a forest. When I entered, it was already over a hundred years old. But today it is gone, destroyed to make way for a suburb. We seminarians were allowed few trips home, no radio, television, or newspapers. The library was small, due not to a lack of resources, but because any book that did not reflect proper orthodoxy, which was most, was banned.

In the seminary, I developed an interest in philosophy when a teacher told us about St. Anselm's "ontological argument" for the existence of God. He told us that down through history the argument had been considered ingenious, but wrong. As a teenager I saw poor Anselm as an underdog and thought how wonderful it would be to prove him right. I tried to learn more about ontology and metaphysics from our library, but to little avail since all books on these subjects were banned. I gleaned a bit from an old encyclopedia and more from books I had smuggled into the seminary with the help of priests on the outside.

I wrote my first "article", a version of Anselm's ontological argument for the existence of God, for a little newsletter the seminarians put out a couple of times before its demise. St. Anselm's argument for the existence of God is purely deductive. It goes like this, using for the most part Anselm's own words (translated by Jonathan Barnes in Barnes, 1972, pp. 88–89):

> Now we believe that [God is] something than which nothing greater can be imagined.
>
> ... it is one thing for a thing to be in the understanding and another to understand that a thing is [exists].

And certainly that than which a greater cannot be imagined cannot be in the understanding alone. For if it is at least in the understanding alone, it can be imagined to be in reality too, which is greater. Therefore if that than which a greater cannot be imagined is in the understanding alone, that very thing than which a greater cannot be imagined is something than which a greater can be imagined. But certainly this cannot be. There exists, therefore, beyond doubt something than which a greater cannot be imagined, both in the understanding and in reality.

We can clearly form the concept of a "being than which a greater cannot be imagined". If this being did not exist in reality, but existed only in our heads, it would not be a "being than which a greater cannot be imagined", since, we could now imagine a greater being, namely one that existed both in reality and in our minds. Therefore, God (or, at least, a being "than which a greater cannot be imagined") must exist. I was thrilled with the pure deductive power of Anselm's argument (and Descartes' later version of such an argument). It seemed that by mere words and the rules of logic, Anselm had conjured up a striking result—the very existence of God.

Many years later, when I had left the seminary and earned my PhD in linguistics at Stanford University (not far from the seminary), this is part of what attracted me to, and made me into, a Chomskian linguist. Chomsky's linguistics, too, was based on deducing powerful conclusions from a small set of abstract basic principles, though in Chomsky's case he added a bit more empirical data to the premises than had Anselm.

From the 1950s on, Chomsky developed a strong deductive argument that human beings acquired their native languages based on a biological capacity for language (e.g., Chomsky, 1957, 1965, 1968, 1975, 1986, 1988, 1995, 2000; see also Gee, 1986; Pinker, 1994). His argument was based on an empirical claim about the "poverty of the stimulus", that is, a claim that the data available to the child in the course of language acquisition could never, in principle, by itself, specify the grammar of the language to which the child was exposed.

Since humans do, of course, acquire their native languages, this meant that language is "innate" in humans in the sense that humans are born with innate knowledge of what a human language can look like. Based on the initial language data to which they are exposed and barring unnatural strictures, language unfolds in humans according to a biological plan, much in the way human feet or hearts develop (of course, one can deform feet by binding them or language by putting children in closets). This implies, of course, that at some suitable level of abstraction all human languages are similar, despite superficial appearances to the contrary.

Chomsky was arguing, therefore, that, at least in regard to language, there is such a thing as "human nature". All humans share the same biological capacity for human language and this is part of what makes them human. Languages cannot differ in any old way, arbitrarily across the board, as the structuralist linguists before Chomsky had believed (e.g., Bloomfield, 1933), but are, at root, basically the "same".

Chomsky also argued (1971, 1975, 1976, 1986, 1987, 1988) that humans may well also have a biological capacity for—a shared inheritance in regard to—things other than language. They may well share, again at a suitable level of abstraction, a common capacity for common sense and ethics. Here, too, there may be more similarities than would appear from a superficial view. This common human capacity for common sense and ethics is what allows all human beings to lead their lives and think for themselves when left suitably free from the strictures and constraints of governments, churches, ideologies, and other institutional forces. These forces often seek to constrain people in the service of those with power and status in society. These forces often serve, much like foot binding, to deform people's natural abilities and inclinations.

Chomsky has claimed that there cannot be a true science of the social and the cultural (1971, 1975, 1976, see especially 1982). For Chomsky, it is just an evolutionary accident that we humans can do science in some areas like physics. Being adept at understanding physics could never have been selected for in evolution, since knowing about things like quarks could never have given anyone a selective advantage in the state of nature. Our ability to do physics must have taken a free ride on some other mental ability that was directly selected for in the sense that the ability to do physics arose because the neural structures that subserve it were accidentally a by-product of this other directly selected for ability—(Pinker, 1994, disagrees and argues that language was directly selected for). Such a "happy" accident did not occur, Chomsky argues, in the case of areas like seeking to understand art or social affairs in a rigorously scientific way. Perhaps, Martian evolution was different and they have a rigorous science of the social, but cannot comprehend physics in any deep way.

However, I have always believed that Chomsky would not have wished there to be a science of the social, even if one could have, in his mind, existed. He believed that if any such science did exist, it would just be used by those in power to manipulate others in the interest of the powerful. Indeed, this is what Chomsky thought of behaviorism, a movement he did not think was scientific (1959), but would not have wished to exist even if he had thought better of it as an intellectual enterprise.

Chomsky, then, can be seen as arguing for a notion of human nature in regard to language and other aspects of human existence. The two sides of the argument are different, of course, since Chomsky is arguing for a linguistic human nature as a professional linguist engaged in science (as he sees it), but more speculatively for a human nature in regard to common sense and ethics (a nature that allows humans to intelligently choose their own destinies in no need of institutional control) as a concerned citizen not then engaged in (what he sees as) rigorous science.

When I took my first job in linguistics, in the School of Language and Communication at Hampshire College in Amherst, Massachusetts, I quickly found out that the notion of human nature was out of favor among social scientists of the 1960s and 1970s. Hampshire had a good many Marxists and Marxist feminists and they abhorred the idea of human nature. They saw it as the historical foundation of racist arguments that some groups of people (e.g., Africans) were "naturally" (that is, in biological terms) inferior to other groups (e.g., Europeans). Of course, Chomsky's notion of human nature is about the important things that all people share as human beings, things sometimes obscured by the work and manipulations of institutions that seek to constrain that nature or transform it.

This is an area where I have, over the years, differed from my more anthropologically and sociologically inspired colleagues. They have sought to stress differences, while I have been more impressed by similarities. For me, people and cultures are more similar than they are different. Thus, what has most interested me is the massive amount of work that people and institutions put, and have put, into making relatively small differences function as large and important ones, usually in the interests of power and privilege for some and not for others.

As an example, consider so-called "Black Vernacular English" ("Ebonics"). In my view, this dialect is, by linguistic standards (certainly in comparison to dialect differences in places like Italy and Germany) trivially different from so-called "Standard English" (and this despite that the fact that it does, indeed, show African influences in its phonology, syntax, and discourse features). What interests me is the massive amount of social and political work that has gone into (and still goes into) making this relatively small difference operate as a major barrier and significant social "problem" when it by no means ever needed to do so. This model seems to me to apply widely to other linguistic, social, and cultural differences.

So, I bought (and buy) Chomsky's argument about human nature, though I now think Anselm's argument (sadly) wrong. Besides making a connection between Anselm and Chomsky, in my youth, I came, many years later, to realize that I had felt, but not acknowledged, a connection between the Catholicism in which I grew up (a particular Orthodox variety) and Chomskian linguistics. In both cases, it was important and consequential that one got recognized, and recognized others, as a Catholic (of the "right" sort) or a Chomskian linguist (of the "right" sort).

Chomskian linguists—many of them then, of course, young, arrogant, and brash—often believed that scholars who pursued social-, culture-, or humanities-oriented work, most especially linguists who did so, were inferior, engaged in a lesser (even silly) enterprise, one that lacked rigor. These issues eventually became even more personal to me. For years after leaving theoretical linguistics to work on the social and cultural aspects of language, I felt two identities inside myself, and one looked down on the other. The theoretical linguist inside me looked down his nose at the sociolinguistic inside me for many years. I knew exactly what attitudes, values, and words to adopt with which to castigate my sociolinguistic self. I was my own tension-filled linguistics department. I don't say that this tension was all bad; in fact, in its own way, it was productive. Indeed, I later came to see it as a dramatic example of what is a typical phenomenon for many people in our society, for example: the middle-class person with working-class origins (a tension I knew as well). Later, when I worked on issues of language, race, and schooling, these sorts of tensions were an obvious part of the analyses.

All of this made me interested in "recognition". I came to see that a great deal of the social work people do is devoted to trying to get recognized, and to recognize others (or refuse to), as having some specific socially situated and consequential identity. Such recognition is open to negotiation, is tension-filled, subject to change and cancellation, in some cases more clear-cut than in others. Whether it is a 5-year-old seeking to get recognized as a "good student" in Ms. Smith's kindergarten, a young Assistant Professor seeking to get recognized as a "respected Chomskian linguist", a Los Angeles cop seeking to get recognized as a "tough cop", or a Native American seeking to get recognized as a "real Indian" (an emic phrase, see Wieder & Pratt, 1990), the process is, at a theoretical level, the same. I later came to call all of these "Discourses" with a capital "D" ("big D Discourses"), using the capital to distinguish Discourse in this sense from "discourse" (with a little "d") which just meant instances of language-in-use (Gee, 1990, 1992, 1999).

Big D Discourses are ways of using language, acting, interacting, valuing, dressing, thinking, believing, and feeling (or displaying these), as well as ways of interacting with various objects, tools, artifacts, technologies, spaces, and times so as to seek to get recognized as having a specific socially consequential identity. Of course, we can recognize people as bidding for and having social identities that we don't ourselves want or know how to enact (e.g., a neo-Nazi or neo-conservative fundamentalist). And, remember, this is all about recognition, and recognition is a probabilistic, negotiated, changeable thing. Someone can get recognized one way on one occasion and not on another (Wieder & Pratt, 1990).

So think of all the "ways with words, deeds, things, thoughts, and feelings" you would have to "pull off" to get recognized in a particular first grade as a "good student" (the issue goes right down to how you hold a pencil!) or "a good initial reader" (it goes right down to what you do with your finger!). Of course, these matters vary with different schools, classrooms, and communities. A first-grade teacher is creating a Discourse in her classroom (a way of being a first-grade student and the various sub-identities like being or not being an "emergent reader" or a "real reader" that this involves), similar to other ones elsewhere, but not identical.

In any Discourse—being a first grader or a cop in L.A.—there are a number of related identities and sub-identities at stake (e.g., "good student", "gifted", "special", "poor reader", etc.; "tough cop", "good cop", "veteran cop", "rookie", "good partner", etc.). These identities form a family that cluster in the Discourse, mutually supporting and reinforcing each other, creating the warp and weave of the Discourse. Note, as well, that Discourses are not like boxes in which something is clearly in or out, but like waves in which it is clear where the middle is, but never really clear where the margins start and stop.

Sharing Time and Discourses

In 1982, I moved from my first academic position at Hampshire College in Amherst, Massachusetts, where I had taught syntactic theory, to a position in applied linguistics in the Applied Psycholinguistics Program at Boston University. This move was an accident twice over. First, it was occasioned by the fact that at Hampshire I had gotten interested in areas like stylistics (linguistics applied to literature) and discourse analysis, both of which were remote from the work in syntax I had been pursuing. I did this to entice students at Hampshire, a liberal college with no grades or course requirements, to take linguistics, hoping to move them from these "soft" areas to the "real" stuff (i.e., syntax). Things worked the other way round, I moved to the "soft" stuff.

Second, I had not realized that the Applied Psycholinguistics Program was in a School of Education (it later moved out). My colleagues told me this was an historical accident and I should just ignore the educators around me. That was hard to do. It quickly became clear to me that these educators were sitting on top of truly "hot" and important issues—issues, as Levi-Strauss might have put it, "good to think with" (in much the way that certain foods are good for your body to eat).

Early in my time at Boston University, my fellow faculty member David Dickinson introduced me to Sarah Michaels, then working at Harvard. Sarah showed me data she and others had collected on first-grade "sharing time" sessions in schools. Sarah and her colleagues had found that some African-American children gave sharing time turns that were quite different from those of the Anglo children in the classrooms (Cazden, 1985; Michaels, 1981, 1985; Michaels & Cazden, 1986; Michaels & Collins, 1984; Michaels & Cook-Gumperz, 1979). These African-American children told what Sarah came to call "topic-associating" stories, while the Anglo children (and some of the other African-American children) told "topic-centered" stories. Topic-associating stories were ones that appeared to move from topic to topic while the unifying theme had to be supplied by the listener. Topic-centered stories (which were usually not really stories, but reports, such as an "event cast" of a trip to a swimming pool, or procedures, such as the steps involved in making a candle) were ones that focused on and developed one unitary topic.

The African-American children's sharing time turns were not well received by their teachers. The teachers thought the children were rambling on and not making sense. They often instituted a rule that each turn had to be about "one important thing" and felt the African-American children often violated this rule. On the other hand, teachers could interrupt and work with the Anglo children, though not the African-American ones, in a sort of dance in which they helped scaffold a piece of language that, while spoken, was explicit and topic-focused in the way in which we expect school-based writing to be. Indeed, Sarah and her colleagues argued that these sharing time sessions were early practice at literacy or literate language for children who could not yet read and write very well.

When I looked at the sharing time data, a number of the African-American stories stood out. They were long, robust, well-organized poetic stories. Unfortunately, the researchers had thrown these out of their data, concentrating on the shorter stories told by the African-American children so as to "control for length", since the Anglo sharing time turns were relatively short (because they were so concise). It appeared to me that many of the shorter African-American turns were cases where children had been stopped by the teacher and told to sit down (for not talking about one important thing) or where the child had started a story, but for one reason or another did not choose to finish it (perhaps, in some cases, because of the teacher's reactions to the story). The stories that were clearly finished did not seem to me to merit the term "topic associating". While they were not literate in the sense of being like an early version of the explicit, concise language we later expect in reports and essays, they were literate in the sense of being early versions of the literary language we expect in poetry and other forms of literary art.

Below I reprint one of these stories that I have used a number of times in my writings (Gee, 1990, 1996, 1999). This is a story by a girl the researchers called "Leona", a little girl about whom a good deal has come to be written by a number of different people over the years:

THE PUPPY STORY

I. Setting

STANZA 1
1. Last yesterday in the morning
2. there was a hook on the top of the stairway
3. an' my father was pickin' me up
4. an I got stuck on the hook up there

STANZA 2
5. an' I hadn't had breakfast
6. he wouldn't take me down
7. until I finished all my breakfast
8. cause I didn't like oatmeal either

II. Catalyst

STANZA 3
9. an' then my puppy came
10. he was asleep
11. he tried to get up
12. an' he ripped my pants
13. an' he dropped the oatmeal all over him

STANZA 4
14. an' my father came
15. an he said "did you eat all the oatmeal?"
16. he said "where's the bowl?"
17. I said "I think the dog took it"
18. "Well I think I'll have t'make another bowl"

III. Crisis

STANZA 5
19. an' so I didn't leave till seven
20. an' I took the bus
21. an' my puppy he always be following me
22. my father said "he—you can't go"

STANZA 6
23. an' he followed me all the way to the bus stop
24. an' I hadda go all the way back
25. by that time it was seven thirty
26. an' then he kept followin' me back and forth
27. an' I hadda keep comin' back

IV. Evaluation

STANZA 7
28. an' he always be followin' me
29. when I go anywhere
30. he wants to go to the store
31. an' only he could not go to places where we could go
32. like to the stores he could go
33. but he have to be chained up

V. Resolution

STANZA 8

34. an' we took him to the emergency
35. an' see what was wrong with him
36. an' he got a shot
37. an' then he was crying

STANZA 9

38. an' last yesterday, an' now they put him asleep
39. an' he's still in the hospital
40. an' the doctor said he got a shot because
41. he was nervous about my home that I had

VI. Coda

STANZA 10

42. an' he could still stay but
43. he thought he wasn't gonna be able to let him go

To any linguist at the time familiar with the literature in sociolinguistics and anthropological linguistics (Bauman, 1986; Bauman & Sherzer, 1974; Finnegan, 1977, 1988; Hymes, 1981; Jackson, 1974; Tedlock, 1983), this story was a quite recognizable linguistic event. First, Leona used some aspects of the (even then) well-studied dialect of Black Vernacular English (Abrahams, 1964, 1970, 1976; Baugh, 1973; Dillard, 1973; Jackson, 1974; Kochman, 1972; Labov, 1972; Smitherman, 1977). For example, the naked "be" in "My puppy he always be following me" in line 21 (repeated in line 28). In Leona's dialect this is a habitual/ durative aspect marker and here means to say that the puppy habitually, as a matter of habit, as part of the puppy's inherent way of acting, continually seeks to follow her (and thereby creates problems and eventually an opposition to the adult discipline of the home that must be resolved).

Second, Leona uses poetic devices that are the hallmark of so-called "oral literature" across the world (devices apparent in adult form in Homer and the Bible, which started as oral stories, see Finnegan, 1977, 1988; Foley, 1988; Havelock, 1976; Hymes, 1981; Ong, 1982; Pattison, 1982; Tedlock, 1983). [Saying that someone is in an "oral culture" does not mean that they and other members of their culture are not literate; it means only that their culture retains a strong allegiance to thematically-based, culturally significant face-to-face story telling.] These devices include repetition, stylistic variation, and syntactic and semantic parallelism, all of which are readily apparent in Leona's stories. For example, notice how in Stanzas 3 and 4 Leona introduces the puppy and the father in parallel ways, first by saying "my puppy/my father came" and then attaching four events to each of the entrances, four acts to the puppy and four pieces of dialogue to the father. This is one of many devices that create an opposition between the youthful puppy that wants to go free and the adult world that wants discipline.

Third, Leona uses a device characteristic of African-American storytelling (and the storytelling of some other cultures). She uses non-narrative material to key the listener into what is the "point" or basic theme of her story. In her case, in this and other of her stories, she does this by exiting the main story line just before her story is about to end and giving the listener some non-narrative information that is the sort of information linguists call "evaluation", i.e., material that signals what makes the story tellable or what its point is (Labov, 1972; Labov & Waletsky, 1967).

Thus, in Stanza 7 we are not given story events (this happened, then this happened), but generalizations (e.g., note, too, the repetition of the habitual/durative "be" and the repetition of "go"). This stanza clearly tells us—which the habitual/durative marker has already signaled—that the theme of the story is the conflict between the puppy (and Leona as a child?) wanting to go free and having, by adult dictate, to be chained up (unfree) [recall the hook earlier in the story]. It is this conflict that must be resolved for the story to be resolved and it is resolved in the last stanzas when an adult authority figure (the doctor) dictates that the puppy cannot "go" (free). [In more adult narratives, evaluation material is often spread out throughout the story, though Leona, when young, tended to concentrate it right before her conclusion.]

The teacher worried about whether or not the puppy was dead (put to sleep), where exactly the puppy was now, and over exactly over how much time these events took place. But these concerns are beside the point in such oral literature stories. Such stories exist primarily to carry themes and develop themes, themes of importance to their tellers and their cultures. They are meant to be exaggerated in ways that bring home those themes (e.g., the hook in the beginning of the story). Leona's theme here—that young things have to follow adult rules (here represented by parents, schools, and doctors) as part and parcel of growing up—is a primordial for children and adults in many cultures.

So Leona has given the teacher a quite recognizable linguistic performance ("oral literature"), one rooted in a long history of African-Americans going back to Africa, one prevalent in many other cultures (though done in somewhat different ways by each), one that in fact, via figures like Homer and Chaucer, is the foundation of Western written literature. Of course, Leona was a young child and, thus, early in her apprenticeship to this cultural verbal style—though quite obviously well on her way.

One thing that went on in classrooms like the one Leona was in was that children like her were misled by the ways in which teachers (and many academics) use the word "story" to cover both narrative verbal texts with plots and oral texts more akin to reports or the news (e.g., going swimming or making candles). Leona thinks the teacher really wants a story and gives her a culturally embedded version of one. But the teacher is actually after a news-like report through which she can scaffold early school-based literate language in the "expository" style (i.e., linear, sequenced, concise, explicit, non-poetic, non-literary, report-like language). Children need practice in many different styles, of course, but such a lack of clarity about goals, practice, and what language means creates a fundamental unfairness, common though it is in schools.

I was first confronted with the sharing time data at a time when I knew nothing about education and had never stepped foot in a public school. I assumed that public schools were all about leveling the playing field. My first thought was: Here is a deep *theoretical* problem. How could a child bring a language practice to school that was so sociohistorically and socioculturally recognizable and significant and yet be construed as a failure, indeed, a failure at language? This seemed to me to be the sort of question that should be central to applied linguistics, though, at that time, such questions were not seen as having anything to do with the field.

I came to view what was happening to Leona as having to do with socially situated identities and tried to capture this through the notion of Discourses (Gee, 1987, 1989, 1990, 1992, 1999). The story is complicated, because it needs to be. Let's start with the idea of a "primary Discourse". Nearly every human being attains a "primary Discourse" early in life as part and parcel of being socialized into a family of a given type (where, of course, what counts as one's "family" varies across people and cultures). For each of us, there are ways with words, deeds, things, thoughts, and feelings that, as children, we associate with being a "person like us" (like our socializing group).

For most people, this primary Discourse eventually becomes the ways with words, deeds, things, thoughts, and feelings that they recruit when they are being (seeking to get recognized as) an "everyday" person, not a specialist of any sort. When we are being "everyday" people (and not acting in special roles like being students and teachers, doctors or scientists, gang members or bird watchers) we are acting within what Habermas (1984) has called our "lifeworld". Each person has a culturally distinctive "lifeworld", a way (really a related set of ways) of being an "everyday" person.

For each of us, our ways of being and acting in our lifeworld originate in and are tied to our primary Discourse, though each of us transforms our primary Discourse through life more or less depending upon how much we have come to disown parts of it under various social, cultural, and political pressures. And, of course, in a pluralistic world you will switch your lifeworld style in interactions with different people. Thus, an African-American may have a different lifeworld style for Black friends than for White ones. But the basic issue is: What are the ways of being, talking, acting, and interacting with which you are most comfortable when you are being informal, seeking just to be an "everyday" person?

Another way to put this is this: humans always balance trying to achieve or show respect (status) and solidarity in their interactions with each other (Milroy, 1987; Milroy & Milroy, 1985). We switch our styles of language, action, and interaction along a continuum, sometimes stressing status (and therefore more "formal") and sometimes stressing solidarity (and therefore more "informal"). For each of us, our primary Discourse (or what we might call later in life, after its various transformations, our lifeworld Discourse) is composed of the ways with words, deeds, things, thoughts, and feelings with which we feel most comfortable when we are seeking primarily to achieve and show solidarity, being "informal", our "everyday" selves.

While Discourses involve not just language, but ways of acting, interacting, thinking, valuing, and coordinating ourselves with things, tools, and technologies, as well, primary/lifeworld Discourses are important from a linguistic perspective. When people are speaking within their primary/lifeworld Discourse, they are using a style of language that linguists refer to as the "vernacular" (Labov, 1972).

Everyone, as they go through life, picks up a variety of different "secondary Discourses", that is, ways with words, deeds, thoughts, feelings, and things that are connected to various "public" institutions beyond the family, institutions such as churches, workplaces, government institutions, and schools. When people act within these Discourses, they are not acting as "everyday" people, but as "specialists" in the sense that they play special roles (play out special identities) as part of the work of these institutions. In the case of secondary Discourses, people are acting and interacting more towards the status side of the status–solidarity divide, putting forward more "formal" styles. They have exited their lifeworlds.

A particular woman, for instance, might be recognized as a business woman, political activist, feminist, church member, National Organization of Women official, PTA member, and volunteer Planned Parenthood counselor, and many more, by carrying out performances that are recognizable within and by these secondary Discourses. Each of these is a way this woman can get recognized as taking on a distinctively "specialist", non-"everyday" (non-lifeworld) identity. While, again, Discourses involve more than language, most secondary Discourses involve styles of language that deviate more or less from anyone's vernacular style of language, even if this only involves distinctive vocabulary.

Schools are filled with secondary Discourses, ranging from being a (recognizable) first-grade student of a certain type, through being a special education student of a certain type, to being a student of mathematics of a certain type. In each case, and many more, the child must act, interact, think, feel, value, use language, and coordinate him or herself with things, tools, and technologies to get recognized as having a given identity (e.g., being "special" or "gifted"; being "good" or "poor" as a math student) or, at least, is institutionally positioned to be expected to do so.

Through the practices of parents and teachers, school-based secondary Discourses come to resonate with, and build on, some children's primary Discourses and not others. Some children come from homes where early versions of school-based practices and their concomitant identities are "filtered" into the child's early socialization into his or her primary Discourse. For example, some parents ask their children at dinner to report on what happened that day and scaffold the child to do so in the sort of concise, linear, and explicit language we associate with school-based literate talk and with many forms of expository school-based writing (Heath, 1983; Ochs, Taylor, Rudolph, & Smith, 1992). This is obviously a practice which resonates with the sorts of sharing time events that Sarah Michaels was studying.

This dinner time "report" is an odd hybrid that (purposely) stands mid-way between school secondary Discourses and the child's acquisition of his or her primary Discourse. That is why I say that a school-based practice is being "filtered" into the home (selective bits of it are incorporated into key moments where the child's initial sense of self in life is being built at home). What is important here is not the practice per se, in my view. Rather, what is important is that such families incorporate a myriad of such early versions of school-based practices into the development of their children's primary Discourses. Such children come to see the ways with words, deeds, things, thoughts, and feelings associated with such practices as part of their core sense of who they are in the world. "People like us" do things like this even when we are just "being ourselves". Such children, early on in school, recognize school as a place and set of practices compatible with, even linked to or associated with, their primary Discourse.

Other children, like Leona, bring equally rich and complex practices from their primary Discourses to school. Their families also sometimes filter bits and pieces of secondary Discourse practices into the socialization of their children. For example, many African-American homes filter into the home-based socialization of their children selective bits of practices associated with church, as did my home when I was young. Even as a pre-school child, I engaged in talk and action at dinner that was connected to religious rituals and this (along with many other things) helped "marry" these practices and their associated attitudes and feelings to my emerging sense of what it meant to be "people like us" (i.e., my primary Discourse).

However, Leona's primary Discourse (and whatever has been filtered into it to give her a head start on certain secondary Discourses) is not recognized by school and built on as a base for the acquisition of school-based secondary Discourses. In turn, Leona does not bring to school practices that get her recognized readily as an "acceptable" student. There is much less resonance, in both directions, between her primary Discourse and school-based secondary Discourses as these are instantiated at the outset of schooling.

Thus, we can say that some families make their children feel that school is for "people like us". On the other hand, for other children, children like Leona, school makes them, from the outset, feel that school is not really for "people like them". In my own case, this sort of conflict was partially resolved because I went to intensely Catholic schools that recognized and built on my non-middle-class, Catholic-focused primary Discourse.

Talk of Discourse is important because it keys us into two things. First, the real action here is at the level of identity formation and the connections (or lack of them) made across identities. The real issue is how people get recognized or fail to get recognized and in what ways. Second, the problem exists at both the micro level of the individual (i.e., Leona and her teachers) and the macro level of institutions. Individual people inhabit Discourses, they act them out. At the same time, most of our Discourses pre-dated our entry into them. They exist (and change) through history. And, in a sense, talk to each other through time. What is happening is happening simultaneously at the individual and the institutional (and sociohistorical) levels and must be analyzed at both levels.

The Reading Wars and Learning as a Discourse Process

Largely because I took an endowed chair in reading at the University of Wisconsin-Madison in 1998, I got caught up in the "Reading Wars" (Coles, 1998). The conflict here is usually seen as "phonics" against "Whole Language", though that considerably oversimplifies the real issues in my opinion. The issues at stake in the "Reading Wars" have turned out to be good ground on which to extend the sort of work I have been discussing. Traditionalists in the reading wars see learning to read as simply gaining certain skills, much as if we saw sharing time as no more than a matter of acquiring skills in regard to delivering reports and event casts. Furthermore, traditionalists view learning to read as what I call an "instructed process", that is, as something that needs to be acquired by being overtly taught (instructed).

Whole language advocates see learning to read as a "natural" process in the way in which people's acquisition of their native language is a "natural" process (see Cazden, 1972, pp. 139–142, for early and critical discussion of the issue). As such, Whole Language advocates argue that people should learn to read not via lots of overt instruction, but through rich immersion in literacy practices. However, as the traditionalists have pointed out, alerted to this fact by linguists, while human beings' acquisition of their native language is biologically supported (and, thus, in that sense, "natural"), the acquisition of literacy is not. Literacy, unlike oral languages, is far too recent on the evolutionary scene to have been incorporated into our biological inheritance.

Does this mean that learning to read is largely a matter of attaining skills through overt instruction? No. Besides natural and instructed learning processes, there are also what we can call "Discourse learning processes". There are some things that are so important to a social or cultural group that the group ensures that everyone who needs to learns them. Take cooking for example. Human cultures have always ensured that people (or, perhaps, only certain people like, unfortunately, in some cultures, women) learn how to cook and cook well enough to keep themselves and others alive and well.

How, for the most part, have people learned to cook in human cultures? Usually not via cooking classes. The process involves "masters" (adults, more masterful peers) creating an environment rich in support for learners (Lave &

Wenger, 1991). Learners observe masters at work. Masters model behavior (e.g., cooking a particular type of meal) accompanied by talk that helps learners know what to pay attention to. Learners collaborate in their initial efforts with the masters, who do most of the work and scaffold the learner's efforts. Texts or other artifacts (e.g., recipes, cook books) that carry useful information, though usually of the sort supplied "on demand" or "just in time" when needed, are often made available. The proper tools are made available, as well, many of which carry "knowledge" learners need not then store in their heads (e.g., pans made of certain materials "know" how to spread heat properly). Learners are given continual verbal and behavioral feedback for their efforts. And, finally, learners are aware that masters have a certain socially significant identity (here, "cook") that they wish to acquire as part and parcel of membership in a larger cultural group. In my view, of course, this last point about identity is crucial.

Processes like learning to cook (or tell stories, give and get gifts, hunt, engage in warfare, set up a household) undoubtedly have their origin in the basic workings of human culture. However, long ago specific groups of human beings learned how to engage in this sort of learning process even when they were not really "cultures". For example, this is how the vast majority of young people today learn to play computer and video games (and the vast majority of them do play such games). People who play video games don't really constitute a "culture" in any classic anthropological sense, though they do constitute a Discourse, because they engage in recognition processes in terms of which they view others as "gamers" of various types.

Let us return for a moment to instructed processes. For most people, learning something like physics is an instructed process they go through in school. However, physicists (masters of physics) long ago realized that if you want someone really to learn physics deeply in the sense of becoming a physicist then, sooner or later, you need to turn learning physics into a Discourse process and not an instructed process (or not just an instructed process). Why? Because it is clear that deep learning works better as a Discourse process than it does as an instructed process. Most humans are not, in fact, very good at learning via overt instruction. For example, most young people would resist learning to play video games via lots of overt instruction—and for a good reason: instruction is a much less efficient process (in all sorts of ways) than learning to play video games via a Discourse process (i.e., via becoming a member of a gamer Discourse).

What does it mean to learn physics as a Discourse process? Much the same as what it meant to learn cooking as a Discourse process. Masters (physicists) allow learners to collaborate with them on projects that the learners could not carry out on their own. Learners work in a "smart" environment filled with tools, technologies, and artifacts that store knowledge and skills they can draw on when they do not personally have such knowledge and skills. Information is given "just in time" when it can be put to use (and, thus, better understood) and "on demand" when learners feel they need it and can follow it. Extended information given out of a context of application (thus not "just in time") is offered after, not before, learners have had experiences relevant to what that information is about. Learners see learning physics as not just "getting a grade" or "doing school", but as part and parcel of taking on the emerging identity of being a physicist.

Thus, to return to the reading wars, children can learn to read in two ways. They can learn via an instructed process concentrating on skills or they can learn via a Discourse practice concentrating on the child's acquiring an identity as a reader of a certain type. A person's identity as a reader is always tied to other identities that person can take on within all their Discourses that recruit literacy in some fashion. This is so because, in Discourse terms, people learn to read specific types of text in specific ways for specific purposes within the specific practices of specific Discourses.

For example, in my youth, my identity as a reader was partly formed by becoming a member of Discourses (including the church in which I grew up, my Catholic elementary school, and my seminary) that saw reading as a "deep" and "sacred" act that gave one access to religious knowledge and other forms of value-laden knowledge. I transferred this same attitude to philosophical texts later on, and, yet later, to texts in theoretical linguistics. In fact, I suppose it was, in part, because these linguistics texts came to seem not value-laden enough that I turned to social, cultural, and educational work.

Does it matter at a practical level whether or not one learns to read through an instructed process or a Discourse process (that is, as part and parcel of acquiring an identity tied to Discourses)? Yes. There is a well known phenomenon called the "fourth-grade slump" (Chall, Jacobs, & Baldwin, 1990). This is the situation where many children seem to be learning to read in the early grades, at least in terms of their test scores, but cannot read well enough later on in school to learn successfully in the content areas like math, science, and social studies. This phenomenon is called the "fourth-grade slump" because, traditionally, children were thought to be learning to read in the first three grades and reading to learn in fourth grade, when content used to "kick in". However, today, school children are exposed to substantive content learning earlier and earlier in school.

Children who learn to read as a Discourse process take on an identity as a school-based reader (and connect that identity in fruitful ways to their out-of-school identities) that ensures that they will not be victims of the fourth-grade slump. I will tell you why I think this is so in a minute. Children who learn to read as a skills-based instructed process apart from such identity formation are often the victims of the fourth grade slump.

Vernacular and Specialist Varieties of Language

My contact with the reading issues—and meditation on things like the fourth-grade slump—led me to see the importance of "specialist" languages associated with secondary Discourses, both in school and in society at large. People think of a language like English as one thing. Actually, it's not one thing, it's many things. There are many different varieties of English. Some of these are different dialects spoken in different regions of the country or by different sociocultural groups. Some of them are different varieties of language used by different occupations or for different specific purposes, for example, the language of lawyers, carpenters, or video game players.

Every human being, early in life, acquires a vernacular variety of his or her native language. This form is used for face-to-face conversation and for "everyday" purposes when people are acting within their lifeworld Discourses. Different groups of people speak different dialects of the vernacular, connected to their families and communities. Thus, a person's vernacular dialect is closely connected to his or her initial sense of self and belonging in life, his or her primary Discourse.

After the acquisition of their vernacular variety has started, people often also go on to acquire various non-vernacular specialist varieties of language used for special purposes within specific secondary Discourses. For example, they may acquire a way of talking (and writing) about fundamentalist Christian theology, video games, or bird watching. Specialist varieties of language are different—sometimes in small ways, sometimes in large ways—from people's vernacular variety of language.

One category of specialist varieties of language is what we can call academic varieties of language, that is, the varieties of language connected to learning and using information from academic or school-based content areas (Gee, 2002; Schleppegrell, 2004; Schleppegrell & Colombi, 2002). The varieties of language used in (different branches of) biology, physics, law, or literary criticism fall into this category. Many people can't stand these varieties of language.

Some texts are, of course, written in vernacular varieties of language, for example, some letters, email, and children's books. But the vast majority of texts in the modern world are not written in the vernacular, but in some specialist variety of language. People who learn to read the vernacular often have great trouble reading texts written in specialist varieties.

Specialist varieties of language, whether academic or not, often have both spoken forms and written ones, and these may themselves differ from each other. For example, a physicist or computer scientist can write in the language of physics or computer science and he or she can talk a version of it, as well.

It is obvious that once we talk about learning to read and talk specialist varieties of language, it is hard to separate learning to read and talk this way from learning the sorts of content or information that the specialist language is typically used to convey. That content is accessible through the specialist variety of language and, in turn, that content is what gives meaning to that form of language. The two— content and language—are married.

Of course, one key area where specialist varieties of language differ from vernacular ones is in vocabulary. But they also differ in syntax and discourse features, as well. For example, suppose someone is studying the development of hornworms (cute green caterpillars with yellow horns). Contrast the vernacular sentence in (1) below with the academic specialist sentence in (2):

1. Hornworms sure vary a lot in how well they grow ("everyday version").
2. Hornworm growth exhibits a significant amount of variation ("academic version").

The specialist version differs in vocabulary (e.g., "exhibits"). But it also differs in syntactic structure, as well. Verbs naming dynamic processes in the vernacular version (e.g., "vary", "grow") show up as nouns naming abstract things in the specialist version ("variation", "growth"). The vernacular sentence makes the hornworms the subject/topic of the sentence, but the specialist sentence makes hornworm growth (a measurable trait for hornworms) the subject/topic. A verb–adverb pair in the vernacular version ("vary a lot") turns into a verb plus a complex noun phrase in the specialist version ("exhibits a significant amount of variation").

Though we do not have space to pursue the matter fully here, specialist varieties of language also differ from vernacular varieties at the discourse level. We can see this even with our two sentences. Note that the specialist version does not allow an emotional word like "sure" that occurs in the vernacular version. We would not usually write or say "Hornworm growth sure exhibits a significant amount of variation". There is nothing wrong with this sentence syntactically. It's just that we don't normally speak or write this way in this variety of language. At the cross-sentential level, specialist languages use many devices to connect, contrast, and integrate sentences across stretches of text that are not used as frequently, nor exactly in the same way, in vernacular varieties of language (like my phrase "at the cross-sentential level" at the beginning of this sentence).

Specialist languages, of course, draw on many of the grammatical resources that exist also in vernacular varieties of language. For example, any vernacular variety of English can make a noun (like "growth") out of a verb (like "grow"). But to know the specialist language in (2) you have to know that this is done regularly in such a variety, you have to know why (what its function is in the specialist language), and you have to know how and why doing this goes together with doing a host of other related things (for example, using a subject like "Hornworm growth", rather than "hornworms", or avoiding emotive words like "sure"). Any variety of a language uses certain patterns of resources and to know the language you have to be able to recognize and use these patterns. This is much like recognizing that the pattern of clothing "sun hat, swim suit, and thongs" means someone is dressed for the beach.

So what's all this got to do with the "fourth-grade slump"? Something has to motivate children to move from lifeworld language like that in (1) and the identities associated with this language to the sort of academic language in (2). This is not an inherently motivating move and many people—including many adults—resist it. There are losses sustained when we move from (1) to (2). We lose hornworms (which are cute) and get an abstract trait of hornworms, namely "hornworm growth (which isn't cute). We lose dynamic processes like "grow" and "vary", which people tend to be intrigued by, and gain abstract processes like "growth" and "variation", which are much less intriguing. We lose emotion ("sure") and gain a bloodless, dispassionate, rational, objective stance. Why would anyone, most especially a child, want to suffer these losses?

Children will only suffer these losses if they see acquiring forms of language like that in (2) as a gain in some sense. And they will see this as a gain if and only if they see the Discourses in which such language is used as valuable and compatible with their other Discourses (most especially their primary Discourses), as well as Discourses in which they will be allowed to function in ways they want to function or feel they need to.

The children who succeed best here are those whose homes filtered into their primary socialization aspects of school-based Discourses, including their language practices (remember the dinner time report). This ties the child's home-based identity to early school Discourses. In turn, the child's identification with these early school-based Discourses makes the child feel motivated when confronted with more mature and more threatening forms of academic language as school goes on. There is a seamless linking of identities and Discourses from home through early schooling and into the content areas of schooling as these get complex in later elementary school, high school, and college.

Academic language is the monster in the closet that each child eventually confronts in school. Some children have seen this monster earlier in their closets at home. If they have had good early schooling, they have played with the monster when it was a baby and they were in the early grades. When they see the full-grown beast, it looks familiar, not too threatening, almost like a member of the family (though, perhaps, one partly gone bad). Children raised on "skills", unprepared to see the monster as part of a family which they must now join or face failure in school, see it as a mountain of disconnected, decontextualized skills which will swamp them.

The bottom line here is this: teaching academic varieties of language outside Discourses that people are acquiring through practice and participation is a sure-fire way to get people to dislike and disidentify with such language and not learn it. Not teaching academic varieties at all is a way to ensure that children who do not have support outside of school for the acquisition of such varieties of language will fail in the content areas (just look at high school textbooks and the varieties of language in which they are written).

Is It Only Poor Children Who Are Failing in School?

At the time that the sharing time data propelled me into work in education, the "hot" question was "Why do so many minority children fail in school?" It seemed like everyone was working on this topic and had a favored answer to it. Some years later, however, based on work in educational cognitive science, it became apparent to me that this was, in part, the wrong question. The question assumes that (many) minority children are failing and that so-called "mainstream" children are succeeding. However, work in educational cognitive science began more and more to show that the so-called successful children often knew only verbal information, but could not apply this information to solve problems (Bruer, 1993; Gardner, 1991). In a real sense, these children didn't really understand what they were learning, beyond being able to give back verbal information about it well enough to pass tests and get "As".

For example, consider the study that showed that students taking a college physics course—students who could write down Newton's Laws of Motion—when asked so simple a question as: "How many forces are acting on a coin when it has been thrown up into the air?" (the answer to which one can actually deduce from Newton's Laws), got the answer wrong (Chi, Feltovich, & Glaser, 1981; see also Gardner, 1991). Leaving aside friction, they claimed that there were two forces operating on the coin, gravity and "impetus", the force the hand has transferred to the coin. Gravity exists as a force, and, according to Newton's Laws, is the sole force acting on the coin when it is in the air (aside from air friction). Impetus, in the sense above, however, does not exist, though Aristotle thought it did and people in their everyday lives tend to view force and motion in such terms quite naturally. These same students did not fare much better after they had completed the course and were in their second physics course. Many studies like this one began to appear, studies that made one believe that, at some level, school wasn't succeeding for the poor *or* the better off. It was not a site for deep learning and understanding.

The problem here seems, to me, to be the fact that schools treat knowledge as something that is general (a matter of principles, rules, and large generalizations) and decontextualized from specific situations, the human body, emotion, human language, and human activity. For school, knowledge exists as ideas, rather general ones, in the head. For humans, however, knowledge, language, perception (including emotion) and action in the world are all tightly connected together.

It used to be, and still is in some quarters, a standard view in psychology that the meaning of a word is some general concept in the head that can be spelled out in something like a definition. For example, the word "bachelor" might be represented by a complex concept in the head that the following definition would capture: "a male who is not married".

However, today there are accounts of language and thinking that are quite different. Consider, for instance, these two quotes from some recent work in cognitive psychology:

> ... comprehension is grounded in perceptual simulations that prepare agents for situated action.
>
> *(Barsalou, 1999a, p. 77)*

... to a particular person, the meaning of an object, event, or sentence is what that person can do with the object, event, or sentence.

(Glenberg, 1997, p. 3)

These two quotes are from work that is part of a "family" of related viewpoints, which for want of a better name, we might call the family of "situated cognition studies" (e.g., Barsalou, 1992, 1999a, 1999b; Brown, Collins, & Dugid, 1989; Clark, 1997; Engeström, Miettinen, & raij Punamaki, 1999; Gee, 1992; Glenberg, 1997; Glenberg & Robertson, 1999; Hutchins, 1995; Lave, 1996; Lave & Wenger, 1991; Wertsch, 1998, and many more). While there are differences among the different members of the family, they share the viewpoint that knowledge and meaning are tied to *people's experiences of situated action in the material and social world*. Furthermore, these experiences are stored in the mind/brain not in terms of language, but in something like dynamic images tied to perception both of the world and of our own bodies, internal states, and feelings:

Increasing evidence suggests that perceptual simulation is indeed central to comprehension.

(Barsalou, 1999a, p. 74)

Let me use a metaphor to make clear what this viewpoint means. Video games like *Deus Ex*, *Half-Life*, *Age of Mythology*, *Rise of Nations*, or *Neverwinter Nights* create visual and auditory worlds in which the player manipulates a virtual character. Such games often come with editors or other sorts of software with which the player can make changes to the game world or even build a new world. The player can make a new landscape, a new set of buildings, or new characters. The player can set up the world so that certain sorts of actions are allowed or disallowed. The player is building a new world, but is doing so by using, but modifying, the original visual images (really the code for them) that came with the game. One simple example of this is the way in which players can build new skateboard parks in a game like *Tony Hawk Pro Skater*. They must place ramps, trees, grass, poles, and other things in space in such a way that they and other players can skateboard the park in a fun and challenging way.

So imagine that the mind works in a similar way. We have experiences in the world, including things we have experienced only in the media. Let us use weddings as an example. These are our raw materials, like the game with which the gamer starts. Based on these experiences, we can build a simulated model of a wedding. We can move around as a character in the model, imaging our role in the wedding, or we can "play" other characters at the wedding (e.g., the minister), imaging what it is like to be that person. The model we build is not "neutral". Rather, it is meant to take a perspective on weddings. It foregrounds certain aspects of weddings that we take as important or salient. It backgrounds other elements that we think are less important or less salient. It leaves some things out all together.

However, we do not build just one wedding simulation and store it away once-and-for-all in our minds. No, what we do, rather, is build different simulations on the spot for different specific contexts we are in. In a given situation or conversation involving weddings, we build a model simulation that fits that context and helps us to make sense of it. Our simulations are specially built to help us make sense of the specific situations we are in, conversations we are having, or texts we are reading. In one case, we might build a simulation that foregrounds weddings as fun, blissful, and full of potential for a long and happy future. In another case, we might build a simulation that foregrounds weddings as complex, stressful, and full of potential for problematic futures.

We also build our model simulations to help us prepare for action in the world. We can act in the simulation and test out what consequences follow, before we act in the real world. We can role-play another person in the simulation and try to see what motivates their actions or might follow from them before we have to respond to them in the real world.

We think and prepare for action with and through model simulations. They are what we use to give meaning to our experiences in the world and to prepare us for action in the world. They are what we use to give meaning to words and sentences. But they are not language. Furthermore, since they are representations of experience (including feelings, attitudes, embodied positions, and various sorts of foregroundings and backgroundings of attention), they are not just "information" or "facts". Rather, they are value-laden, perspective-taking "games in the mind".

Of course, talking about simulations in the mind is a metaphor that, like all metaphors, is incorrect if pushed too far (see Barsalou, 1999b, for how a similar metaphor can be cashed out and corrected by a consideration of a more neurally realistic framework for "perception in the mind"). Nonetheless, this viewpoint leads us to see that meaning is not about general definitions in the head. It is about building specific game-like simulations (wherein we can act or role-play other people's actions) for specific contexts.

This is true even for words that seem so clearly to have precise definitions, like the word "bachelor". For example, what model simulation(s) would you bring to a situation where someone said of a woman, "She's the bachelor of the group"? I would build a simulation in which the woman was attractive, at or a little over marriageable age, perhaps a bit drawn to the single life and afraid of marriage, but open to the possibilities. I would see myself as acting in various ways towards the woman and see her responding in various ways. The fact that the woman is not an "unmarried man" does not stop me from giving meaning to this utterance. You, having had different experiences than me, would form a different sort of simulation. Perhaps the differences between my simulation and yours are big, perhaps they are small. They are small if you and I have had similar experiences in life and larger if we have not.

Once we see the importance to comprehending oral and written language of being able to simulate experiences, we can see the importance of supplying all children in schools the range of necessary experiences with which they can build good and useful simulations for understanding things like science. But this is just what schools usually do not do. They seek to offer, for the most part, purely verbal (informational) understandings cut off from the wealth of embodied experiences that would give this verbal information real meaning and value. Privileged children can often gain many important school-enhancing experiences outside of school, using their families' resources to make up for the experience deficit they face at school.

These three themes came, to me, to seem importantly interconnected in thinking about schools and learning more generally: the role of Discourses in enacting and recognizing identities; the challenges of specialist languages, especially academic varieties of language in school; and the necessity of situated embodied experiences (and not just verbal information) as a foundation for learning.

New Capitalism and Popular Culture

Two larger contexts eventually came, to me, to seem crucial to these three themes (Discourses, academic languages, and situated cognition). One was the nature of our "new capitalist" high-tech global world as an economic system. The other was the changing nature of culture and technology, especially in regard to literacy and language practices.

My book with Glynda Hull and Colin Lankshear (*The New Work Order*, 1996) discusses the change in our economy from the old industrial economy to the new economy based on technology, service work, and knowledge work. The production of commodities (standardized products that nearly everyone could afford) was crucial to the old capitalism. Think of Henry Ford's famous remark that you could get a Ford in any color you wanted as long as it was black. Even as cars became more variable, the vast majority of people bought one based on price and functionality.

But, thanks to the world-wide spread of knowledge and technology, nearly every country on the globe can and does produce commodities today (Thurow, 1999). This has led to an overproduction of such commodities as cars, bicycles, and televisions, intense competition, lower levels of profit, and a shift of manufacturing jobs to "developing" countries. The new capitalism in "developed" countries is focused around the creation of new knowledge, technologies, designs, and services for consumers seen as occupying different "niches" or identities. What makes a company profitable is not selling something like a car as a commodity, but selling the car as a sign of one's special identity, e.g., the sort of people who drive a Hummer as against the sort that drive a new VW bug. Services play the same role, speaking to people's niche identities and lifestyles.

Over the last few years, in part in concert with the New London Group (1996), of which I was a member, I have argued that the notion of *design* (Kress, Jewitt, Ogborn, & Tsatsarelis, 2001; Kress & Van Leeuwen, 2001) is central to understanding and surviving in the new capitalism. There are three types of design that reap large rewards in the new capitalism: the ability to design, understand, and act within new *identities*, *affinity groups*, and *networks*. These three types are all deeply inter-related (Gee 2000–2001).

Let's start with designed *identities*. One type of design typical in the new capitalism (Rifkin, 2000) is the ability to design products, services, or experiences so that they create or take advantage of a specific identity connected to specific sorts of consumers. In turn, businesses seek through the design of such identities to contract an ongoing *relationship* with the consumer in terms of which he or she can be sold ever newer variations of products and services or from which information can be leveraged for sale to other businesses. The product or service itself is not the important element here. After all, many products (as commodities) are getting cheaper and cheaper to make and many services don't involve any material things at all (Thurow, 1999). What is important is the identity and relationship that are associated with the product or service.

Let me give just one example, typical of a myriad of others. Consider the Web site "palm.com", the site of the Palm™ company, which sells handheld computer organizers. A series of rotating pictures at the top of the site clearly signals the sort of identity the company wants the consumer to assume (e.g., "Find yourself on the road to independence", associated with a picture of the open road, or "Find yourself on the road to freedom", associated with a picture of downhill skiing, or "Follow Wall Street from your street", associated with a picture of the Wall Street sign). Furthermore, the site contains a link to the "The Palm Community", where consumers can swap stories, chat with other palm users, contribute to a discussion board, give advice to other users, get information on related products and links, download free software, and sign up for a free e-mail newsletter. The Palm™ company is contracting an ongoing relationship with their consumers, placing them in relationship to (networking them with) each other, and creating an affinity group (see next section).

The Palm™ company is creating not just an identity, but is doing so through creating an "affinity group". Affinity groups are increasingly important today, both in business and politics (Beck, 1999; Beck, Giddens, & Lash, 1994; Rifkin, 2000). Greens, Saturn owners, members of an elite guarded-gate community, users of Amazon.com, skate boarders, poetry rave fans, or Pokémon fanatics all are members of affinity groups within which they share practices, patterns of consumption, and ongoing relationships to specific businesses and organizations. In an affinity group, people form affiliations with each other, often at a distance (that is, not necessarily face-to-face, though face-to-face interactions can also be involved), primarily through shared practices or a common endeavor (which entails shared practices), and only secondarily through shared culture, gender, ethnicity, or face-to-face relationships (see Rose, 1997, for an important discussion of the relationships between affinity groups as a contemporary form of organization and activism and social class).

In an affinity group, knowledge is often both *intensive* (each person entering the group brings some special knowledge) and *extensive* (each person shares some knowledge and functions with others). In an affinity group knowledge is also often *distributed* across people, tools, and technologies, not held in any one person or thing, and *dispersed*, that is people in the group, using modern information and communication technologies, can draw on knowledge in sites outside the group itself (though, thanks to modern technology, in a sense nothing is really outside the group. It's all a matter of links in a network).

Finally, in an affinity group, much knowledge is often *tacit*, that is built up by daily practice and stored in the routines and procedures of the people who engage in the practices of the group. Such knowledge is not easily verbally explicated. New members acquire such tacit knowledge by guided participation in the practices of the group, not primarily through direct instruction outside these practices. The guidance they receive comes both from more advanced members, but also from various objects, tools, and technologies, many of which are designed to facilitate and supplement members' knowledge and skills.

Finally, let me turn to designing *networks*. Another crucial aspect of design in the new capitalism is *networking* people and organizations (Kelly, 1998). Networking involves designing communicational links between people and organizations. It also crucially involves creating links between people and various sorts of tools and technologies. These tools and technologies not only help create the communicational links that constitute networks, they are themselves nodes in the network in which knowledge is stored and across which it is distributed (together with people's minds).

In fast changing times and markets, the more nodes to which one is connected, the more information one receives and the faster one can adapt and change. Networks harness the power of *unfamiliarity*. If people or organizations are networked only with people or organizations like themselves, then everyone in the network pretty much knows what everyone else knows and there is nothing very new to be learned. In slow changing times, this is fine—maybe even good— since a common core of knowledge can be ever refined. On the other hand, if people or organizations are networked with diverse others, then they are going to learn and keep learning new things, things not already in their own repertoire of knowledge and skills. In a fast changing world, the power of network links to unfamiliar people and organizations is crucial.

Networks that leverage the power of unfamiliarity often have to be large and diffuse, and many of the links are relatively weak links, unlike the strong bonds that people tend to have with those with whom they are familiar and with whom they share a good deal. We come, more and more, to live in a world of many weak links, rather than a few strong ones. This is aided and abetted by the increased *mobility* of many people in the new capitalism, people who move, either physically or virtually, from place to place, creating multiple diffuse weak links to other people and organizations (Bauman, 1998). In fact, in the new capitalist world, mobility is a form and source of power. The mobile classes often leave it to the locals (people who cannot get out or who have few links beyond their area) to clean up (or live with) the messes they have left behind.

Meditation on the new capitalist world leads us to see, I believe, that schools as they are currently constituted are not preparing people—and most especially children who do not get such preparation at home—for our "new times", to understand, critique, and engage with design, affinity groups, and networking with diverse others (Gee, 2000, 2002; Gee, Allen, & Clinton, 2001; Gee & Crawford, 1998). Thus, in today's schools, old inequities remain, but new ones are arising, as well.

And this brings me to my last topic, namely, the ways in which learning outside of school, in these "new times", is outpacing learning inside schools. Some years after studying the new capitalism, I came to see—largely thanks to interacting with my now sixteen-year-old son, Sam—that the popular cultural practices in which children engage today are not only more complex than were those of my childhood, but often more complex than what goes on in school, especially in our return to "the basics" and skill-and-drill. Thus, I have devoted some of my recent work to computer and video games, arguing that young people see in these often long, complex, and difficult games better approaches to learning than they see in school (Gee, 2003). After all, if a computer or video game, which can take 50 or more hours to play, can't get learned and learned well, the company that makes it will go broke.

But let me use another example here, not video games directly, but Pokémon ("Pocket Monsters"), odd looking little creatures that human trainers care for. Pokémon can fight each other, but losers don't die, they just fall asleep. Typical of today's popular culture, which tends to be multi-modal and multi-tasking, Pokémon appear on cards, as plastic figures, in video games, and in television shows and movies.

There are a great many Pokémon now. But let's just consider the Pokémon world as of the time the Nintendo Game Boy games *Pokémon Red*, *Blue*, and *Yellow* were out, the late 1990s. At the time, there were 150 Pokémon. They all had polysyllabic names, ranging from Aerodactyle through Nidoran to Wartortle. Each Pokémon name stands not for just an individual Pokémon, but a type. A child can collect several Aerodactyles or Nidorans in a game.

Each Pokémon falls into one of 16 types (Bug, Dark, Dragon, Electric, Fighting, Fire, Ghost, Grass, Ground, Ice, Normal, Poison, Psychic, Rock, Steel, and Water) that determine how the Pokémon fights. There are actually more than sixteen types, since some Pokémon are mixed or hybrid types, but let's leave that aside. Take Charmander, a Pokémon that looks something like an orange dinosaur with fire coming out of its long tail, as an example. Charmander is a Fire type and has such attack skills as Ember, Leer, Flamethrower, and Fire Spin.

Many, but not all, Pokémon, can evolve, as they gain experience, into one or two other Pokémon. Thus, Charmander can evolve into Charmeleon. Charmander and Charmeleon look alike except that Charmeleon has horns. In turn, Charmeleon can eventually evolve into Charizard, who looks like Charmeleon with wings.

Each Pokémon has a set of attack skills that determines how it fights against other Pokémon. For example, Charmander has the following attack skills (some of which are obtained only when the player's Charmander advances to a certain skill level by winning battles in the game): Scratch, Growl, Ember, Leer, Rage, Slash, Flamethrower, and Fire Spin. Some Pokémon have a somewhat shorter list of attack skills, many have a longer list. Let's for simplicity's sake say that each Pokémon has eight possible attack skills.

What does a child have to know to name and recognize Pokémon? The child has to learn a system, the Pokémon system. And that system is this: 150 Pokémon names; 16 types; 2 possible other Pokémon a given Pokémon can evolve into; 8 possible attack skills from a list of hundreds of possible skills. The system is $150 \times 16 \times 2 \times 8$, and, of course, we have simplified the real system greatly. I know of no evidence that mastering the Pokémon universe differs by the race, class, and gender of children. Poor children do it as well as rich, if they have access to the cards, games, or figures.

Now, consider the following paradox. School traditionalists claim that the big problem in our schools is that we need to teach "phonics skills" (the mapping between sounds and letters) more overtly and intensively. When children learn phonics, they are faced with a system of 44 phonemes (the basic speech sounds in English) coupled with 26 letters of the alphabet. That is, the children need to learn which (one or more) of 44 sounds each of the 26 letters can be associated. This system is pitifully smaller than the Pokémon system. Yet, in the case of learning to read at school, we need to spend billions of dollars on government-sponsored reading initiatives (like those in the No Child Left Behind legislation) to teach children to match these 44 phonemes and 26 letters. Furthermore, in the case of learning to read in school, but not in the case of learning Pokémon, race and class make a big difference, since poor children and children from some minority groups, on average, learn to read in school less well than more privileged children.

Many people confronted with the Pokémon argument say something like this: "But Pokémon is entertaining and motivating. School can't compete with that". So, are we to conclude that science, for instance, one of human beings' most spectacular achievements, is neither fun nor motivating? You won't get very far convincing any good scientist of this. But, be that as it may, the real problem is this: We all know that if we turned Pokémon into a school curriculum, as such curricula exist today, then certain children—many of them poor children—would all of a sudden have trouble learning Pokémon. Pokémon is organized around identity (e.g., one is a Pokémon trainer), affinity groups (e.g., kids interact with Pokémon websites), and networking (e.g., trading).

So what is it about school that it manages to transform children who are good at learning (witness Pokémon, witness Leona's sharing time story), regardless of their economic and cultural differences, into children who are not good at learning, especially, but not only, if they are poor or members of certain minority groups? But this is where we started.

Implications for Research and Intervention

I have never kept track of work that uses my work and so cannot talk in specifics about research projects and educational interventions that have used my work. I have over the years purposely not paid attention to this, because I have argued in my work that frameworks like mine (or any others) about how language and literacy learning ought to work must be adapted and customized by others for their own uses up to the point where the framework becomes their own and not mine.

However, I have over the last few years moved to the study of digital media and learning, precisely because I think digital media can allow us to design the sorts of learning I advocate, learning that I call situated/sociocultural learning (Gee, 2004). "Situated" means the learning is based on (often collaborative) problem-solving in specific contexts with clear goals for action. "Sociocultural" means that learning always involves networking people in ways that create new social identities and honor and use old ones. I do not believe digital media is necessary for such learning, but only that it can enhance such learning in some contexts. I have also argued that learning in popular culture today using digital media like video games is often a better representation of situated/sociocultural learning than we see in many of our schools. In Gee (2007) and Gee and Hayes (2010, 2011) I spell out as specifically as I can what applied research on situated/sociocultural learning and successful examples of it in practice look like.

References

Abrahams, R. D. (1964). *Deep down in the jungle: Negro narrative folklore from the streets of Philadelphia*. Hatboro, PA: Folklore Associates.

Abrahams, R. D. (1970). *Positively black*. Englewood Cliffs, NJ: Prentice Hall.

Abrahams, R. D. (1976). *Talking black*. Rowley, MA: Newbury House.

Barnes, J. (1972). *The ontological argument*. London, UK: Macmillan.

Barsalou, L. W. (1992). *Cognitive psychology: An overview for cognitive scientists*. Hillsdale, NJ: Lawrence Erlbaum.

Barsalou, L. W. (1999a). Language comprehension: Archival memory or preparation for situated action. *Discourse Processes, 28*, 61–80.

Barsalou, L. W. (1999b). Perceptual symbol systems. *Behavioral and Brain Sciences, 22*, 577–660.

Baugh, J. (1973). *Black street speech: Its history, structure and survival*. Austin: University of Texas Press.

Bauman, R. (1986). *Story, performance, and event: Contextual studies of oral narrative.* Cambridge, UK: Cambridge University Press.

Bauman, R., & Sherzer, J. (Eds.). (1974). *Explorations in the ethnography of speaking.* Cambridge, UK: Cambridge University Press.

Bauman, Z. (1998). *Globalization: The human consequences.* Cambridge, UK: Polity Press.

Beck, U. (1999). *World risk society.* Oxford, UK: Blackwell.

Beck, U., & Giddens, A., & Lash, S. (1994). *Reflexive modernization: Politics, traditions and aesthetics in the modern social order.* Stanford, CA: Stanford University Press.

Bloomfield, L. (1933). *Language.* London, UK: Allen & Unwin.

Brown, A. L., Collins, A., & Dugid, P. (1989). Situated cognition and the culture of learning. *Educational Researcher, 18,* 32–42.

Bruer, J. T. (1993). *Schools for thought: A science of learning in the classroom.* Cambridge, MA: MIT Press.

Cazden, C. B. (1972). *Child language and education.* New York, NY: Holt, Rinehart and Winston.

Cazden, C. B. (1985). Research currents: What is sharing time for? *Language Arts, 62,* 182–188.

Chall, J. S., Jacobs, V., & Baldwin, L. (1990). *The reading crisis: Why poor children fall behind.* Cambridge, MA: Harvard University Press.

Chi, M. T. H., Feltovich, P. J., & Glaser, R. (1981). Categorization and representation of physics problems by experts and novices. *Cognitive Science, 13,* 145–182.

Chomsky N. (1957). *Syntactic structures.* The Hague, The Netherlands: Mouton.

Chomksy, N. (1959). Review of *Verbal Behavior,* by B. F. Skinner. *Language, 35*(1), 26–57.

Chomksy, N. (1965). *Cartesian linguistics.* New York, NY: Harper and Row.

Chomksy, N. (1968). *Language and mind.* New York, NY: Harcourt, Brace and Jovanovich.

Chomksy, N. (1971). *Problems of knowledge and freedom: The Russell lectures.* New York, NY: Pantheon.

Chomksy, N. (1975). *Reflections on language.* New York, NY: Pantheon Books.

Chomksy, N. (1976). Problems and mysteries in the study of human language. In A. Kasher (Ed.), *Language in focus: Foundations, methods and systems. Essays in memory of Yehoshua Bar-Hillel.* Dordrecht, The Netherlands: D. Reidel.

Chomksy, N. (1982). *Noam Chomsky on the generative enterprise: A discussion with Riny Huybregts and Henk van Riemsdijk.* Dordrecht, The Netherlands: Foris Publications.

Chomksy, N. (1986). *Knowledge of language: Its nature, origin, and use.* New York, NY: Praeger.

Chomksy, N. (1987). *On power and ideology: The Managua lectures.* Boston, MA: South End Press.

Chomksy, N. (1988). *Language and problems of knowledge: The Managua lectures.* Cambridge, MA: MIT Press.

Chomksy, N. (1995). *The minimalist program.* Cambridge, MA: MIT Press.

Chomksy, N. (2000). *New horizons in the study of language and mind.* Cambridge, UK: Cambridge University Press.

Clark, A. (1997). *Being there: Putting brain, body, and world together again.* Cambridge, MA: MIT Press.

Coles, G. (1998). *Reading lessons: The debate over literacy.* New York, NY: Hill and Wang.

Dillard, J. L. (1973). *Black English: Its history and usage in the United States.* New York, NY: Random House.

Engeström, Y., Miettinen, R., & raij Punamaki, R. L. (Eds.). (1999). *Perspectives on activity theory.* Cambridge, UK: Cambridge University Press.

Finnegan, R. (1977). *Oral poetry*. Cambridge, UK: Cambridge University Press.

Finnegan, R. (1988). *Literacy and orality*. Oxford, UK: Basil Blackwell.

Foley, J. M. (1988). *The theory of oral composition*. Bloomington: University of Indiana Press.

Gardner, H. (1991). *The unschooled mind: How children think and how schools should teach*. New York, NY: Basic Books

Gee, J. P. (1986). Toward a realistic theory of language acquisition. *Harvard Educational Review, 56*, 52–68.

Gee, J. P. (1987). What is literacy? *Teaching and Learning, 2*, 3–11.

Gee, J. P. (1989). Literacy, discourse, and linguistics: Essays by James Paul Gee [special issue, edited by C. Mitchell]. *Journal of Education, 171*(1).

Gee, J. P. (1990). *Social linguistics and literacies: Ideologies in discourses*. London, UK: Taylor and Francis [2nd ed., 1996].

Gee, J. P. (1992). *The social mind: Language, ideology, and social practice*. New York, NY: Bergin & Garvey.

Gee, J. P. (1996). *Social linguistics and literacies: Ideology in discourses* (2nd ed.). London, UK: Taylor & Francis.

Gee, J. P. (1999). *An introduction to discourse analysis: Theory and method*. London, UK: Routledge.

Gee, J. P. (2000). Teenagers in new times: A new literacy studies perspective. *Journal of Adolescent & Adult Literacy, 43*(5), 412–420.

Gee, J. P. (2000–2001). Identity as an analytic lens for research in education. *Review of Research in Education, 25*, 99–125.

Gee, J. P. (2002). Literacies, identities, and discourses. In M. Schleppegrel & M. C. Colombi, (Eds.), *Developing advanced literacy in first and second languages: Meaning with power* (pp. 159–175). Mahwah, NJ: Lawrence Erlbaum.

Gee, J. P. (2003). *What video games have to teach us about learning and literacy*. New York, NY: Palgrave/Macmillan.

Gee, J. P. (2004). *Situated language and learning: A critique of traditional schooling*. London, UK: Routledge.

Gee, J. P. (2007). *Good video games and good learning: Collected essays on video games, learning, and literacy*. New York, NY: Peter Lang.

Gee, J. P., Allen, A-R., & Clinton, K. (2001). Language, class, and identity: Teenagers fashioning themselves through language. *Linguistics and Education, 12*, 175–194.

Gee, J. P., & Crawford, V. (1998). Two kinds of teenagers: Language, identity, and social class. In D. Alverman, K. Hinchman, D. Moore, S. Phelps, & D. Waff (Eds.), *Reconceptualizing the literacies in adolescents' lives* (pp. 225–245). Hillsdale, NJ: Lawrence Erlbaum.

Gee, J. P., & Hayes, E. R. (2010). *Women as gamers: The Sims and 21st century learning*. New York, NY: Palgrave/Macmillan.

Gee, J. P., & Hayes, E. R. (2011). *Language and learning in the digital age*. London, UK: Routledge.

Gee, J. P., Hull, G., & Lankshear, C. (1996). *The new work order: Behind the language of the new capitalism*. Boulder, CO: Westview.

Glenberg, A. M. (1997). What is memory for. *Behavioral and Brain Sciences, 20*, 1–55.

Glenberg, A. M., & Robertson, D. A. (1999). Indexical understanding of instructions. *Discourse Processes, 28*, 1–26.

Habermas, J. (1984). *Theory of communicative action* (Vol. 1, T. McCarthy, Trans.). London, UK: Heinemann.

Havelock, E. (1976). *Preface to Plato*. Cambridge, MA: Harvard University Press.

Heath, S. B. (1983). *Ways with words: Language, life, and work in communities and classrooms.* Cambridge, UK: Cambridge University Press.

Hutchins, E. (1995). *Cognition in the wild.* Cambridge, MA: MIT Press.

Hymes, D. (1981). *"In vain I tried to tell you": Essays in native American ethnopoetics.* Philadelphia: University of Pennsylvania Press.

Jackson, B. (1974). *"Get your ass in the water and swim like me": Narrative poetry from black oral tradition.* Cambridge, MA: Harvard University Press.

Kelly, K. (1998). *New rules for the new economy: Ten radical strategies for a connected world.* New York, NY: Viking.

Kochman, T. (Ed.). (1972). *Rappin' and stylin' out: Communication in urban black America.* Urbana: University of Illinois Press.

Kress G., Jewitt, C., Ogborn, J., & Tsatsarelis, C. (2001). *Multimodal teaching and learning: The rhetorics of the science classroom.* London, UK: Continuum.

Kress, G., & Van Leeuwen, T. (2001). *Multimodal discourse: The modes and media of contemporary communication.* London, UK: Arnold.

Labov, W. (1972). *Language in the inner city: Studies in Black English vernacular.* Philadelphia: University of Pennsylvania Press.

Labov, W., & Waletsky, J. (1967). Narrative analysis: Oral versions of personal experience. In J. Helm (Ed.), *Essays on the verbal and visual arts* (pp. 12–44). Seattle: University of Washington Press.

Lave, J. (1996). Teaching, as learning, in practice. *Mind, Culture, and Activity, 3*, 149–164.

Lave, J., & Wenger, E. (1991). *Situated learning: Legitimate peripheral participation.* New York, NY: Cambridge University Press.

Michaels, S. (1981). "Sharing time": Children's narrative styles and differential access to literacy. *Language in Society, 10*, 423–42.

Michaels, S. (1985). Hearing the connections in children's oral and written discourse. *Journal of Education, 167*, 36–56.

Michaels, S., & Cazden, C. (1986). Teacher/child collaboration as oral preparation for literacy. In B. Schieffelin (Ed.), *Acquisition of literacy: Ethnographic perspectives* (pp. 132–154). Norwood, NJ: Ablex.

Michaels, S., & Collins, J. (1984). Oral discourse styles: Classroom interaction and the acquisition of literacy. In D. Tannen (Ed.), *Coherence in spoken and written discourse* (pp. 219–244). Norwood, NJ: Ablex.

Michaels, S., & Cook-Gumperz, J. (1979). A study of sharing time with first-grade students: Discourse narratives in the classroom. In *Proceedings of the Fifth Annual Meetings of the Berkeley Linguistics Society* (pp. 647–660). Berkeley, CA: Berkeley Linguistics Society.

Milroy, L. (1987). *Language and social networks* (2nd ed.). Oxford, UK: Blackwell.

Milroy, J., & Milroy, L. (1985). *Authority in language: Investigating language prescription and standardisation.* London, UK: Routledge.

New London Group. (1996). A pedagogy of multiliteracies: Designing social futures. *Harvard Educational Review, 66*, 60–92. [Reprinted in B. Cope & M. Kalantzis (Eds.). (1999). *Multiliteracies: Literacy learning and the design of social futures* (pp. 9–37). London, UK: Routledge.]

Ochs, E., Taylor, C. Rudolph, D., & Smith, R. (1992). Storytelling as a theory-building activity. *Discourse Processes, 15*, 37–72.

Ong, W. J. (1982). *Orality and literacy: The technologizing of the word.* London, UK: Methuen.

Pattison, R. (1982). *On literacy: The politics of the word from Homer to the age of rock.* Oxford, UK: Oxford University Press.

Pinker, S. (1994). *The language instinct: How the mind creates language.* New York, NY: William Marrow.

Rifkin, J. (2000). *The age of access: The new culture of hypercapitalism where all of life is a paid-for experience.* New York, NY: Jeremy Tarcher/Putnam.

Rose, F. (1997). Toward a class-cultural theory of social movements: Reinterpreting new social movements. *Sociological Forum, 12*(3), 461–493.

Schleppegrell, M. (2004). *The language of schooling.* Mahwah, NJ: Lawrence Erlbaum.

Schleppegrell, M., & Colombi, M. C. (Eds.). (2002). *Developing advanced literacy in first and second languages.* Mahwah, NJ: Lawrence Erlbaum.

Smitherman, G. (1977). *Talkin and testifin: The language of Black America.* Boston, MA: Houghton Mifflin.

Tedlock, D. (1983). *The spoken word and the work of interpretation.* Philadelphia: University of Pennsylvania Press.

Thurow, L. C. (1999). *Building wealth: The new rules for individuals, companies, and nations in a knowledge-based economy.* New York, NY: Harper Collins.

Wertsch, J. V. (1998). *Mind as action.* Oxford, UK: Oxford University Press.

Wieder, D. L., & Pratt, S. (1990). On being a recognizable Indian among Indians. In D. Carbaugh (Ed.), *Cultural communication and intercultural contact* (pp. 45–64). Hillsdale, NJ: Lawrence Erlbaum.

5

A POSTCOLONIAL PERSPECTIVE IN APPLIED LINGUISTICS

Situating English and the Vernaculars

Vaidehi Ramanathan

Increasing discussions around English being a "world" language (Brutt-Griffler, 2002) and the instrumental role it plays in globalization force us now to take stock of the "dominating" role that English seems to be assuming. Scholarship in this realm ranges from researchers questioning mediums-of-instruction policies, to ways in which English operates to create inner and outer circles in different countries, to how it gets positioned vis-à-vis local, "vernacular" languages (Alidou, 2004). Regardless of how scholars are positioned in the debate, much of the research seems to draw from and is connected to issues in implicit and explicit English language policies—state-wide, nation-wide, and institutional—and ways in which they impact a variety of teaching and learning contexts. Such views, while valuable, can be seen to run the risk of rendering language policies around English and local languages as abstract entities partially formulated behind closed doors, and formalized in documents without paying much heed to local realities. In the area of postcolonial scholarship, issues of language policies around English and the vernaculars assume particular hues, given historical, political, cultural and geographic tropes, with colonial policies still in place.

However, grounded perspectives of postcolonial engagements—everyday engagements by teachers and learners—prod us to consider ways in which policies are not just top-down mandates that happen to us humans, shaping our engagements in the world, but live, dynamic forces that find their viability and articulation in the most local of spaces: in institutions, pedagogic practices, school settings, teacher-education programs, and disciplinary orientations (Ramanathan, 2005a, 2005b; Tollefson, 1991, 2002). Such views have tended to remain largely marginalized in West-based applied linguistic research, but they are crucial to consider since many of our students in (West-based) ESL classrooms are from formerly colonized countries (India, Sri Lanka, Pakistan, Bangladesh, Nigeria,

South Africa, Zimbabwe to name a few) and bring with them learning experiences that need to be a part of our MA-TESOL and other teacher-education programs. In what follows, I offer a few grounded sketches of postcolonial realities based in key educational sites in the city of Ahmedabad, Gujarat, India, where I completed my K-12 and some of my graduate school education. But before that I offer some necessary background regarding key tenets of the postcolonial framework, and how I got started in my long-term endeavor in Gujarat.

What Is Postcolonialism?

In simple terms, postcolonialism refers to points of view of people from formerly colonized countries regarding their colonial past. In terms of scholarship, it manifests itself as 'speaking back' to colonial powers, often in the language of colonizer. European colonial powers had assumed the right to take over entire countries—almost all of them non-Western—and sought to rationalize their take-over in terms of prevailing discourses that viewed non-Western peoples as "inferior, child-like or feminine, incapable of looking after themselves (despite having done so perfectly well for millennia) and requiring the paternal rule of the West for their own interests (today they are deemed to require 'development')" (Young, 2003, p. 2). Atrocities committed by colonial powers in the defense of building empires varied in different countries, with some cataclysmic events spurring local 'subjects' towards fighting for independence. Within the Indian context, the Jallianwalla Bagh massacre of 1919, where General Dyer opened fire on an unarmed crowd of 20,000 people, was a pivotal moment for freedom fighters such as Gandhi, Tagore and Andrews (see Ramanathan, 2009, for details) who sought to overturn colonial rule (Indian Independence was won in 1947).

The policies and mandates that the English colonial powers set in place especially in the field of education were in many instances, in the South Asian context (of India, Pakistan, Sri Lanka and Bangladesh), ones of "Divide and Rule." This was a mode of operating that the Raj (as the English colonial power is known in S. Asia) devised so as to rule more effectively. The Raj needed Indians to run their Empire and so offered English education to small numbers of Indians that would help them in this endeavour. This one colonial policy took root and went very deeply into the South Asian ideological space to where English-medium education was deemed as having more cultural capital and symbolic power than an education in the vernaculars (Gee, 1990; Kalantzis & Cope, 2002; McCarty, 2002, 2005; Hawkins, 2004), an ideology that is very visible, enacted and real today. The general importance accorded to English and the extent to which it pervades the everyday life of the postcolonial person, has, from the point of view of some scholars, rendered the postcolonial identity "hybrid." Indeed, authors such as Verma (2010) write about 'forked tongues' and the general deracination a person educated in the English-medium feels because he/she does not have as intimate a connection with their local vernacular as they do with English (and so by extension may be seen to feel "less Indian"). Postcolonial scholarship often refers to this amalgam as being 'hybridised' because a variety of colonial and vernacular resources inform personal identities. (Formerly colonized countries have also been called the 'subaltern' since they remained on the margins of dominant hegemonic power structures).

My entry into my long-term endeavour in my home town ironically began in the U.S. when I was taking a seminar by Prof. James Paul Gee at the University of Southern California. In 1989, we were reading his book *Social Linguistics and Literacies* (in proof form since his book hadn't yet emerged in print) wherein he seemed to crystallize for me something I knew to be unerringly correct, but had not been able to articulate. I was working on a project for one of my qualifying papers—on two stories, one told by a little white child called Sandy, and another by little black child called Leona—wherein I argued that mainstream listeners were able to parse and comprehend Sandy's story with more ease than Leona's (see Ramanathan-Abbott, 1993), thereby underscoring a point that Gee (1990) himself was making regarding mainstream U.S. teachers not being able to hear their non-mainstream students. Prof. Gee was my mentor through my doctoral work (which I did in an area unrelated to literacy; on the sociolinguistic dimensions of Alzheimer discourse, as a matter of fact), and his views on narrative, literacy, and socio-politics heavily shaped my thinking. When I introduced a couple of chapters of his book to teachers in Ahmedabad, their responses were similar to mine, and that contributed to the impetus for starting my project.

I began my project in Ahmedabad by going back to the college where I received my undergraduate degree. I knew the principal and the teachers, I was familiar with the curriculum, the hallways, canteens and basketball courts were old haunts of mine. Being immersed again in this context not only allowed me to address policies that had changed, but I was able to start relating issues that came up in this one institution to others in the city, and before long to those in non-formal educational domains as well. My early steps and some incipient ideas that had remained inchoate in Prof. Gee's 1989 class had taken on a life of their own and had a propelling energy for which I could take little credit, since it emerged from the collective ideas of teachers, principals, students, textbooks, exam responses, media write-ups, interviews, field notes, documentaries. It is snapshots of this endeavour to which I now turn.

English- and Vernacular-Medium Education in India: Colonial Vestiges, Neo-Colonial Laminations

Issues of Data and Method

My extended endeavour with English- and vernacular-medium teachers and students in Ahmedabad, Gujarat has to do with partially addressing ways in which colonial policies assume neo-colonial laminations in current postcolonial India.

Sixty-five years as India is from Independence from the Raj, the country has begun to rethink and change colonial education policies. But many colonial mandates remain and my engagements in this space have been about addressing how everyday lived realities get negotiated.

My data—accumulated over a decade now—comprises a range of materials gathered in and with a variety of peoples in different institutions in Ahmedabad. Ahmedabad's population is approximately 4.5 million, and most everybody speaks at least two languages. The official languages in the state and city are Gujarati, Hindi and English (although there are sizeable pockets of populations speaking a variety of other Indian languages), and all three are taught at the K-12 level (more on K-12 language policies presently). In the space of formal learning, my work is in three institutional sites:

1. a middle-class, EM Jesuit liberal arts institution (where I attended college);
2. an upper-class, EM business college that encourages only English language use in its classes; and
3. a very poor, VM women's college where instruction is dominantly in Gujarati, including the teaching of English literature.

Data from these institutions included extensive interviews with students, faculty and administrators, copies of pedagogic materials, texts, exams, student responses, and countless hours of classroom observations and field notes. Also part of this project are occasional individual and group meetings with both EM and VM teachers to discuss concerns about curriculum, especially the adapting of West-based ELT materials partially made available by the British Council, and some of which I supply (when asked) in the Indian setting.

My data from non-formal educational domains comes from two sites, both of which embody Gandhian notions of 'Non-cooperation':

1. an extra-curricular program run out of the women's college (mentioned above) that caters to addressing concerns of civic change, and
2. the Gandhi Ashram (which was historically Gandhi's home/office and continues to engage in Gandhian projects and be a source of Gandhianism in the state).

Data from these sites include extended interviews with key people running various civic projects in the city, field notes on workshops, and a variety of historical materials written by and to Gandhi (letters, memos, bulletins) that is available in the Ashram and at the Rhodes House library in Oxford University (see Ramanathan, 2009, for a discussion of some of this correspondence). My juxtaposing data from formal and non-formal domains of education is deliberate. If we turn our gaze to issues in the community, very different laminations of 'education' emerge that cast differing light on inequities in the formal realm.

Sites That Reproduce the English-Vernacular Divide: Tracking Policies, Inequities in Textbooks

Most K-12 students in India get slotted into what are called "Vernacular-medium" (VM; Gujarati in the present case) and "English-medium" (EM) tracks of schooling (see Ramanathan, 2005a, for a detailed discussion of inequities perpetuated by such tracking). Constitutionally, the Indian government promises the availability of an education in the mother tongue (in the 21 official languages) as well as an education in English (where English is the medium of instruction). In Gujarat, English is introduced as a foreign language in grade 5 in the Gujarati-medium classes, and Gujarati is introduced at the same grade level in English-medium classes. Hindi is introduced in grade 4 and Sanskrit in grade 7 in both mediums and all EM and VM students have to learn these through grade 12. If policies existed in vacuums, this scene might be regarded as reasonably egalitarian; after all, students in both streams are becoming literate in several languages, with multilingualism being institutionally validated and legitimized.

But, as we know, educational policies and enactments of and around them, have rings of divisiveness and exclusionism that surround them (Hornberger & Johnson, 2007; King, 2001; McCarty, 2005; Shohamy, 2006). Equity in this context, as indeed in many parts of the world, is directly tied to which kind of student is ready for college. Colleges in India, for the most part (except for a few liberal arts colleges), are in the English-medium, which of course means that students with vernacular-medium backgrounds (where they have had access to a few hours of English instruction a week) have to compete with their EM counterparts (for whom English is almost a first language) in colleges and beyond. And given our globalizing world, inequities relating to who has access to English (Gee, 2003), and how access to it opens other communal doors (jobs, interviews), this plays itself out in most differentiated ways (Morgan & Ramanathan, 2009).

One key site where this gulf is very evident is in the English language textbooks that are available to students in the two different tracks. Towards underscoring how the two tracks of education produce two very different 'literate in English' candidates, I offer below two tables that lay out the 'minimal levels of learning' (MLLs) (somewhat comparable to what in the California context is referred to as K-12 'standards') for English language learning in the two mediums. (I do need to note here that there has been a concerted effort to change state-wide educational policies to where English might now be introduced in the first grade instead of the fifth). For now, though, the present policies are still the norm.

Two noticeable writing-related differences in Table 5.1 are: 1) writing for vernacular-medium students is presented as a discrete skill and is addressed separately from reading, a feature that contrasts with writing and reading being presented as conjoined entities for EM students, and 2) that writing for EM students is essayist in orientation from early on: "writing paragraphs on given topics" (vs. "gaining the basic mechanics of English writing ... with proper

TABLE 5.1 Divergent MLLs for VM and EM Students

	Excerpts from MLL from English textbooks used in the **Gujarati-medium**	*Excerpts from MLL from English textbooks used in the* **English-medium**
Grade 5	<u>Writing</u>: Gains control of the basic mechanics of writing in English like capital letters, small letters, punctuation, writing neatly on a line with proper spacing. Transcribes words, phrases and sentences in English. Produces words and spells them correctly. Writes numbers up to 50, telephone numbers, road signs.	<u>Reading and writing</u>: Reading textual material and writing answers to questions based on and related to the text. Reading and interpreting and offering comments on maps and charts. Reading children's literature and talking about it. Writing paragraphs on given topics. Reading and writing simple recipes.
Grade 6	<u>Reading</u>: Reads aloud simple sentences, poems, dialogues and short passages with proper pauses. Reads and follows given directions. Reads numbers up to a hundred. <u>Writing</u>: Writes with proper punctuation marks. Writes words and sentences neatly on a line with proper spacing, punctuation marks, and capitalization. Writes answers to questions based on text material.	<u>Reading and writing</u>: Reading textual material and writing answers to questions based on the text. Reading and interpreting simple abbreviations. Reading narrative prose and adventure stories and talking about them. Writing/building stories based on given questions/points. Reading and using the telephone directory.
Grade 7	<u>Reading</u>: Reads aloud simple sentences. Finds key words and phrases from a text. <u>Writing</u>: Writes words and sentences and paragraphs dictated with correct spellings, proper punctuation marks. Learns to write words and sentences neatly on a line with proper spacing and punctuation. Writes answers to questions based on the text.	<u>Reading and writing</u>: Reading textual material and writing answers based on the text. Writing essays based on the text. Reading literary stories and prose lessons. Reading simple passages of reflective prose. Reading and interpreting common instructions such as railway timetables.
	From: Purani, Salat, Soni, and Joshi (1998), pp. 1–3 (for grades 5, 6 and 7 respectively).	From: Purani, Salat, Soni, and Joshi (1998), p. 2 (for grades 5, 6, 7 respectively).

TABLE 5.2 A Partial List of Contents, Grades 6, 8, and 10

	VM List of Contents	*EM List of Contents*
Grade 6	Welcome, friends A Fancy Dress Show A Seashore A Park A Village Fair In the School Compound What time is it now? The Environment Day	A Voyage to Lilliput Farewell to the Farm The Changing World Abraham Lincoln (Parts 1 and 2) Don Quixote Meets a Company of Actors The Poet's House Woodman, spare that tree! City streets and country roads

Grade 8	GM (no authors provided)
	Poetry: (optional)
	Rhyme
	Rhyme
	Rhyme
	Only one Mother
	The Picnic
	Two Birds
	Prose: Let's begin
	Hello! I am Vipul
	A Railway Station
	At the Zoo
	On the Farm
	Good Manners
	In the Kitchen
		Poetry: Under the Greenwood Tree: William
		  Shakespeare
		She Dwelt among the Untrodden Ways:
		  William Wordsworth
		To a Child Dancing in the Wind: W. B. Yeats
		The Listeners: Walter de la Mare
		Coming: Phillip Larkin
		A Blackbird Singing: R. S. Thomas
		Prose: Little Children Wiser than Men: Leo
		  Tolstoy
		Do You Know?: Clifford Parker
		My Financial Career: Stephen Leacock
		The Lady Is an Engineer: Patricia Strauss
		The Judgment Seat of Vikramaditya: Sister
		  Nivedita

Grade 10	Poetry (optional)
	Laughing Song: Blake
	In the night: Naidu
	Wander Thirst: Gerald
	  Gould
	The secret of the
	  machines: Rudyard
	  Kipling
	Prose (no authors
	  provided)
	An act of Service
	Strange but true
	Have you heard this one?
	Vaishali at the police
	  station
	Prevention of cruelty to
	  animals
	The Indian village—then
	  and now
		Poetry:
		Blow, Blow, Thou Winter Wind: Shakespeare
		London: Blake
		Upon Westminster Bridge: Wordsworth
		To—: Shelley
		La Belle Dame Sans Merci: Keats
		The Professor: Nissim Ezekeil
		The Fountain: Lowell
		Prose:
		Ramanujam: C. P. Snow
		On Saying Please: A. G. Gardener
		The Home Coming: Tagore
		Andrew Carnegie: E. H. Carter
		A Day's Wait: Hemingway
		After Twenty Years: O. Henry
		Vikram Sarabhai: M. G. K. Menon

	From: Thakker, P. (1999).	From: Vamdatta, Joshi, & Patel (2000), p. 44.

spacing" for the VM student), or writing essays based on texts (vs. learning to write words and sentences neatly for the VM student).

These unequal levels of literacy across the two mediums are evident in the very divergent kinds of English language readings for the two tracks for students. Table 5.2 offers a partial list of topics addressed in the English language textbooks used in each track.

Several interesting features emerge from a close comparison of the partial list of contents in the two sets of textbooks. VM texts with their general focus on survival English emphasize how language is used in particular Indian contexts (at the park, at the zoo, or sending a telegram). The readings in EM texts, in contrast, are more cosmopolitan, drawing as they do from a variety of texts, including essays and short readings on Abraham Lincoln in grade 6, to those by Stephen Leacock and Tolstoy in grade 8, to ones by Hemingway and Tagore in grade 10. Poetry, a genre that draws heavily on metaphorical use of language, is relegated to the "optional" category in VM texts (indeed, prefaces to the textbooks say that poetry for VM students is to be regarded as "supplementary reading"). Poetry is part of the mandated EM curriculum.

At a somewhat superficial level the above tables could be read as snippets of 'evidence.' However, it is their positioning in larger cultural and political inter-locking chains (that include snobberies, pedagogies, ideologies) that contribute to sedimenting these inequities in the formal realm.

Non-Formal Education, Civic Engagements, Efforts at Equality

Such instances of the 'divide' necessarily force one to raise the question of: what can be done to make language-education issues more equitable? Is it the case that as researcher I am focusing only on inequities? Have I been blind to how ordinary, everyday shifts happen and to what extent did my EM background keep me from seeing transformations? Teachers, while heavily influenced by policies and mandates, are thinking agents who make choices, who choose to act in ways that are sometimes diametrically opposed to official rules, and who are motivated by codes of individual ethics—sometimes rationalized in religious terms, sometimes philosophic—and who stare fearlessly back at inequity and move towards dissolving it one very small grain at a time. It was when one of the teachers at the low-income women's college introduced me to some of his students working in non-formal education projects that I realized the extent to which the EM part of my background had superseded the vernacular parts of me (at least as far as this research endeavour was concerned), and kept me myopic. I turn now to addressing Gandhianism and non-formal learning, and ways in which grassroots efforts at empowerment happen by drawing on the most local and available of resources, namely the vernaculars. As we will see, both instances laminate 'learning' differently from the formal realm and make us pay heed to institutionalized schooling policies that supply us only with the narrowest understandings about inequity and learning.

While it may seem as if I am taking a major detour in the following section, it is necessary background by which to understand civic engagement, alternate literacies, and the value of non-formal education.

Some Communal Issues in Ahmedabad: Setting the Backdrop for Non-Formal Education

In 2001 and 2002 two devastating events occurred that impacted the city of Ahmedabad in traumatic ways.[1] The first was a 7.9 earthquake in 2001 and the second, gory Hindu–Muslim riots in 2002. The earthquake of 2001, that occurred around 9:00am on January 26, (about the time that most educational institutions in the city were holding Republic Day celebrations), had its epicenter in the small town of Bhuj, about 200 miles from Ahmedabad. An estimated 17,000 bodies were recovered, more than 30,000 people were reported dead or missing, 166,000 or more were injured, and over a million homes were destroyed. The devastation in Ahmedabad, needless to say, was extensive, with school buildings crushing little children, flats and apartments coming down on families getting ready to start their day, and businesses being decimated.

As if this were not enough, the following year, on February 27, 2002, the city broke out into the worst Hindu–Muslim riots in recent years. The events allegedly unfolded like this (there is a lot of room for debate here about how planned or accidental the whole scenario was. Indeed, the case is still pending the courts): 58 Hindu pilgrims returning from Ayodhya (a Hindu holy site) had their train cabin set ablaze outside Ahmedabad. The train had made a scheduled stop, during which a scuffle between some of the pilgrims and a tea vendor began, started to escalate, and eventually culminated in the train compartment going up in blazes and the pilgrims being burnt to death (allegedly by a group of Muslims). This led to a vicious collective anger on the part of the hardline Hindus that resulted in a horrendous week of rioting where Muslim homes were burnt, businesses looted, women raped, and children killed. More than 1,000 Muslims died.

While I cannot come close to accounting for the numerous local ways in which various groups in the city of Ahmedabad leapt into action,[2] including the group of teachers I work with, I shall devote myself to explaining in some detail the work of two endeavours committed to communal and educa-tional change in very different ways (see Ramanathan, 2006a, for a detailed discussion). My point here is to underscore how vernacular resources—typically seen as 'backward,' rabid, fundamentalist, nativist (a colonial legacy that the EM press has tended to assume)—become a most valuable well of resources for reconstructing lives and communities. Learning and teaching in these contexts assume very different hues that complicate our collective notions of devaluing the vernacular.

Gandhian Ideologies in Two Settings: Gandhi's Views on Non-Formal Education, Community Service, and Non-Cooperation

Because both institutions echo Gandhian views in a variety of direct and indirect ways, I would like to provide in this section a brief and interconnected understanding of those aspects of Non-Cooperation that are most relevant to the issues at hand. While world history documents Non-Cooperation in terms of civil disobedience, Satyagraha and non-violence, there are a host of details in this philosophy that are pertinent to the present discussion, including: 1) the value of harnessing the vernaculars (including those of promoting vernacular-medium education), 2) the importance of community service being an integral part of a basic education, and 3) promoting non-formal education that encourages a healthy development of civic citizenship.

Each of these ideals gets encased in the larger rhetorical strain of "Non-cooperation," which Gandhi advocated during his struggles for Indian Independence (see Ramanathan 2006a, 2012, for a detailed discussion), and which people at the two institutions interpret and enact differently. The following are some excerpts from his writings on this topic:

On Vernacular (and English) Education:

1. I hold it to be as necessary for the urban child as for the rural to have the foundation of his development laid on the solid work of the mother-tongue. It is only in unfortunate India that such an obvious proposition needs to be proved (Gandhi in *Harijan*, 9–9–'39, edited by Kumarappa, 1954, [Gandhi 1954]).

2. . . . The only education we receive is English education. Surely we must show something for it. But suppose we had been receiving during the past fifty years education through our vernaculars, what should we have today? We should have a free India, we should have our educated people, not as if they were foreigners in their own land, but speaking to the heart of the nation; they would be working amongst the poorest of the poor, and whatever they would have gained during the past fifty years would be a heritage for the nation . . . (Gandhi, cited in Kumarappa, 1954, p. 13 [Gandhi, 1954]).

On (Non-)Formal Education:

1. . . . But unless the development of the mind and body goes hand in hand with a corresponding awakening of the soul, the former alone would prove to be a poor lop-sided affair. By spiritual training I mean

education of the heart. A proper and all-around development of the mind, therefore, can take place only when it proceeds *pari passu* with the education of the physical and spiritual faculties of the child. They constitute an indivisible whole. According to this theory, therefore, it would be a gross fallacy to suppose that they can be developed piecemeal or independently of one another (Gandhi, 1954, p. 25).

2. By education I mean all-round drawing out of the best in children—body, mind, and spirit. [Formal] Literacy is not the end of education nor the beginning. It is only one of the means whereby men and women can be educated (Gandhi, 1954, p. 25).

3. [Non-formal education] . . . will check the progressive decay of our villages and lay the foundation for a juster social order in which there is no unnatural division between the 'haves' and the 'havenots' and everybody is assured a living wage and the rights to freedom. . . . It will provide a healthy and a moral basis of relationship between the city and village and will go a long way towards eradicating some of the worst evils of the present social insecurity and poisoned relationship between the classes (Gandhi, 1954, p. 25).

Fundamentals of Basic Education:

1. All education to be true must be self-supporting, that is it will pay its expenses excepting the capital . . .

2. In it the cunning of the hand will be utilized even up to the final stage, that is to say, hands of pupils will be skillfully working at some industry for some period during the day.

3. All education must be imparted through the medium of the provincial language.

4. In this there is no room for giving sectional religious training. Fundamental universal ethics will have full scope.

5. This education whether it is confined to children or adults, male or female, will find its way to the homes of the pupils.

6. Since millions of students receiving this education will consider themselves as of the whole of the India, they must learn an interprovincial language. This common inter-provincial speech can only be Hindustani written in Nagari or Urdu script. Therefore, pupils will have to master both scripts (Gandhi, 1954, p. 56).

Gandhi's views above have to be interpreted in the political context in which they were made. From approximately 1920–1947, Gandhi's views were decidedly nationalistic, since he and his allies were trying to rally the country toward destabilizing the Raj, and toward gaining Indian independence. Because his views on the above issues were directly anti-English—since he felt that the language divided the country—his championing of the vernaculars sits in a polarized position (somewhat simplistic by today's standards) vis-à-vis English. While Gandhi's message of non-violence seems to be ironically completely forgotten in Gujarat, given the recent horrific riots, the larger strain of non-cooperation still resonates. As we will see, non-cooperation in the two endeavours discussed presently is directed against perceived social forces that preserve inequities. The steadfast way in which both projects work at bridging perceived gulfs is reminiscent of Gandhi's insistence on being 'civil' and of responding to tyranny by searching for non-violent, effective alternatives.

The Two Endeavours: Drawing on Non-Cooperation to Expand "Education" and Civic Engagement

The National Social Service Scheme at the Women's College

Located in the inner-city, the women's college is a low-income Gujarati-medium liberal arts college in downtown Ahmedabad where much of the rioting of 2002 occurred. In my previous writing (Ramanathan, 2006a) regarding this college, I have discussed ways in which the National Social Service (NSS)—a nation-wide, Gandhian, social service organization—a chapter of which is in this school, engages many of the institution's female students in extracurricular activities that directly target community needs. Begun in commemoration of Gandhi's centennial year in 1969, the organization encourages students to volunteer time toward social projects, including those relating to literacy, health, sanitation, women and children's welfare, AIDS awareness, drug addiction awareness, human rights, and national integration.[3] Added to this list are the recent projects that address the needs of families most affected by the two events. While I have addressed ways in which this extra-curricular project harnesses a variety of vernacular resources in some detail elsewhere (Ramanathan, 2006a), I will for the purposes of the present discussion attempt to make this point by drawing primarily on interview data with Mr. N.,[4] the key person that runs this project endeavour (I do need to note here that all my interviews were in Hindi and Gujarati and that I have translated the excerpts below for the present argument; see Ramanathan, 2006b, for a discussion on tensions with translations).

Mr. N., a teacher of 19th century British literature, began this project more than 15 years ago with a commitment to translating the best of Gandhi's ideals—of service, self-respect, valuing the vernacular backgrounds of his students—to specific contexts of practice. Realizing that he operates in a space where speaking openly of socio-political issues is most incendiary—in downtown Ahmedabad where much of the rioting occurred, in a very poor, diverse college with students from both Hindu and Muslim (as well as other) backgrounds—this man works toward expanding his view of education by connecting it to issues of 'citizenship,' taking pride in being 'Gujarati,' and relying on what is currently within one's reach to ply instruments of change. When asked about why the classroom was not a viable sphere for his message, he said:

> The classroom is the most incendiary place to raise community issues ... you see, the students come from such different backgrounds, with such divergent points of view, how can I bring up political and community issues, especially now when everyone, but everyone is reeling from the riots? Some of my students have lost their homes, some family members. *But I will say this: I know that I want to address these issues somehow; I want them to know that education is not only about what they learn and what we teach in classes about Dryden and Congreve, it is about participating in the community.* It is about taking the best of literary values—connecting to other humans—and living them. So rather than be overtly political about it, I channel their and my energy in my projects where the focus is on the community, regardless of who the members of the community are, and I have both Muslim and Hindu students working in these projects.
>
> (*Faculty Interview,*[5] *2: 2, June 2, 2004)*

When the earthquake hit, he organized his students into groups that went out and worked in the community: in communal kitchens for people that were left homeless, in contacting municipal authorities for clean drinking water, and in getting blankets and warm clothes because it was winter. Because the riots occurred around the time that many of the students were to take their final university exams, and because the exam centers were far away and there was curfew in town, he organized buses that would take students from riot-affected areas to the exam centers.

As he explains in the excerpt above, "education" for him is more about "connecting to other humans" than it is about what is taught and learned in the classroom, and moving toward this end without engaging in divisive political rhetoric is instrumental in his mission, since his focus is on "what needs to get done, what the reality in front of me is like" (Faculty Interview, 2: 5). One way that he works toward this goal is by emphasizing in his workshops (for NSS volunteers) what being "Gujarati" means: its diversity (the fact that it is a native language for a diverse set of people including Hindus, Sikhs, Muslims, Parsis, Christians, and Jews), the fact that it is home to other migrant Indians (like my family who are originally Tamilian but who have settled in Gujarat), the fact that it is the birthplace of Gandhi who represented the last word on community service, non-formal education, and above all Hindu–Muslim unity. As he says,

My job is to create a space whereby such sentiments and values about community participation can flourish. The last 3 or 4 years have been so painful for so many people in this state. I want to be able to say that when my students graduate they do so with some pride and awareness of the ties that bind them to their fellow citizens. That the riots should have happened here in Gandhi's home state, when his life's actions centered around Hindu–Muslim unity—how do I not get my Gujarati students to see that irony? My problem is: how do I get them to realize this inductively? How can I make that realization happen quietly, without dogma, without saying too much?

(Faculty Interview, I, 2: 7)

One way by which he communicates his message indirectly is by not speaking about NSS issues in the classroom, or in corridors where students abound, but by relying on his NSS student-volunteers to "spread the word" as indeed they do. As he explains:

It is crucial that this work not become a dogma ... given my position, my speaking of it directly runs that risk. I speak of it in workshops, I organize their camps, I attend the training sessions with them; I want to do all that, but I will not seek students out by speaking of it directly. They have to want to do this work. The value of non-formal education is that it remain 'non-formal.' You take it into the classroom and it is gone. Pfff ... like that! They have to hear of this community work from other involved students; they have to see their classmates being fulfilled by this.

(Faculty Interview, I, 2: 13)

Echoes of Gandhi's views on non-formal education are obvious here, as indeed is the Gandhian insistence on proceeding with such work diligently and without fuss. While non-formal education has traditionally been conceived of as an educational alternative operating outside the constraints of the classroom, the changes that such education seems to seek eventually make their way to classrooms.

Education and Community at the Gandhi Ashram

This theme of quietly working on community problems and of viewing such work as integral to larger understandings of education is most resonant in the Gandhi Ashram, which houses a program called *Manav Sadhna* (*MS; Human Improvement*). The Gandhi Ashram in Ahmedabad is the largest of Gandhi's ashrams, since this particular one served as his headquarters during the struggle for Independence. On the banks of the river Sabarmati, the ashram is located on spacious grounds. One side holds his library and archival materials about him, and on the doorway to this section is a huge tribute to Martin Luther King. The other side of the ashram has what used to be his living quarters: his spinning wheel, his desk, rooms of his closest allies. The ashram, even today, is a place that welcomes the poorest of the poor and offers a haven and rehabilitation for those seeking it.

All work that goes on in the Gandhi Ashram seems to embody quintessential "Gandhian" ideals of self-reliance, cross-religious unities, non-formal and basic education, coupled with a thick strain of quiet non-cooperation. Begun by three people—Jayesh Patel, Anar Patel, and Viren Joshi[6]—in 1991, *Manav Sadhna* today runs more than 20 well-developed community-oriented programs. Born and raised in the ashram because his father was a staunch Gandhian follower, the first of the three has Gandhi 'in his bones,' so to speak and much of what follows in this section is drawn from my interviews with him, from participating in workshops he has led, and from interviews with other people at the ashram with whom he has put me in touch.

While there are several similarities between the NSS work of Mr. N. and the projects of *MS*—both have strong Gandhian strains, both enhance the vernaculars, both are community oriented—there are interesting differences. Unlike the project run by Mr. N. where civic engagement is parallel to formal, classroom-based learning, the focus of the projects at the Gandhi Ashram is on interpreting all education as 'civic education' and on attending to the most basic of human needs (food, clothing, shelter) before addressing any issues related to formal learning. Also, unlike the NSS project, the children that the Ashram caters to are the extremely poor. When I spent time at the ashram in May and June 2004, Jayesh recalled how the three of them began their program with the explicit aim of working with the poorest persons they could find. While he narrated this to me in Gujarati, I am presenting it below in translation. (I need to note here that I am deliberately choosing to present extensive, fuller quotes to mitigate the loss already encountered in translation, a process that necessitates the adding of more layers of 'distance' from the very first layer of the narrator's recounting and my interpreting in Gujarati, to my then presenting and interpreting this narrative in academic English).

> ... the three of us had noticed that a lot of village people, because of a scarcity of resources in villages—equipment, money, water—migrate to the cities and they live in slums. And we found that mothers work as cleaners/maids in people's homes, fathers work in pulling handcarts and they send their children out to pick rags. The childhoods of these children are completely lost. Middle-class children have all they could possibly have but these others have no opportunities and we decided we wanted to work with these children. Think globally, act locally ... so the three of us started our work. The three of us took along biscuits, chocolates, some clothes and we set out in a rickshaw and went to the Naranpura crossroads. I still remember this and there we saw two children working in a tea stall, making

tea, and serving it to customers. We asked the tea-stall owner if we could sit with the children and chat with them. Hope you don't mind. We started talking to the children who were clearly suspicious of us. "Who are these people who are asking me all these questions," they thought. We told the children, "we came to be friends with you. Will you share a meal with us?" The children said yes. . . . and when we got to know them, we gave them clothes, cut their nails, shampooed their hair, got them shoes. We went again in a few days, and by then, these children had talked about what we had done for them with their friends and before long they would wait for us to come, calling "Jayeshbhai Virenbhai." . . . We soon realized it was getting very difficult for us to cater to all the children there and so asked "will you come to the Gandhi Ashram? We have a campus there and we can introduce you to people there. Can you come once a week?" Our very first program was "Back to childhood" in '91. While we had each done work with children before this, but this was our first Manav Sadhna project. Soon thereafter, the children started coming, first 10, then 15 . . . they seemed to enjoy coming here. We used to give them baths, clothes and then began helping them with their homework. You'll see some of them today . . . they've grown but are still here. They were dirty, unbathed, with unwashed clothes . . . we showered them with care, told them stories, prayed with them, showed them films and sang songs with them. We did a lot through play and then would eat together with them . . .

(Jayesh Patel, Gandhi Ashram: 2, June 3, 2004)

As Jayesh explained to me: "for us education is community work; if schooling does not teach you to connect with your fellow humans, then what good is it?" (June, 3, 2004).

Like the NSS-related work at the women's college, *MS* is committed to working with and around social stratifications, including Hindu–Muslim tensions, some of which were exacerbated during the quake (and very definitely during the riots; indeed, there had been reports that particular groups of peoples, including Muslims, did not get the aid they needed). Jayesh, Viren, Anar and the *MS* volunteers began working with some very poor destitute villages in a corner of Kutch (not far from the epicenter), with 80 percent of its population being Muslim, and with the Hindu population migrating. Almost all the homes had been decimated. As Jayesh explains:

There was almost nothing left there. We wanted to do something about this. *We did an initial analysis and educated ourselves of their needs*: broken down homes, no resources, no fodder or water for livestock, the general geographical conditions of the place (frequent cyclones and hurricanes). Over the last few years we have reached a point where it is self-sufficient, stopped migration, worked out Hindu–Muslim tensions to where during the recent riots, not one of these 47 villages reported anti-Hindu, anti-Muslim incidents.

(Jayesh Patel, Gandhi Ashram, 4, June 3, 2004)

This close attention to "educating oneself," of figuring out and questioning one's own default assumptions has echoes of Gandhi's non-cooperation, and finds interesting articulation in the idea that we each need to 'not cooperate' with our default views but attempt to step outside them by 'educating ourselves' by learning from others. A point that illustrates this best has to do with *MS*'s work in a set of villages after the massive earthquake and ways in which they went about educating themselves about the lives of the villagers after paying close attention to the needs of the local people, and by drawing extensively on their valued, vernacular ways of living. Robin Sukhadia, with whom I have been in email contact, and who has worked with *MS* in some of these villages, explains on his website the conflicts many of the villagers experienced between the modern kinds of houses that were being built for them after the quake and the 'traditional' homes they were used to and wanted:

There has been tremendous financial and infrastructural support pouring into Kutchh after the earthquake, and so many NGOs and international agencies and religious organizations have come here to build homes and rebuild this area ... new hospitals have been built, new roads, new homes, but sadly, it seems to me, that many of these projects (which are funded mainly from abroad) have very insensitively proceeded with building living "communities" without much thought as to the traditional way of life here ... and it seems that many of the villagers and farmers who lost everything here, do not wish to live in homes that resemble city homes and pre-fabricated enclaves ... the villagers, who have lived off the land for generations, have nowhere to put their cattle, to grow their crops, or to stay connected to the land in these new homes ... sadly many of the homes are empty because the villagers have decided it is better to be homeless than succumb to these imposed forms of living which are being built in the name of service to the poor but ... *MS*'s approach here, thankfully, has been very different. They have, instead of imposing designs and architects, rather empowered the local communities to design their own homes in their traditional methods ... they have built *Bhungas*, beautiful, mud-based round buildings that have been in use for hundreds of years here ... not surprisingly, these structures were the only ones that survived the earthquake ... they are very practical and make sense for this environment. So, *Manav Sadhna* provided the guidance for the reconstruction of their homes, and the community ... [look at] what happens in the name of service. ...

(Robin Sukhadia, cited in Ramanathan, 2006a)

The idea of drawing on, listening to, and educating oneself about what a community needs permeates all aspects of *MS*'s projects and is a key issue in the orientation workshops (for *MS* volunteers) that I participated in. Not only are the volunteers—all of whom are Gujarati—reminded of and educated in Gandhi's ideals in the workshops, but they are encouraged to make connections between the work they do and the specific Gandhian ideals they are enacting. So, whether it is working in a very poor Urdu-medium Muslim school (that municipal authorities have largely ignored) or finding clothes and food supplies for a very poor farmer who is suffering the consequences of a bad crop and little rain, or organizing the celebrations of a key religious holiday (Hindu, Muslim, Christian, Jewish, Sikh, Parsi), among others, the volunteers are provided platforms and contexts whereby both their conceptual understanding of Gandhi and their practice are extended and looped into each other. As one of the volunteers tells me: "these workshops are not just about educating ourselves about Gandhi, but about bringing our work back to Gandhi ... we go out and do Gandhi's work, but we each have to come back to Gandhi ..." (V 2: 2, Jun 11, 2004).

Interestingly, politically- and community-oriented as all of this work by *MS* is, there is little or no reference to political events, and ways in which they have exacerbated social/religious stratifications in the city. When discussing the work done by MS volunteers after the riots, no overt mention was made of Gujarat's chief minister (who has been accused of not doing enough to protect the Muslims) or of the incendiary rhetoric of the ruling BJP state government. The idea that "there is a job to be done" and "I have to do it" (Jayesh Patel: 5, June 10, 2004) seems to be a dominant theme, and non-cooperation during this time was and still is enacted in terms of steadfastly engaging in the opposite of all riot-related acts: of making shelter, finding lost relatives, distributing food and clothes, finding employment for the numerous widowed women, providing a haven for orphaned children. While all of the volunteers at *MS* are engaged in various riot-related projects, it is with the children that they are most concerned. As Jayesh explains:

> If we wish to reach the parents, we have to start with children. It is only through our work that we pass on our message. We cannot formally teach anybody anything; we can only do. In the end, everything we learn goes back to the community. Why not start with the community in the first place? Why not start with children?
>
> *(Jayesh Patel, p. 6, June 3, 2004)*

Clearly, distinctions between 'civic engagement' and 'education' have blurred here; they are in this context almost synonymous.

Winding Down: Articulating Implications

Moving away from the locality of these scenes to the more generalized space of research frameworks, we can see that juxtaposing skeins of formal and non-formal education permits hues around the Vernaculars that otherwise tend to remain hidden. The Vernaculars, while devalued in the formal realm, become the very resources by which communities heal themselves. This irony is a subtext that flows thickly through many issues around English and the Vernaculars in S. Asia, and is integrally tied to the postcolonial research framework. It is to the specifics of this framework and how it has helped my endeavour that I now turn.

First, since this framework involves 'speaking back' to colonial powers, it ushers in history, a discipline that has been generally regarded as marginal to applied linguistics. After all, in order to gain a fuller sense of how I am today—where I fit, how I see myself, others, our planet—I had to gain a fuller sense of historical conditions that brought me to my present, a historical sense that exceeded the history I was taught in K-12. I had to educate myself about colonial documents, especially as they pertained to language teaching, largely separatist schooling policies for Indians and the English, ways in which Indian history until 1947 was told to Indians by British historians (which, as I mentioned earlier, was by and large unkind), the efforts of Indian historians writing Indian history, and how my own family background had differing relations vis-à-vis the English (both of my grandfathers worked for the Raj, but one was a staunch Gandhian, the other an Anglophile). History, then—personal, national, international—is crucial in the postcolonial endeavour.

The second key point that this framework implies is a deep commitment to recognizing how history plays itself out in contexts of inequity. Within applied linguistics, this could mean identifying ways in which unjust conditions get reproduced in everyday interactions (the consistent use of a certain dismissive or patronizing tone in interactions with poorer VM students, for instance), connections between these 'smaller' contexts and other structural inequities (reproduced in textbooks, or in the low expectations on the part of teachers regarding VM students), and then further out into the larger culture (ideologies perpetuated by the media that equates EM people with 'sophistication' and the VM with being 'backward'). Bringing the past into understanding inequity in the present permits insights into colonizing policies that still hold sway; being alert to cross-questioning our own assumptions permits us to address shifts and transformations.

Growing into this multi-pronged awareness also raises consciousness regarding disputes and conflicts around ownership and claiming the right to speak for one's self about one's past. And this is where the third point about this research framework comes in. On the one hand is the wresting back of historiography from 'colonial powers,' and assuming the right to claim reception; on the other, it is also about recognizing that there are others who are already doing so (VM teachers and students in this case) but are doing so in ways, languages and forms that we have remained blind to because we have collectively bought into status-quo ways of being, thinking, believing, living, that keep our vision blinkered. In my own case, it wasn't until I turned my gaze to issues in the community that I began to connect to the vernacular part of me. Doing so allowed me to acknowledge the efforts of Mr. N. and *Manav Sadhna,* whose efforts are as much about achieving the right to claim a space and understanding of one's history—through enactments of Gandhianism—as is my own writing about these issues. The workshops with these teachers have, over the years, made me ever conscious of how critical work happens on the sidelines, in unexpected ways, and in manners that defy definition or categorization. It is in not-cooperating with our own default assumptions that we render ourselves open to seeing the hierarchies in languages, peoples, and literacies, and it is in this way that this framework is ultimately ethical, since its focus is integrally on changing our own perspectives as it validates those of others that are waiting to be acknowledged and heard.

Notes

1   Some of what follows has appeared in Ramanathan (2005a, 2006a).
2   Some activist groups in Ahmedabad include:
   a) Janvikas: an organization which focuses on the empowerment and development of NGOs in Gujarat.
   b) Janpath Citizens Initiative: a coalition of over 200 local grassroots NGOs coming together in the days following the Gujarat quake.
   c) Navsarjan Trust: led by Martin Macwan: an organization representing Dalit rights in India.
   d) Rishta: A Gujarat Jesuit writers' cell—engaged in a series of workshops for the development of vernacular media, especially for Christian and Muslim youth.
   e) *Manav Sadhna*: Run out of the Gandhi Ashram.
3   Yearly camps and training are offered for all volunteers for a minimal fee as well as extended camps for college-going youth. Themes of some camps in the last few years have been "Youth for sustainable development," Youth for wasteland development," and Youth for greenery."
4   Towards preserving the identities of people, I am using initials that are pseudonyms.
5   Faculty Interview; GA to Gandhi Ashram.
6   I am using their real names since this is their preference. They wish to be identified this way, especially if it is in the context of raising awareness of Gandhianism, which this paper partially intends.

References

Alidou, H. (2004). Medium of instruction in postcolonial Africa. In J. Tollefson & A. Tsui (Eds.), *Medium of instruction policies: Which agenda? Whose agenda?* Mahwah, NJ: Lawrence Erlbaum Associates.

Brutt-Griffler, J. (2002). *World English: A study of its development.* Clevedon, UK: Multilingual Matters.

Gandhi, M. K. (1954). *Medium of instruction* (B. Kumarappa, Trans.). Ahmedabad, India: Navjivan Publishing House.

Gee, J. P. (1990). *Social linguistics and literacies: Ideologies in discourses.* Bristol, PA, Falmer Press.

Gee, J. P. (2003). Opportunity to learn: A language-based perspective on assessment. *Assessment in Education, 10*(1), 27–46.

Hawkins, M. (Ed.). (2004). *Language learning and teacher-education.* Clevedon, UK: Multilingual Matters.

Hornberger, N., & Johnson, D. (2007). Slicing the onion ethnographically: Layers and spaces in multilingual language education policy and practice. *TESOL Quarterly, 41*(3), 509–532.

Kalantzis, M., & Cope, B. (2002). Multicultural education: Transforming the mainstream. In S. May (Ed.), *Critical multiculturalism: Rethinking multicultural and antiracist education* (pp. 245–276). Philadelphia, PA: Falmer Press.

King, K. A. (2001). *Language revitalization processes and prospects: Quichua in the Ecuadorian Andes.* Clevedon, UK: Multilingual Matters.

McCarty, T. (2002). Between possibility and constraint: Indigenous language education, planning, and policy in the United States. In J. Tollefson (Ed.), *Language policies in education: Critical issues* (pp. 285–307). Mahwah, NJ: Lawrence Erlbaum Associates.

McCarty, T. (Ed.). (2005). *Language, literacy and power in schooling.* Mahwah, NJ: Lawrence Erlbaum Associates.

Morgan, B., & Ramanathan, V. (2009). Outsourcing, globalizing economics, and shifting language policies: Issues in managing Indian call centres. *Language Policy, 8*(1), 69–80.

Purani, T., Salat, J., Soni, P., & Joshi, S. (1998). *English readers.* Gandhinagar, India: Gujarat State Board of Textbooks.

Ramanathan-Abbott, V. (1993). An examination of the relationship between social practices and the comprehension of narratives. *Text, 13*(1), 117–141.

Ramanathan, V. (2005a). *The English-vernacular divide: Post-colonial language policies and practice.* Cleveland, UK: Multilingual Matters.

Ramanathan, V. (2005b). Situating the researcher in research texts: Dilemmas, questions, ethics, new directions. *Journal of Language, Identity, and Education, 4*(4), 291–297.

Ramanathan, V. (2006a). Gandhi, non-cooperation and socio-civic education: Harnessing the vernaculars. *Journal of Language, Identity, and Education, 5*(3), 229–250.

Ramanathan, V. (2006b). Of texts AND translations AND rhizomes: Postcolonial anxieties AND deracinations AND knowledge constructions. *Critical Inquiry in Language Studies, 3*(4), 223–244.

Ramanathan, V. (2009). Silencing and languaging in the assembling of the Indian nation-state: British public citizens, the epistolary form, and historiography. *Journal of language, identity, and education, 8*, 203–219.

Ramanathan, V. (2012). Rethinking discourses around the English-Cosmopolitan correlation: Scenes from formal and non-formal educational contexts. In M. Martin Jones, A. Blackledge, & A. Creese (Eds.), *The Routledge handbook of multilingualism* (pp. 66–82). New York, NY: Routledge.

Shohamy, E. (2006). *Language policy: hidden agendas and new approaches.* New York, NY: Routledge.

Thakker, P. (Ed.). (1999). *English, Standard 8.* Gandhinagar, India: Gujarat State Board of Textbooks.

Tollefson, J. W. (Ed.). (1991). *Planning language, planning inequality.* London, UK: Longman.

Tollefson, J. W. (Ed.). (2002). *Language policies in education: Critical issues.* Mahwah, NJ: Lawrence Erlbaum Associates.

Vamdatta, D., Joshi, P., & Patel, Y. (Eds.). (2000). *English, Standard 10.* Gandhinagar, India: Gujarat State Board of Textbooks.

Verma, P. (2010). *Becoming Indian: The unfinished revolution of culture and identity.* New Delhi, India: Penguin India

Young, R. (2003). *Postcolonialism: A short introduction.* Oxford, UK: Oxford University Press.

6

"MULTILITERACIES"

New Literacies, New Learning

Bill Cope and Mary Kalantzis

This paper examines the changing landscape of literacy teaching and learning, revisiting the case for a "pedagogy of multiliteracies" first put by the New London Group in 1996. It describes the dramatically changing social and technological contexts of communication and learning, develops a language with which to talk about representation and communication in educational contexts, and addresses the question of what constitutes appropriate literacy pedagogy for our times.

Introduction

The New London Group[1] first came together in the mid-1990s to consider the state and future of literacy pedagogy. After a meeting in September 1994, the New London Group published an article-long manifesto (New London Group, 1996) and then a book (Cope & Kalantzis, 2000b) outlining an agenda for what we called a "pedagogy of multiliteracies". Experts, colleagues and friends, all with a concern for language and education, we had set aside that initial week in 1994 to talk through what was happening in the world of communications and what was happening (or not happening but perhaps should happen) in the teaching of language and literacy in schools.

During that week, we used what then seemed to be a daringly novel mix of technologies: a portable computer with a data projector and screen. With these, we jointly built a schema—a series of headings and notes—that was to be the structure and argument of the 1996 article and the 2000 book. Not much more

Chapter 6 is reprinted from 'Multiliteracies: New Literacies, New Learning' by Bill Cope & Mary Kalantzis (2009). In *Pedagogies: An International Journal*, 4(3), pp. 164–195 (Taylor & Francis Ltd, www.tandfonline.com, reprinted by permission of the publisher).

than a decade later, portable computers are called "laptops". The term "data projector" has also entered our language more recently. Back then, the machine in question, a very expensive glass-screened device that you laid on a conventional overhead projector was only known by its forgettable brand name. Today, such tools of text and talk are commonplace, even though they are now nearly always framed by the "bullet point" lists of PowerPoint "slides" in a didactic "presentation" rather than the scrolling text of a word processor that we used as our joint thinking and writing tool over that week.

Using these then-unusual technologies, we did another strange thing for a group of academics. We committed ourselves to a collaborative writing exercise which involved, not two or three people, but 10. During the week, we had to listen hard to what other people had to say, pick up on the cadences in their arguments, capture the range of perspectives represented by the members of the group, negotiate our differences, hone the key conceptual terms and shape a statement that represented a shared view at the common ground of our understandings.

Since 1996, we have often come together in a virtual sense, worked together on various projects and published together. Members of the New London Group have also met annually at the International Conference on Learning: in Townsville, Australia, 1995; Alice Springs, Australia, 1997; Penang, Malaysia, 1999; Melbourne, Australia, 2000; Spetses, Greece, 2001; Beijing, China, 2002; London, UK, 2003; Havana, Cuba, 2004; Granada, Spain, 2005; Montego Bay, Jamaica, 2006; and Johannesburg, South Africa, 2007. Numerous new relationships have been formed and old ones consolidated at these conferences, and many publications have followed in the *International Journal of Learning* (www.Learning-Journal.com). The intellectual genesis of this vibrant conference and the journal can be traced back to the New London Group. For the most part, the New London Group has continued to work together. We have met irregularly and in different combinations. We have created networks and affiliations and worked in joint projects with new colleagues in their varied institutions and national settings. Ideas have developed, friendships have deepened and relationships have spread to encompass new people and exciting endeavours.

Beyond this personal experience of the life of ideas, none of us could have predicted the reach and influence that the multiliteracies idea would have way beyond our own circles of personal and professional association. Even the idea of a "Google search" was unimaginable in the mid-1990s. However, a search on Google in 2009 showed that more than 60,000 web pages mentioned "multiliteracies", an unusually accurate figure because we coined the word during our New London meeting to capture the essence of our deliberations and our case.

In the initial article and book, we presented "a pedagogy of multiliteracies" as a programmatic manifesto. The world was changing, the communications environment was changing, and it seemed to us that to follow these changes literacy teaching and learning would have to change as well. This was the gist of our argument. The details are in an analysis of the questions of "why", "what" and "how" of literacy pedagogy.

To the "why" question, we responded with an interpretation of what was happening to meaning making and representation in the worlds of work, citizenship and personal life that might prompt a reconsideration of our approaches to literacy teaching and learning. We were interested in the growing significance of two "multi" dimensions of "literacies" in the plural—the multilingual and the multimodal. Multilingualism was an increasingly significant phenomenon that required a more adequate educational response in the case of minority languages and the context of globalization (Cazden, 2006b; Ismail & Cazden, 2005). We also felt that discourse differences within a language had not been adequately taken into account. Central to our broader interpretation of multilingualism was the burgeoning variety of what Gee (1996) calls "social languages" in professional, national, ethnic, subcultural, interest or affinity group contexts. For all the signs that English was becoming a world language, it was also diverging into multiple Englishes. Whereas traditional literacy curriculum was taught to a singular standard (grammar, the literary canon, standard national forms of the language), the everyday experience of meaning making was increasingly one of negotiating discourse differences. A pedagogy of multiliteracies would need to address this as a fundamental aspect of contemporary teaching and learning.

In response to the question of "what", we spoke of the need to conceive meaning making as a form of design or active and dynamic transformation of the social world, and its contemporary forms increasingly multimodal, with linguistic, visual, audio, gestural and spatial modes of meaning becoming increasingly integrated in everyday media and cultural practices. These constituted the second of the "multis"—the inherent multimodality of contemporary forms of representation. As a consequence, the traditional emphasis on alphabetical literacy (letter sounds in words in sentences in texts in literatures) would need to be supplemented in a pedagogy of multiliteracies by learning how to read and write multimodal texts that integrated the other modes with language.

To the question of "how", we analysed the limitations both of traditional literacy teaching that set out to transmit language rules and instil good practice from literary models ("overt instruction"), and progressivisms that considered the immersion or natural learning models that worked for oral language learning to be an adequate and sufficient model for literacy learning ("situated practice"). Instead, we suggested that a pedagogy of multiliteracies would involve a range of pedagogical moves, including both "situated practice" and "overt instruction", but also entailing "critical framing" and "transformed practice".

Do these generalizations still hold? So much has happened over the past decade and a half. When we met in 1994, email was new; the web was barely known and it was impossible to imagine its impact; almost no one had mobile telephones; and writing on a phone or using a phone to take photographs were unthinkable. Now we live in a world of iPods, wikis, blogs and SMS messages. Not even nameable a decade ago, these are just a few of the new spaces in which representation now occurs.

With these new communication practices, new literacies have emerged. They are embodied in new social practices—ways of working in new or transformed forms of employment, new ways of participating as a citizen in public spaces, and even perhaps new forms of identity and personality.

This article revisits the propositions in the original article and book in the light of the remarkable changes that have occurred in the world since the mid-1990s, as well as what we and other colleagues have learnt from extensive and intensive experiences of testing the ideas in the manifesto in school realities. Rather than write a blow-by-blow analysis of what is the same and what has changed in the world and our collective and various views of the world, we have decided to put the case afresh. We have found that the basic shape of our original position has stood the test of time. In fact, it has proved to be a useful guide to understanding and practice—the centrality of diversity, the notion of design as active meaning making, the significance of multimodality and the need for a more holistic approach to pedagogy. However, the original case does need to be restated in the light of experience, its examples updated, its language adapted to contemporary circumstances and its pedagogical agenda sharpened in the context of today's politics of education.

This article was drafted by Mary Kalantzis and Bill Cope after canvassing the original members of the New London Group for their current reflections and reviewing their subsequent writings. We also spent several very productive days with Courtney Cazden in Melbourne in January 2006. The text was then reviewed and commented upon by the original members of the New London Group.

The "Why" of Multiliteracies

First, why literacy? Or even more fundamentally, why education (in which literacy is a "basic")? On this front, not much has changed in the years since we first wrote. The two sides of the political spectrum, characterized loosely as "left" and "right", remain poles apart in what they see as the appropriate role of literacy learning in society, and indeed, education in general.

There is no dispute, however, that education provides access to material resources in the form of better paid employment; it affords an enhanced capacity to participate in civic life; and it promises personal growth. Upon education still rests one of the key promises of modern societies. People of the right call this promise "equity". They say that the world is inevitably and irreducibly unequal. However, inequality is not unjust insofar as education is one of society's "opportunities". It is free and compulsory, and through education, people can become anything they like and succeed on their own terms—if they have the will and the "ability", that is. Education is one of the key sources of social equity. People of the left, however, maintain that the goal of education is equality. Whether their vision is wishful or utopian, nothing less than equality is an acceptable objective, even if, in the short term, all that can be achieved in education is to pursue an ongoing struggle to reduce the gap between the haves and the have-nots—hence the compensatory programmes, the remedial curriculum for children who have been "left behind" and the special efforts made in schools in poor neighbourhoods.

Whether the rhetoric is based on notions of equity or equality, education continues to fail to meet these promises. If it could provide either greater equity or equality, it is doing neither. The gap between the rich and the poor is growing, and even when the poor sometimes become slightly less poor, it is rarely because education has improved. Maybe it is a delusion to think that education could ever be an instrument that ameliorates society's most fundamental ills. Nevertheless, education—and literacy teaching in particular—does continue to make such promises.

But an odd thing has happened over the past decade. Education has become a more prominent topic in the public discourse of social promise. The expectations of education have been ratcheted up in the rhetoric of the right as much as that of the left. More than ever before, our political leaders are saying that education is pivotal to social and economic progress. They express this in the rhetoric of the "new economy" and "knowledge society". Business leaders also tell us that knowledge is now a key factor of production and a fundamental basis of competitiveness at the personal, enterprise and national levels. As knowledge is the result of learning, education is more important than ever. This does not necessarily translate into greater public investment in education (a business-like approach, one would think) but today's rhetoric about the importance of education does give educators greater leverage in the public discourse than we had a decade ago (Kalantzis & Cope, 2006, 2012b).

And literacy education in particular? What is its role in underwriting equity/equality in the knowledge society, or even investment in the "knowledge economy"? How is that tug of war playing out in reality as well as in teaching and learning practices? To answer these questions, we will look once again at what is happening at work, in the public lives of citizens and the personal lives and identities of people (see Table 6.1).

Workers

In our original formulations, we contrasted the new capitalism with the old. The old capitalism was a place of rigid hierarchy, a top-down discourse of discipline and command and an ever-finer division of labour which deskilled workers. Meanwhile, school was a place that inculcated rudimentary "basics". Literacy, in fact, was two of the "three R's": reading and writing (the third "R" being "rithmetic"). Children memorized spelling lists and learnt parts of speech and correct grammar. School was a universe of straightforward right and wrong answers, authoritative texts and authoritarian teachers. The underlying lesson of

TABLE 6.1 The "Why" of Multiliteracies: Our Changing Times

	Recent pasts	*Near futures*
Workers	Hierarchical command structures	Human capital, value in "intangibles"
	De-skilling	> Knowledge economy
	Discipline	Learning is critically related to work
	Rudimentary basics	New lines of inequality
Citizens	Command politics	Neoliberalism
	The "nanny state"	> Globalism
	Nation-state cultural and linguistic uniformity	Self-governing communities
Persons	Command personalities and compliant personalities	> Rebalancing of agency
	Pressures to homogeneity	Deep diversity

the basics was about the social order and its sources of authority, a lesson that was appropriate for a society that expected its workers to be passively disciplined.

The trends in the "new capitalism" we described in the initial multiliteracies paper have, if anything, accelerated over the ensuing decade, or at least they have in the more prosperous parts of advanced economies. As befits the public rhetoric about the knowledge economy, human capital is now presented as the key to having a "competitive edge", whether that be the skills and knowledge of an individual seeking employment, the aggregate of human capital in an enterprise, or the international competitiveness of a regional or national workforce in the world economy. This is one of a number of intangibles that have come to figure as of equal or sometimes even greater importance than fixed capital. Others include intellectual property, technological know-how, business processes, organizational flexibility, corporate memory, brand identity, design aesthetics, customer relationships and service values. These intangibles are all the stuff of learning, whether it is informal or tacit learning in the corporate culture, explicit learning via knowledge management in the "learning organization", or human qualities that can be acquired in formal institutions of education or special training programmes (Kalantzis, 2004).

The everyday life experience of work has also changed in new economy organizations. Replacing the hierarchical command structures of the old workplace are the horizontal relations of teamwork. Replacing the logic of the division of labour and deskilling is the logic of "multiskilling" or creating the rounded and flexible worker whose skills repertoire is ever-broadening. Replacing mass production of uniform products is customization of products and services for niche markets, each representing a kind of identity in the commodity space of the new capitalism. Replacing the orders of the boss are "flattened hierarchy" and the supposedly self-motivating dynamics of belonging to the corporate culture, enacting its vision and personifying its mission. Replacing the formalities of the old primary discourses of command are the informalities of an apparent egalitarianism—the conversational meetings and chatty emails instead of the stiff old memos, the chummy retreats that aim to build interpersonal relationships and the training sessions that build corporate culture instead of the deference one used to show to the boss. Replacing self-interest and competition are relationships of sharing and collaboration, exemplified in open source software that is socially constructed and freely available. And replacing line management are relationships of pedagogy: mentoring, training and managing corporate knowledge in the learning organization. These kinds of changes, surely, provide educators reason to claim to be a central part of the main game of the new economy.

In this interpretation of the dynamics of today's capitalism, how do we create a literacy pedagogy that promotes a culture of flexibility, creativity, innovation and initiative? Even more clearly than was the case in the mid-1990s, the old literacy and its underlying moral economy are no longer adequate on their own. In the pedagogy of multiliteracies, we have attempted to develop a literacy pedagogy that will work pragmatically for the new economy. It should also have the most ordinarily conservative of reasons for existence: that it will help students get a decent job, particularly if the dice of opportunity seem to be loaded against them. Literacy needs much more than the traditional basics of reading and writing the national language: in the new economy workplace, it is a set of supple, variable, communication strategies, ever-diverging according to the cultures and social languages of technologies, functional groups, types of organization and niche clienteles.

Equally plausible is another, perhaps more sanguine reading of today's capital-ism, born of the global convulsions of the last decade and the transformations that have occurred in the economy and education. In this reading, we should be under no illusions about the liberatory potential of the new economy or even about how "new" it is. The discourses and practices of today's workplace can equally be read as a highly sophisticated form of co-option—the co-option of teamwork, vision and mission and corporate culture, for instance, in which everyone is sup-posed to personify the enterprise, to think, will and act the enterprise. The more you feel you belong to this kind of enterprise, the more its inequalities—its iniqu-ities indeed—recede into the inevitability of common sense. And a lot of people are left out of the new economy: the service workers in hospitality and catering who wash dishes and make beds; the illegal immigrants who pick fruit and clean people's houses; and the people who work in old-style factories in China or call centres in India. Patterns of exclusion remain endemic. Even in the heart of the new economy, those who do not manage to clone to the corporate culture and buy into its feigned egalitarianism—people who find their difference makes them an outsider, however subtle—find their aspirations to social mobility hitting "glass ceilings". In this case, a pedagogy of multiliteracies may go one step further to help create conditions of critical understanding of the discourses of work and power, a kind of knowing from which newer, more productive and genuinely more egalitarian working conditions might emerge (Cope & Kalantzis, 1997, 2000b; Gee, 2000, 2002; Gee, Hull, & Lankshear, 1996; Kalantzis, 2004).

Citizens

Now that the dust has settled after the Cold War, the last years of the twentieth century represent a turning point in the history of the nation-state and the nature of the relationship of states to citizenries. The welfare state had been the capitalist world's answer to communism. And twentieth-century capitalism felt it had to afford a programme of redistributive justice, a large and expensive "nanny" state that blunted its sharper edges and worst inequalities.

Over the past decade, states in capitalist societies have begun a conscious programme of retreat, shrinking the state and reducing the scale of their welfare programmes. They have developed policies of deregulation in which professional and business communities create their own standards of operation. They have privatized formerly public assets, selling them to corporations. These changes have been articulated through the ideology of "neoliberalism", whose key mantra is that small states afford citizens greater liberty. In this theory, society is created through the market and the state should stay out of social and economic affairs to as great a degree as possible. Every tax cut, every programme cut, is made in the name of this neoliberal interpretation of liberty.

These developments can be observed in schools as shrinking state funding, pressure for teaching to become a self-regulating profession, self-managing schools that are run more like businesses or corporations, and increasing numbers of private schools and even privately owned for-profit schools. Education is conceived more as a market than a service provided to citizens by a welfare state. In the context of the shrinking state, its role is being reduced to the most basic of basics—literacy as phonics and numeracy as algorithmic procedures—on the assumption that the market can do the rest for those who can afford the tuition fees and find value for their money.

Today's state of affairs can be interpreted in two ways. The first interpretation is bleak—one set of evils is being replaced by another, albeit quite different, set. The spread of the ideology and practices of the market exacerbates inequality. Neoliberalism in practice reduces the quality and status of education for many, particularly those who have no alternative except public schooling.

Since our initial observation of these trends, and without denying their veracity, we would also like to suggest a parallel, strategic interpretation. As the state shrinks, we witness the rise of self-governing structures in civil society. The Internet is governed, not by any state or coalition of states, but by the World Wide Web Consortium, a group of interested experts and professionals who cohere around elaborate processes of consensus building and decision-making. Professional standards are increasingly being developed by the professions themselves (teaching less so than other professions, but it may be a worthwhile agenda for teachers to take increasing control of their own standards) and organizations such as schools, which were formerly the objects of command at the nether reaches of bureaucratic hierarchy, increasingly have to regard themselves as sites of self-managing corporate bodies.

For better, at the same time, as for worse, the old top-down relationship of state to citizen is being replaced by multiple layers of self-governing community, from the local to national and global levels. Old schooling inculcated loyalty to the nation-state. We would argue that today, new schooling needs to promote a very different kind of citizenship—an active, bottom-up citizenship in which people can take a self-governing role in the many divergent communities of their lives—the work teams, their professions, neighbourhoods, ethnic associations, environments, voluntary organizations and affinity groups (Kalantzis, 2000). Some of these may be local and physically co-located; others may be dispersed, virtual or even global.

To the extent that these self-governing spaces in civil society are opened up by government retreat and tax cuts, they may be doomed to penury and failure. They may also contribute to a dangerous fragmentation into a not-so-civil society. This is the basis of the case against neoliberalism. Its long-term success as a strategy for governance is by no means assured, and its desirability is, to say the least, debatable.

Either way, the old literacy is no longer adequate either to support decentralized governance along neoliberal lines or a civil society capable of making reasonable demands of its state. The multiliteracies approach suggests a pedagogy for active citizenship, centred on learners as agents in their own knowledge processes, capable of contributing their own as well as negotiating the differences between one community and the next.

Persons

Perhaps even more central to the case for multiliteracies today is the changing nature of everyday life itself over the past decade. We are in the midst of a profound shift in the balance of agency, in which as workers, citizens and persons we are more and more required to be users, players, creators and discerning consumers rather than the spectators, delegates, audiences or quiescent consumers of an earlier modernity. Albeit in fits and starts, the command society is being displaced by the society of reflexivity. For instance, take something so ordinary and pervasive as narrative. In everyday family and community life, the narratives of gaming have become an even bigger business than Hollywood over the past decade. From the most impressionable of ages, children of the Nintendo, PlayStation and Xbox generation have become inured to the idea that they can be characters in narratives, capable of determining or, at the very least, influencing the story's end (Gee, 2003, 2005). They are content with being no less than actors rather than audiences, players rather than spectators, agents rather than voyeurs and users rather than readers of narrative. Not content with programmed radio, these children build their own playlists on their iPods. Not content with programmed television, they read the narratives on DVDs and Internet-streamed video at varying depth (the movie, the documentary about the making of the movie) and dip into "chapters" at will. Not content with the singular vision of sports telecasting on mass television, they choose their own angles, replays and statistical analyses on interactive digital TV (Kalantzis, 2006a).

Old logics of literacy and teaching are profoundly challenged by this new media environment. They are bound to fall short, not only disappointing young people whose expectations of engagement are greater, but also for failing to direct their energies to the developing of the kinds of persons required for the new domains of work, citizenship and personality (Yelland, 2006).

The trends, of course, are contradictory. For every moment in which agency is passed over to users and consumers, power is also centralized in ways that have become more disturbing with time. The ownership of commercial media, communications channels and software platforms is becoming alarmingly concentrated (Jenkins, 2004). Besides, to what extent are the new media that engage user agency (such as games) providing an escape from reality instead of a preparation for it? And for every dazzling new opening to knowledge and cultural expression in the new "gift economy" of the Internet—Google is a prime example of this—there are disturbing new possibilities for the invasion of privacy, cynically targeted advertising and control over knowledge sources and media (Lanchester, 2006).

One thing is clear, however. Diversity is pivotal in today's life-worlds—much more profoundly and pervasively so than the straightforward demographic groupings that underwrote an earlier identity politics of gender, ethnicity, race and disability, which were the forms of politics that first unsettled the hoped-for homogeneity of mass society and the nation-state. The moment one allows any more scope for agency, one finds oneself facing layers upon layers of difference—in workplaces, markets, self-governing communities, amongst, between and within personalities. One discovers existing agencies in the massively plural, and not the fabrications and falsifications of the command society with its one people, one state nationalism, its regime of mass production and uniform mass consumption and the pretensions to cultural homogeneity of the old mass media and mass culture. These go far deeper than simple demographics and uncover deep differences of experience, interest, orientation to the world, values, dispositions, sensibilities, social languages and discourses. And insofar as one person inhabits many lifeworlds (home, professional, interest, affiliation), their identities are multilayered. Diversity, in fact, has become a paradoxical universal. The kind of person who can live well in this world is someone who has acquired the capacity to navigate from one domain of social activity to another, who is resilient in their capacity to articulate and enact their own identities and who can find ways of entering into dialogue with and learning new and unfamiliar social languages (Cope & Kalantzis, 1998). One of the fundamental goals of a pedagogy of multiliteracies is to create the conditions for learning that support the growth of this kind of person: a person comfortable with themselves as well as being flexible enough to collaborate and negotiate with others who are different from themselves in order to forge a common interest.

Whether it be in the domains of governance, work or cultural life, the homogenizing command society is tending to give way to the society of diversity and reflexivity—or so we might say in one reading of our contemporary situation. In another reading, we might experience these same phenomena as fragmentation, egocentrism, randomness, ambiguity and anarchy. Or we might pronounce it a mere illusion in the context of the centralization of knowledge economy power in the hands of fewer people. In any of these views, the ramifications for teaching and learning are enormous. A pedagogy of multiliteracies can be agnostic about the stance learners and teachers may wish to take in relation to changing social conditions. For example, they might take the route of compliance or that of critique. If they take the former route, education will help them develop capacities that will enable them to access the new economy and share in its benefits. Or they may reject its values and their consequences in the name of an emancipatory view of education's possibilities. Whichever stance they take, their choices will be more explicit and open to scrutiny.

Over the past decade and a half, we have tried to track, document and reflect on enactments of multiliteracies in action. As a consequence, we have witnessed the huge variations in interpretation that have resulted: from "makeover" practices that bolt the new onto the old to breakthrough learning relationships that are genuinely innovative. Whatever the path, schooling in general and literacy pedagogy in particular, cannot afford to ignore the trajectories of change. They need to be able to justify the pedagogical paths they choose to take.

The "What" of Multiliteracies

Since the publication of the initial multiliteracies paper, we have attempted to articulate further and to apply the pedagogy of design and multimodality. Since that time, our tone and emphasis have changed. Three major innovations over that time have been to focus less on the teachable specificities of meaning-system and more on the heuristics of learners' discovering specificities amongst the enormously varied field of possibly-relevant texts; to develop a theory of semiotic transformation as a theory of learning itself; and to reconfigure the modalities of multimodality.

In a pedagogy of multiliteracies, all forms of representation, including language, should be regarded as dynamic processes of transformation rather than processes of reproduction. That is, meaning makers are not simply replicators of representational conventions. Their meaning-making resources may be found in representational objects, patterned in familiar and thus recognizable ways. However, these objects are reworked. Meaning makers do not simply use what they have been given: they are fully makers and remakers of signs and transformers of meaning.

The pedagogical implications of this shift in the underlying conception of meaning making (semiosis) are enormous. In the old literacy, learners were passive recipients or at best, agents of reproduction of received, sanctioned and authoritative representational forms. The logic of literacy pedagogy was one that made it an instrument of social design that buttressed a regime of apparent stability and uniformity. In contrast, a pedagogy of multiliteracies requires that the enormous role of agency in the meaning-making process be recognized, and in that recognition, it seeks to create a more productive, relevant, innovative, creative and even perhaps emancipatory, pedagogy. Literacy teaching is not about skills and competence; it is aimed at creating a kind of person, an active designer of meaning, with a sensibility open to differences, change and innovation. The logic of multiliteracies is one that recognizes that meaning making is an active, transformative process, and a pedagogy based on that recognition is more likely to open up viable life courses for a world of change and diversity.

Designing Meanings

When developing the key ideas for a pedagogy of multiliteracies a decade ago, we sought to replace static conceptions of representation such as "grammar" and "the literary canon" with a dynamic conception of representation as "design". This word has a fortuitous double meaning, simultaneously describing intrinsic structure or morphology and the act of construction. Design in the sense of construction is something you do in the process of representing meanings—to oneself in sense-making processes such as reading, listening or viewing, or to the world in communicative processes such as writing, speaking or making pictures. The multiliteracies view of design has three aspects (see Table 6.2): *Available Designs* (found representational forms); the *Designing* one does (the work you do when you make meaning, how you appropriate and revoice and transform *Available Designs*); and *The Redesigned* (how, through the act of Designing, the world and the person are transformed).

Available Designs are the found or discernible patterns and conventions of representation. There are many ways to describe similarities and dissimilarities in meaning making, including mode (such as linguistic, visual, audio, gestural, tactile

TABLE 6.2 The "What" of Multiliteracies: Designs of Meaning

Available Designs	Found and findable resources for meaning: culture, context and purpose-specific patterns and conventions of meaning making.
Designing	The act of meaning: work performed on/with Available Designs in representing the world or other's representations of it, to oneself or others.
The Redesigned	The world transformed, in the form of new Available Designs, or the meaning designer who, through the very act of Designing, has transformed themselves (learning).

and spatial), genre (the shape a text has) and discourse (the shape meaning making takes in a social institution) (Gee, 1996; Kress, 2003). It was the project of old literacy teaching to create a definitive catalogue of useable and advisedly useful conventions of meaning, conveniently confined to a standard national form of written language. In the contemporary domains of work, citizenship and everyday life, however, relevant conventions are hugely variable and inherently dynamic. This is even more so now than was the case in the mid-1990s. They are hugely variable across modes (for instance, the deep multimodality of contemporary communications channels and technologies) and between diverging social languages (for instance, of affinity, profession, expertise, ethnicity, subculture and style). Catalogues of convention can only ever be partial and they embody an understanding of agency ("Here is the catalogue, so you should learn it") which, if our analysis of changing work, citizenship and personal life is correct, becomes less and less germane to our changing times.

Rather than address the specificities of meaning-making systems (which we tended to do earlier), we propose that the conventions of any domain be addressed with open-ended questions about meaning, such as:

- Representational: to what do the meanings refer?
- Social: how do the meanings connect the persons they involve?
- Structural: how are the meanings organized?
- Intertextual: how do the meanings fit into the larger world of meaning?
- Ideological: whose interests are the meanings skewed to serve?

A pedagogy of multiliteracies speaks to the question of conventions in meaning, not to tell of their morphology in a formalistic fashion but in order to describe their open-ended and shifting representational processes and account for their purposes. These processes have a cultural and situational basis. Their regularities are the reason for their context-specific legibility; their unfamiliarity is what we need to deal with when we cross into a new domain. Our aim is not simply to teach the structures or forms of modalities, or genres or discourses because in today's world especially, that can only open up the receding horizons of complexity and diversity. Rather, it is to design learning experiences through which learners develop strategies for reading the new and unfamiliar, in whatever form these may manifest themselves. Instead of simply telling learners of authoritative designs, it asks the question of design, or the relation of meaning form to meaning function. In addressing this question, learners may be able draw upon various metalanguages describing the forms of contemporary meaning—professional and specialist, for instance—and from these construct their own frames of functional explanation.

Designing is the act of doing something with Available Designs of meaning, be that communicating to others (such as writing, speaking, making pictures), representing the world to oneself or others' representations of it (such as reading, listening or viewing). Against the inert notions of acquisition, articulation, competence or interpretation that underpin the old literacy teaching, a pedagogy of design recognizes the role of subjectivity and agency in this process. The meaning-maker-as-designer draws selectively from the infinite breadth and complexity of Available Designs in the many domains of action and representation that make up the layers of their past and new experience. The act of representation is interested and motivated. It is directed, purposive and selective. It is an expression of an individual's identity at the unique junction of intersecting lines of social and cultural experience. In Designing, the meaning maker enacts a new design. However, in putting Available Designs to use, they are never simply replicating found designs, even if their inspiration is established patterns of meaning making. What the meaning maker creates is a new design, an expression of their voice which draws upon the unique mix of meaning-making resources, the codes and conventions they happen to have found in their contexts and cultures. The moment of design is a moment of transformation, of remaking the world by representing the world afresh. Creativity, innovation, dynamism and divergence are normal semiotic states. This is a prospective view of semiosis, a view that puts imagination and creative reappropriation of the world at the centre of representation and thus learning. In contrast, the old literacy required of its teachers and learners a retrospective view of meaning that relied on the successful transmission and acquisition of received conventions and canons. Repetition, replication, stability and uniformity had to be imposed by the old literacy, against the grain of the human-semiotic nature of Designing.

The Redesigned is the residue, the traces of transformation that are left in the social world. The texts of Designing become The Redesigned, new resources for meaning in the open and dynamic play of subjectivities and meanings. One person's Designing becomes a resource in another person's universe of Available Designs. This is how the world is left changed as a consequence of the transformational work of Designing. In the life of the meaning maker, this process of transformation is the essence of learning. The act of representing to oneself the world and others' representations of it transforms the learner him- or herself. The act of Designing leaves the designer Redesigned. As the designer makes meanings, they exert their subjectivity in the representational process, and as these meanings are always new ("insights", "expressions", perspectives"), they remake themselves. The result of their representational work and their exertion of subjectivity is transformed subjectivity—and thus learning (Cope & Kalantzis, 2000a; Kress, 2000a, 2003). This development of a theory of learning in which transformation or redesign is a pivotal microdynamic is one of the key developments in the multiliteracies theory since the mid-1990s.

Modalities of Meaning

Of all the changes currently underway in the environment of meaning-design, one of the most significant challenges to the old literacy teaching is the increasing multimodality of meaning. Traditionally, literacy teaching has confined itself to the forms of written language. The new media mix modes more powerfully than was culturally the norm and even technically possible in the earlier modernity that was dominated by the book and the printed page. Through the theorizations and curriculum experimentations of the past decade and a half, we have reconfigured the range of possible modalities. We have separated written and oral language as fundamentally different modes (Kress, 2003), added a tactile mode and redefined the contents and scope of the other modes.

- Written language: writing (representing meaning to another) and reading (representing meaning to oneself)—handwriting, the printed page, the screen.
- Oral language: live or recorded speech (representing meaning to another); listening (representing meaning to oneself).
- Visual representation: still or moving image, sculpture, craft (representing meaning to another); view, vista, scene, perspective (representing meaning to oneself).
- Audio representation: music, ambient sounds, noises, alerts (representing meaning to another); hearing, listening (representing meaning to oneself).
- Tactile representation: touch, smell and taste: the representation to oneself of bodily sensations and feelings or representations to others that "touch" one bodily. Forms of tactile representation include kinaesthesia, physical contact, skin sensations (temperature, texture, pressure), grasp, manipulable objects, artefacts, cooking and eating, aromas.
- Gestural representation: movements of the hands and arms, expressions of the face, eye movements and gaze, demeanours of the body, gait, clothing and fashion, hairstyle, dance, action sequences (Scollon, 2001), timing, frequency, ceremony and ritual. Here gesture is understood broadly and metaphorically as a physical act of signing (as in "a gesture to . . .") rather than the narrower literal meaning of hand and arm movement.
- Representation to oneself may take the form of feelings and emotions or rehearsing action sequences in one's mind's eye.
- Spatial representation: proximity, spacing, layout, interpersonal distance, territoriality, architecture/building, streetscape, cityscape, landscape.

We have also undertaken new work on the capacity of different modes to express many of the same kinds of things; that is, the representational potentials that are unique unto themselves. In other words, between the various modes, there are inherently different or incommensurate affordances as well as the parallel or translatable aspects of the representational jobs they do.

On the side of parallelism, a grammar of the visual can explain the ways in which images work like language. For example, action expressed by verbs in sentences may be expressed by vectors in images. Locative prepositions in language are like foregrounding or backgrounding in images. Comparatives in language are like sizing and placement in images. The given and the new English clause structures are like left/right placement in images (in the cultures of left to right viewing, at least), and the real/ideal in language is like top/down placement in images (Kress, 2000b; Kress & van Leeuwen, 1996). The process of shifting between modes and re-representing the same thing from one mode to another is known as synaesthesia, and representational parallels make it possible.

By and large, traditional literacy does not recognize or adequately use the meaning and learning potentials inherent in synaesthesia. It tries to confine itself to the monomodal formalities of written language, as if the modality of written language could be isolated as a system unto itself. This was always a narrowing agenda. Today, even more than a decade ago, such narrowing is unrealistic given the multimodal realities of the new media and broader changes in the communications environment.

However, the consequences of narrowing of representation and communic-ation to the exclusive study of written language (sound-letter correspondences, parts of speech and the grammar of sentences, literary works and the like) are more serious than its still powerful, though declining, relevance to contemporary condi-tions. Synaesthesia is integral to representation. In a very ordinary, material sense, our bodily sensations are holistically integrated, even if our focus of meaning-making attentions in any particular moment might be one particular mode. Gestures may come with sound; images and text sit side by side on pages; architectural spaces are labelled with written signs. Much of our everyday representational experience is intrinsically multimodal. Indeed, some modes are intrinsically close to others—so close in fact that one easily melds into the others in the multimodal actualities of everyday meaning. Written language is closely connected to the visual in its use of spacing, layout and typography. Spoken language is closely associated with the audio mode in the use of intonation, inflection, pitch, tempo and pause. Gesture may need to be planned or rehearsed, either in inner speech (talking to oneself) or by visual-ization. Children have natural synaesthetic capacities, and rather than build upon and extend these, over a period of time school literacy attempts to separate them to the extent even of creating different subjects or disciplines—literacy in one cell of the class timetable and art in another (Kress, 1997).

The different modes of meaning are, however, not simply parallel, and this is something we have come to recognize more clearly in the work we have done over the past decade. Meaning expressed in one mode cannot be directly and completely translated into another. The movie can never be the same as the novel. The image can never do the same thing as the description of a scene in language. The parallelism allows the same thing to be depicted in different modes, but the meaning is never quite the same. In fact, some of the differences in meaning potential afforded by the different modes are fundamental. Writing (along the line, sentence by sentence, paragraph by paragraph, one page after the next) sequences elements in time and so favours the genre of narrative. Image collocates elements according to the logic of simultaneous space, and so favours the genre of display. Writing's intrinsic temporality orients it to causality; image to location. Written language is open to a wide range of possible visualizations (e.g., is the movie how you visualized things when you were reading the book?). The words have to be filled in with visual meaning. Visuals, however, require that the viewer creates order (time, causation, purpose, effect) by arranging elements that are already visually complete (Kress, 2003). In other words, reading and viewing require different kinds of imagination and transformational effort in the re-representation of their meanings to oneself. They are fundamentally different ways of knowing and learning the world.

This paradoxical mix of parallelism and incommensurability between modalities is what makes addressing multimodality integral to the pedagogy of multiliteracies. In the face of the *back-to-basics* movement, we would put the case that synaesthesia is a pedagogical move that makes for powerful learning in a number of ways. Some learners may be more comfortable in one mode than another. It may be their preferred mode of representation—what comes to them easiest, what they are good at, the mode in which they best express the world to themselves and themselves to the world. One person may prefer to conceive a project as a list of instructions; another as a flow diagram. The parallelism means that you can do a lot of the same things in one mode that you can do in the next, so a pedagogy that restricts learning to one artificially segregated mode will favour some types of learners over others. It also means that the starting point for meaning in one mode may be a way of extending one's representational repertoire by shifting from favoured modes to less comfortable ones. If the words do not make sense, the diagram might, and then the words start to make sense. However, the incommensurability of modes works pedagogically, too. The words make sense because the picture conveys meaning that words could never (quite or in a completely satisfactorily way) do. Conscious mode switching makes for more powerful learning. If the multiliteracies agenda captures some generalities of multimodality that extend beyond the contemporary moment, changes in the contemporary communications environment simply add urgency to the call to consciously deploy multimodality in learning. We are in the midst of a seismic shift in communications, from the world told through the medium of writing on the page of the book, magazine or newspaper, to the world shown through the medium of the visual on the screen. There was a compelling linearity to the traditional page of written text. Its reading path was clear, even if one had to fill in what the referents of the words looked and felt like. The lexis of writing may have demanded some semantic filling, but its syntax was clear. In the case of images, the elements of meaning (lexis) are given but, despite some loose reading conventions (left to right, top to bottom) influenced by the culture of reading scripts that run this way, the reading path is more open than that of writing. The syntax is in the hands of the viewer (Kress, 2003). In this regard, in the construction of the text, the balance of agency in meaning construction has shifted in favour of the viewer.

Webpages today are full of written text, but the logic of their reading is more like the syntax of the visual than that of the written language. Reading the screen requires considerable navigational effort. Today's screens are designed for many viewing paths, allowing for diverse interests and subjectivities amongst viewers, and the reading path they choose will reflect the considerable design effort the viewer has put into their reading. In fact, the common-sense semantics is telling— "readers" of books have become "users" now that they are on the web. Nor is this shift only happening on the web: printed pages more and more resemble screens. The mix of image, caption, list and breakout box is such that the reading paths of the image are now to be found on the page—the science textbook, the glossy magazine, the contemporary newspaper or the instruction manual, for instance. And where writing is found, visual supports allow a simplified syntax for the writing itself, for instance in the form of a decreasing clausal complexity. This decreasing complexity of writing, however, is compensated for by an increasingly complex multimodality (Kress, 2003).

The reasons for this change are in part practical and material. The elementary modular unit in the manufacture of traditional pages was the character "type" of Gutenberg's printing press. It was not easy to print images on the same page as typography. The elementary modular unit of today's digit media, however, is the pixel, the same unit from which images are rendered. In fact, this process is longer than the history of digitization. It started with lithographic printing—the application of photographic processes to printing in the mid-twentieth century (Cope & Kalantzis, 2004). Today, even sound is rendered from the same source as pixels—the bits and bytes of digitized information storage. This means that the practical business of doing multimodality is easy now, and because it is, we are using the affordances of the complementary modes to ease the semantic load that had been placed on written language. However, in so doing, we have created new complexities in multimodal representation. It is time to accord this the same earnest attention that literacy teaching has applied to language.

For every shift in the direction of the visual in the new communications environment, however, there are other returns to writing—email, SMS and blogging, for instance. This was unimaginable when we first wrote the multiliteracies manifesto. None of these forms, however, are simply returns. They all express new forms of multimodality—the use of icon in SMS and the juxtaposition of image in MMS (Multimedia Message Service; sending images with text); the layout of blog pages and email messages; and the trend in all of these new forms of writing to move away from the grammar of the mode of writing to the grammar of the mode of speaking. Then there is the deep paradox of the "semantic web" in which images, sound and text are only discoverable if they are labelled. The semantic web of the presently emerging Internet is built on a kind of multimodal grammar ("structural and semantic mark-up", semantic schemas or ontologies) by way of running commentary on the images, sound and writing that this mark-up labels (Cope, Kalantzis, & Magee, 2011). Whichever way we look, written language is not going away. It is just becoming more closely intertwined with the other modes, and in some respects becoming more like them. The trend to multimodality we predicted in the first multiliteracies article has been confirmed, even if the specifics of the changes, and the intensity and speed of change, were inconceivable.

The "How" of Multiliteracies

Meanwhile, what is happening in schools? What have we been doing differently in literacy teaching in recent years? One kind of answer is, depressingly, not much. There is a deadening institutional inertia in schools and their disciplines, in the heritage physical architecture of school buildings and the institutional architecture of educational bureaucracy.

Another kind of answer has been to go back to the basics. This is a move in which conservative activists have, in many places, succeeded in reversing the slow march of progressivist curriculum reform over the course of the twentieth century that started with the influence of educationists such as Dewey and Montessori from that century's beginning. A third kind of answer is to move forward and to redesign pedagogy for our changing times. The experimental practices of a pedagogy of multiliteracies have been one such attempt to move forward.

The back-to-basics movement has had considerable success in taking education back over the past decade to what appears, in the retrospective view of its advocates, to be the halcyon days of traditional schooling. One mark of its success has been the imposition of high stakes standardized testing in which once again the school undertakes the process of social sifting and sorting against a singular and supposedly universal measure of basic skills and knowledge. Another sign of the success of this movement is the return to didactic "skill and drill" curriculum that jams content knowledge to fit the tests.

In literacy, the skill and drill regime starts with phonics. There is some merit in sound-to-letter correspondence but not enough to warrant its fetishization by the back-to-basics people as one of the keys to literacy. When they come to write in English, children encounter 44 sounds and the 26 letters that represent these sounds. Meanwhile, in the motivating spaces of contemporary child culture (such as Pokémon or video games), children quickly master immensely more complex systems without instruction by a teacher (Gee, 2004b). The horizons of phonics are set so low and the results so easy to measure that it is not hard to show improved results, even amongst children who come from communities and cultures that historically have not achieved at school.

Then comes the "fourth-grade slump" where the test results return to form (Gee, 2004b). The problem is that writing is not a transliteration of speech, as the phonics people simplistically imply. It is a different mode with a significantly different grammar (Kress, 2003). Some kinds of learners seem to "get it"; others do not. The more academic modes of written language make intuitive sense to some but not others. Some can relate to the distinctive forms of written language as a cultural move—being a scientist and writing like one, or being an author and writing like one. Learning to write is about forming an identity; some learners can comfortably work their way into that identity and others cannot, and the difference has to do with social class and community background. In the long run, phonics fails to achieve this and thus fails learners who do not come from cultures of writing. Perhaps these learners may have been able to extend their repertoires into the mode of writing and its cultures if the starting point had been other modes, and the entry points to literacy had been activities of synaesthesia that were more intellectually stimulating and motivating than sound–letter correspondences? Perhaps a pedagogy that built on the multifarious subjectivities of learners might work better than drilling to distraction the ones who do not immediately "get" the culture of writing?

Meanwhile, we are supposed to be creating learners for the knowledge economy, for new workplaces that place a premium on creativity and self-motivation and for citizenship that devolves regulatory responsibility to many layers of self-governing community. This economy is a lifeworld in which the balance of agency has shifted towards users, customers and meaning makers and in which diversity (not measurable uniformity) prevails. Just as the Iraq war may have increased the global incidence of terror in the name of a War on Terror, so the back-to-basics people in education may be misreading entirely what society needs from education, even from the most conservative, systems-bolstering point of view. In short, they might be wrong.

If there is a method in the apparent madness, it may be that back-to-basics is education on the cheap in the era of neoliberalism (Apple, 2006). The powers-that-be may have no intention of matching all the fine political talk about the knowledge society with commensurate additional resourcing for education. Phonics and tests are all that the political system and the electorate wants to pay for, and quality, high-end education that moves beyond the horizons of didactic, mass production, uniform, easy-to-measure teaching is something the user will have to pay for. Anything more than the basics is only for those who can afford it. This is a bleak scenario and it seems a politically wiser strategy to try to take system promises about things such as the knowledge society, at their word.

For instance, didactic teaching promotes mimesis—the transmission and acquisition of the rules of literacy. Teaching is a process of transmission. Cultural stability and uniformity are the results. By contrast, a pedagogy of multiliteracies is characteristically transformative as it builds on notions of design and meaning-as-transformation. Transformative curriculum recognizes that the process of designing redesigns the designer (Kalantzis, 2006b; Kalantzis & Cope, 2012a). Learning is a process of self-re-creation. Cultural dynamism and diversity are the results.

We would argue that such a transformative pedagogy is based both on a realistic view of contemporary society (how does schooling offer cultural and material access to its institutions of power?) and on an emancipatory view of possible paths to improvement in our human futures (how can we make a better, more equal, less humanly and environmentally damaging world?). Insofar as these two goals might at times be at odds, a transformative pedagogy could be used to support either view. Then, it is up to the learner to make of the pedagogy what they will, be that a sensible conservatism (sensible for being realistic about the contemporary forces of technology, globalization and cultural change) or an emancipatory view that wants to make a future that is different to the present by addressing its crises of poverty, environment, cultural difference and existential meaning (Kalantzis, 2006a).

The transformative pedagogy of multiliteracies identifies four major dimensions of pedagogy that we originally called situated practice, overt instruction, critical framing and transformed practice. In applying these ideas to curriculum realities over the past decade, we have reframed these ideas somewhat and translated them into the more immediately recognizable pedagogical acts or "knowledge processes" of *experiencing, conceptualizing, analysing* and *applying* (Kalantzis & Cope, 2005). We have also come to characterize the process of moving backwards and forwards across and between these different pedagogical moves as *weaving* (Luke, Cazden, Lin, & Freebody, 2005).

- *Experiencing:* Human cognition is situated. It is contextual. Meanings are grounded in the real world of patterns of experience, action and subjective interest (Gee, 2004a, 2006). One of the pedagogical weavings is between school learning and the practical out-of-school experiences of learners. Another is between familiar and unfamiliar texts and experiences. These kinds of cross-connections between school and the rest of life are "cultural weavings" (Cazden, 2006a; Luke et al., 2005). Experiencing takes two forms:
  - o *Experiencing the known* involves reflecting on our own experiences, interests, perspectives, familiar forms of expression and ways of representing the world in one's own understanding. In this regard, learners bring their own, invariably diverse knowledge, experiences, interests and life-texts to the learning situation.
  - o *Experiencing the new* entails observing or reading the unfamiliar, immersion in new situations and texts, reading new texts or collecting new data. Learners are exposed to new information, experiences and texts, but only within the zone of intelligibility and safety, sufficiently close to their own lifeworlds to be at least half meaningful in the first instance, yet potentially transformative insofar as the weaving between the known and the new takes the learner into new domains of action and meaning (Kalantzis & Cope, 2005).
- *Conceptualizing:* Specialized, disciplinary and deep knowledges based on the finely tuned distinctions of concept and theory typical of those developed by expert communities of practice. Conceptualizing is not merely a matter of

"teacherly" or textbook telling based on legacy academic disciplines, it is a knowledge process in which the learners become active conceptualizers, making the tacit explicit and generalizing from the particular.

o *Conceptualizing by naming* involves or draws distinctions of similarity and difference, categorizing and naming. Here, learners give abstract names to things and develop concepts (Vygotsky, 1962).

o *Conceptualizing with theory* means making generalizations and putting the key terms together into interpretative frameworks. Learners build mental models, abstract frameworks and transferable disciplinary schemas. In the same pedagogical territory, didactic pedagogy, would lay out disciplinary schemas for the learners to acquire (the rules of literacy, the laws of physics and the like). Conceptualizing requires that learners be active concept and theory-makers. It also requires weaving between the experiential and the conceptual (Kalantzis & Cope, 2005). This kind of weaving is primarily cognitive, between Vygotsky's world of everyday or spontaneous knowledge and the world of science or systematic concepts, or between Piaget's concrete and abstract thinking (Cazden, 2006a).

• *Analysing:* Powerful learning also entails a certain kind of critical capacity. "Critical" can mean two things in a pedagogical context—to be functionally analytical or to be evaluative with respect to relationships of power (Cazden, 2006a). Analysing involves both of these kinds of knowledge processes.

o *Analysing functionally* includes processes of reasoning, drawing inferential and deductive conclusions, establishing functional relations such as between cause and effect and analysing logical and textual connections. Learners explore causes and effects, develop chains of reasoning and explain patterns in text.

o *Analysing critically* (that is, more critically than functionally) involves evaluation of one's and other people's perspectives, interests and motives. In these knowledge processes, learners interrogate the interests behind a meaning or an action, and their own processes of thinking (Kalantzis & Cope, 2005). This critical kind of weaving works bi-directionally between known and new experiences, and between prior and new conceptualizations (Cazden, 2006a).

• *Applying*:

o *Applying appropriately* entails the application of knowledge and under-standings to the complex diversity of real world situations and testing their validity. By these means, learners do something in a predictable and expected way in a "real world" situation or a situation that simulates the "real world".

o *Applying creatively* involves making an intervention in the world which is truly innovative and creative and which brings to bear the learner's interests, experiences and aspirations. This is a process of making the world anew with fresh and creative forms of action and perception. Now learners do something that expresses or affects the world in a new way, or that transfers their previous knowledge into a new setting (Kalantzis & Cope, 2005). This weaving can take many forms, bringing new experiential, conceptual or critical knowledge back to bear on the experiential world.

These pedagogical orientations or knowledge processes are not a pedagogy in the singular or a sequence to be followed. Rather, they are a map of the range of pedagogical moves that may prompt teachers to extend their pedagogical repertoires. Didactic teaching emphasizes the overt instruction of conceptual, disciplinary schemas at the expense of other pedagogical orientations. Progressivisms that focus on grounded learner activity locate themselves in experiential activities and often at the expense of deep conceptual work. Transformative pedagogy adds analysis and application to the mix.

In the last decade, there has been increasing recognition of the need to integrate both experiencing and conceptualizing, the first two of the pedagogical processes identified in the multiliteracies schema. At least in many English-medium countries, the "reading wars" between "phonics" and "whole language" have been replaced by an emphasis on "balanced literacy"—even though perhaps it is replaced more in rhetoric than in practice in every classroom. However, the critical literacy implied by analysing has had less uptake in either of its meanings, perhaps because of its latent possibility of arousing controversies. Applying in the sense of transformed practice has faced greater barriers. Paradoxically, in many countries, the arguments for educational reform that rest on fears of economic competition lead to programmatic statements about the importance of fostering entrepreneurship, creativity, problem-posing as well as problem-solving—all forms of applying in a properly transformative sense. Intervening to effect such changes requires overcoming schools' notorious resistance to change and overcoming the more specific problem of opening up entrenched didactic teaching practices, which is in some contexts exacerbated by large class sizes. In such cases, any opening up must not simply be to didactic teaching's opposite (a "progressive" over-reliance on experiencing) but to a repertoire of the four learning processes for students and complementary teaching strategies for teachers.

Using the heuristic of the different pedagogical orientations to reflect on their practice, teachers may find themselves to have been unreflectively caught in the rut of one or more of the knowledge processes, or in knowledge processes that do not align in practice with the stated goals of learning. It is useful to be able to unpack the range of possible knowledge processes to decide and justify what is appropriate for a subject or a learner, to track learner inputs and outputs, and to extend the pedagogical repertoires of teachers and the knowledge repertoires of learners. A pedagogy of multiliteracies suggests a broader range of knowledge processes be used, and that more powerful learning arises from weaving between different knowledge processes in an explicit and purposeful way (see Table 6.3).

TABLE 6.3 The "How" of Multiliteracies: The Microdynamics of Pedagogy

Pedagogical orientations: 1996 formulation	Knowledge processes: 2006 reformulation
Situated practice	Experiencing ...the Known ...the New
Overt instruction	Conceptualizing ...by Naming ...with Theory
Critical framing	Analysing ...Functionally ...Critically
Transformed practice	Applying ...Appropriately ...Creatively

A pedagogy of multiliteracies also opens access to powerful learning to a broader spread of learners in a world where diversity is becoming all the more critical. The old learning of the command society could at least try to get away with a one-size-fits-all approach. However, as soon as agency is rebalanced and we have to take learner subjectivities into account, we encounter a panoply of human differences that we simply cannot ignore any longer—material (class, locale), corporeal (race, gender, sexuality, dis/ability) and circumstantial (culture, religion, life experience, interest, affinity). In fact, not dealing with difference means exclusion of those who do not fit the norm. It means ineffectiveness, inefficiencies and thus wasted resources in a form of teaching that does not engage with each and every learner in a way that will optimize their performance outcomes. It even cheats the learners who happen to do well—those whose favoured orientation to learning the one-size-suits-all curriculum appears to suit—by limiting their exposure to the cosmopolitan experience of cultural and epistemological differences so integral to the contemporary world (Kalantzis, 2006a).

A pedagogy of multiliteracies allows alternative starting points for learning (what the learner perceives to be worth learning, what engages the particularities of their identity). It allows for alternative forms of engagement, such as the varied experiences that need to be brought to bear on the learning, the different conceptual bents of learners, the different analytical perspectives the learner may have on the nature of cause, effect and human interest, and the different settings in which they may apply or enact their knowledge. It allows for divergent learning orientations (preferences, for instance, for particular emphases in knowledge making and patterns of engagement). It allows for different modalities in meaning making, embracing alternative expressive potentials for different learners and promoting synaesthesia as a learning strategy. It also reflects a rebalancing of agency in the recognition of active "design" and inherent learning potentials in the representational process: every meaning draws on resources of the already designed world of representation; each meaning maker designs the world afresh in a way that is always uniquely transformative of found meanings. They then leave a representational trace to be found by others and transformed once again (Cope & Kalantzis, 2000b). Finally, a transformative pedagogy allows for alternative pathways and comparable destination points in learning (Kalantzis & Cope, 2004, 2005). The measure of success of transformative pedagogy is equally high performance learning outcomes that can produce comparable social effects for learners in terms of material rewards and socially ascribed status (Kalantzis, 2006b).

Multiliteracies in Practice

This updated and revised restatement of the multiliteracies agenda is grounded in more than 10 years of practical intervention, research and theoretical work. It now remains to mention some of this work briefly. As some of this has been discussed or referenced above or will be featured in the other articles in this special issue, we will mention just three groups of educators who have developed systematic interventions and research programmes around multiliteracies: Denise Newfield and the late Pippa Stein at the University of the Witwatersrand, South Africa; Eleni Karantzola and Evangelos Intzidis at the University of the Aegean, Greece; and Ambigapathy Pandian and Shanthi Balraj at the Universiti Sains Malaysia, Penang, Malaysia.

Newfield and Stein's work began with the launching of the MA in English Education at the University of the Witwatersrand in 1997, in which the then-recently published multiliteracies article (New London Group, 1996) was prescribed. The multiliteracies framework soon became an anchor for the students' work. In the ensuing years, the multiliteracies pedagogy assumed an ever more central place in pre-service and in-service teacher education courses at the University of the Witwatersrand. Members of the research team began implementing the pedagogy in a range of educational contexts—at primary, high school and tertiary levels, in English literacy, language and literature classrooms, in science, art and visual literacy classrooms—both in well- and under-resourced contexts. Teachers were excited by their pedagogic experiments and would meet regularly to discuss and display what learners were producing under the influence of the new pedagogy.

Newfield and Stein report that multiliteracies has been taken up and extended in South Africa in powerful ways, focusing on identity work in relation to the apartheid past, and in relation to human rights, diversity, multilingualism and multiple epistemologies. The ever-expanding group has worked with indigenous knowledge systems, cultural practices and languages, within a critical framework that takes account also of school and global literacies.

Marion Drew and Kathleen Wemmer's work with first-year audiology students had the students studying textbooks and visiting local *sangomas* (traditional doctors). Joni Brenner and David Andrew based their class assignments for visual literacy students on local craft forms, such as the *Minceka*, a traditional cloth worn by women in the Limpopo province. Tshidi Mamabolo's foundation students at Olifantsvlei Primary School made dolls based on traditional South African fertility figures in their literacy classroom. Robert Maungedzo's disaffected high school students moved from a position of refusal to unstoppable creativity, engaging in a range of semiotic activity from cloth making and praising in indigenous languages to writing stories and poems in English. The students produced powerful hybrid, syncretic texts that speak of themselves as "new South Africans", and which reflect on themselves in relation to past, present and future. This has been a project of giving voice to the marginalized and dispossessed, and of extending the semiotic repertoire of the already voiced.

For Newfield, Stein and their group, the multiliteracies agenda has spoken to the post-apartheid historical moment in South Africa, with its progressive and democratic constitution and revised national curriculum. It cohered with and helped give shape to emerging curricular principles, such as democratic practice, multilingualism, multiculturalism and notions pertaining to textual multiplicity. South African educators and academics took it up and inflected it in powerful ways that expressed the particularities of South Africa in the post-1994 decade of freedom and democracy (Newfield, 2005; Newfield & Stein, 2000; Newfield et al., 2001; Stein, 2003; Stein & Newfield, 2002a, 2002b, 2003). In recognition of the enormous interest in the multiliteracies work in South Africa, the International Conference on Learning was held in Johannesburg at the University of the Witwatersrand in 2007.

The multiliteracies notion was introduced to Greece with a number of presentations from 1997 by Mary Kalantzis at conferences and teacher training programmes initiated by Gella Varnava-Skoura at the University of Athens and Tassos Christidis at the Centre for the Greek Language at the University of Thessaloniki. Building on these relationships, the International Conference on Learning was subsequently held in Spetses, Greece in July 2001 (Kalantzis & Cope, 2000, 2001).

Karantzola and Intzidis began research work in 1997 on the design of multi-modal meaning in curriculum resources used in Greek compulsory education (Karantzola & Intzidis, 2001a). They went on to examine the implementation of multiliteracies pedagogy across the curriculum, with a particular emphasis on teaching science in secondary education (Karantzola & Intzidis, 2000, 2001b).

In a project lasting from 1997 to 2000, Karantzola and Intzidis implemented multiliteracies theory to develop an alternative language curriculum for "night high schools" and "second chance schools". Amongst the products of this initiative were collaboratively produced newspapers at each school. In 2000, this work won the first prize in the Hellenic Ministry of Education and Religious Affairs National Competition for Innovation. From this, they went on in a joint project with Mary Kalantzis to assist in the redevelopment of Greece's adult education system for the General Secretariat for Adult Education in the Hellenic Ministry of Education and Religious Affairs. This work has ranged from giving shape to the overall policy framework for adult education in Greece to the implementation of multiliteracies pedagogy in adult education centres across the country (Karantzola, Kondyli, Intzidis, & Lykou 2004a; 2004b). Most recently, Karantzola and Intzidis have been involved in the establishment of the Literacy Research Network at the University of the Aegean to provide a research focus in the field of adult education and to offer a focal point in the struggle against social exclusion by promoting lifelong learning to the general population. Finally, a Greek language edition of the multiliteracies book (to be published by Routledge) is forthcoming, with additional Greek case studies by Karantzola and Intzidis.

In Malaysia, Pandian and Balraj were attracted to the multiliteracies pedagogy from the perspective of their multilingual, multi-ethnic and multi-religious setting, together with dramatic developments in the use of information and communication technologies in Malaysia. These technologies were being promoted as indispensable tools for individuals to lead their learning, economic and social life in the changing times. In this context, the multiliteracies framework advanced by the New London Group offered a useful viewpoint for thinking about the provision of education that would equip students with the knowledge and skills necessary to be active and informed citizens and workers in a changing world—a world of diversity and one in which our means of communication and access to information are changing rapidly.

The multiliteracies research in Malaysia began in 1997, and in 1999 the International Learning Conference brought key members of the original New London Group to Penang. From this the International Literacy Research Unit was created, formalising the relationships and developing the basis of an international research program (Kalantzis & Cope, 1999; Kalantzis & Pandian, 2001; Pandian, 1999, 2001, 2003, 2004a, 2004b). The research has covered two major areas: the teaching of English in Malaysia, and, more recently, the "learning by design" pedagogy, based on the four pedagogical orientations proposed by the New London Group. The learning by design work has involved teachers and students producing dynamic and exciting multimodal texts, closely related to their own communities and life experiences, whilst at the same time extending their communicative repertoires (Pandian & Balraj, 2005).

Conclusion

After a decade and a half, an enormous body of work has emerged around the notion of multiliteracies. Although the changes of the past decade have been huge, we have found that the core concepts developed in the mid-1990s have stood the test of time. In this restatement, we have refined and reformulated the original concepts in the light of subsequent events, further research and trialling of the key ideas in educational practice.

There have been both intellectual continuity and change in the development of a pedagogy of multiliteracies over the past decade. After all, some significant degree of change is what we would expect when we hold to a theory of representation in which transformation is fundamental and stability in the forms of meaning is almost invariably an illusion.

Acknowledgements

In writing this revised paper we also involved colleagues with whom we have developed close working relations as they have tested and extended the multiliteracies ideas over the past 10 years: Denise Newfield and the late Pippa Stein of the University of the Witwatersrand, South Africa; Ambigapathy Pandian and Shanthi Balraj of Universiti Sains Malaysia, Penang, Malaysia; and Vangelis Intzidis and Eleni Karantzola of the University of the Aegean, Rhodes, Greece. We want to thank the other members of the New London Group for their comments and suggestions, and Nicola Yelland for her suggestion that it was time to write it.

Note

1   Few members of the New London Group are still in the positions they were in 1996. Courtney Cazden has retired from the Graduate School of Education, Harvard University, USA, but remains as active as ever as Charles William Eliot Professor Emerita. Bill Cope is Research Professor in the Department of Educational Policy Studies, University of Illinois, Urbana-Champaign. Norman Fairclough has retired from Lancaster University, UK, and now lives and writes from Bucharest. Jim Gee is Mary Lou Fulton Presidential Professor of Literacy Studies at Arizona State University, USA. Mary Kalantzis is Dean of the College of Education, University of Illinois, Urbana-Champaign. Gunther Kress is Head of the Department of Culture, Language and Communication at the Institute of Education, University of London. Allan Luke is a Research Professor at the Queensland University of Technology, Australia. Carmen Luke is a Professor in the Centre for Critical and Cultural Studies, University of Queensland, Australia. Sarah Michaels is at the Hiatt Center for Urban Education, Clark University, USA. Martin Nakata is Director of Indigenous Academic Programs at Jumbunna Indigenous House of Learning, University of Technology, Sydney, Australia.

References

Apple, M. W. (2006). Understanding and interrupting neoconservatism and neoliberalism in education. *Pedagogies: An International Journal, 1*(1), 21–26.

Cazden, C. B. (2006a, January). *Connected learning: "Weaving" in classroom lessons.* Paper presented at the Pedagogy in Practice 2006 Conference, University of Newcastle, New South Wales, Australia.

Cazden, C. B. (2006b). [Review of the books *Language policies and language education: The impact in East Asian countries in the next decade* and *English language teaching in East Asia today: Changing policies and practices*]. *Asia Pacific Journal of Education, 26*, 120–122.

Cope, B., & Kalantzis, M. (1997). *Productive diversity: A new approach to work and management.* Sydney, Australia: Pluto Press.

Cope, B., & Kalantzis, M. (1998). Multicultural education: Transforming the mainstream. In S. May (Ed.), *Critical multiculturalism* (pp. 245–274). London, UK: Falmer Press.

Cope, B., & Kalantzis, M. (2000a). Designs for social futures. In B. Cope & M. Kalantzis (Eds.), *Multiliteracies: Literacy learning and the design of social futures* (pp. 203–234). London, UK: Routledge.

Cope, B., & Kalantzis, M. (Eds.). (2000b). *Multiliteracies: Literacy learning and the design of social futures*. London, UK: Routledge.

Cope, B., & Kalantzis, M. (2004). Text-Made text. *E-Learning, 1*, 198–282.

Cope, B., Kalantzis, M., & Magee, L. (2011). *Towards a semantic web: Connecting knowledge in academic research*. Cambridge UK: Woodhead Publishing.

Gee, J. P. (1996). *Social linguistics and literacies: Ideology in discourses*. London, UK: Taylor and Francis.

Gee, J. P. (2000). New people in new worlds: Networks, the new capitalism and schools. In B. Cope & M. Kalantzis (Eds.), *Multiliteracies: Literacy learning and the design of social futures* (pp. 43–68). London, UK: Routledge.

Gee, J. P. (2002). New times and new literacies: Themes for a changing world. In M. Kalantzis, G. Varnava-Skoura, & B. Cope (Eds.), *Learning for the future*. Melbourne, Australia: Common Ground.

Gee, J. P. (2003). *What video games have to teach us about learning and literacy*. New York, NY: Palgrave Macmillan.

Gee, J. P. (2004a). *Game-like situated learning: An example of situated learning and implications for opportunity to learn*. Unpublished manuscript, University of Wisconsin.

Gee, J. P. (2004b). *Situated language and learning: A critique of traditional schooling*. London, UK: Routledge.

Gee, J. P. (2005). *Why video games are good for your soul: Pleasure and learning*. Melbourne, Australia: Common Ground.

Gee, J. P. (2006). *Are video games good for learning?* Unpublished manuscript, Games and Professional Simulation Group, University of Wisconsin.

Gee, J. P., Hull, G., & Lankshear, C. (1996). *The new work order*. Boulder, CO: Westview.

Ismail, S. M., & Cazden C. B. (2005). Struggles for indigenous education and self-determination: Culture, context, and collaboration. *Anthropology and Education Quarterly, 36*, 88–92.

Jenkins, H. (2004). The cultural logic of media convergence. *International Journal of Cultural Studies, 7*, 33–43.

Kalantzis, M. (2000). Multicultural citizenship. In W. Hudson & J. Kane (Eds.), *Rethinking Australian citizenship* (pp. 99–110). Melbourne, Australia: Cambridge University Press.

Kalantzis, M. (2004). Waiting for the barbarians: "Knowledge management" and "learning organisations". *International Journal of Knowledge, Culture and Change Management, 4*, 1823–1827.

Kalantzis, M. (2006a). Changing subjectivities, new learning. *Pedagogies: An International Journal, 1*(1), 7–12.

Kalantzis, M. (2006b). Elements of a science of education. *Australian Educational Researcher, 33*(2), 15–42.

Kalantzis, M., & Cope, B. (1999). Multiliteracies. In A. Pandian (Ed.), *Global literacy: Vision, revisions and vistas in education* (pp. 1–12). Serdang, Malaysia: Universiti Putra Malaysia Press.

Kalantzis, M., & Cope, B. (2000). Multiliteracies: Rethinking what we mean by literacy and what we teach as literacy in the context of global cultural diversity and new communications technologies. In A.-F. Christidis (Ed.), *"Strong" and "weak" languages in the European Union: Aspects of linguistic hegemonism* (pp. 667–679, English; pp. 80–96, Greek).Thessaloniki, Greece: Centre for the Greek Language.

Kalantzis, M., & Cope, B. (2001). Polugsammatsmoi [Multiliteracies]. In A.-F. Christidis (Ed.), *Egkyklopaidikos odhgos gia ti Glossa* (pp. 214–217).Thessaloniki, Greece: Centre for the Greek Language.

Kalantzis, M., & Cope, B. (2004). Designs for learning. *E-Learning, 1*, 38–92.

Kalantzis, M., & Cope, B. (2005). *Learning by design.* Melbourne, Australia: Victorian Schools Innovation Commission.

Kalantzis, M., & Cope, B. (2006). *The learning by design guide.* Melbourne, Australia: Common Ground.

Kalantzis, M., & Cope, B. (2012a). *Literacies.* Cambridge UK: Cambridge University Press.

Kalantzis, M., & Cope, B. (2012b). *New learning: Elements of a science of education.* Cambridge UK: Cambridge University Press.

Kalantzis, M., & Pandian, A. (Eds.). (2001). *Literacy matters: Issues for new times.* Penang, Malaysia: Universiti Sains Malaysia.

Karantzola, E., & Intzidis, E. (2000). Multiliteracies and multimodalities: Narrative and conceptual visual representations. *Glossikos Ypologistis, 1*, 119–124.

Karantzola, E., & Intzidis, E. (2001a). Multimodality across the curriculum. In M. Kalantzis (Ed.), *Languages of learning: Changing communication and changing literacy teaching* (pp. 9–12). Melbourne, Australia: Common Ground.

Karantzola, E., & Intzidis, E. (2001b). Interrelations among texts, diagrams and photographs: Multimodal designs of meaning in science teaching. *Glossikos Ypologistis, 2*, 199–203.

Karantzola, E., Kondyli, M., Intzidis, E., & Lykou, C. (2004a). Literacy for active citizenship: Methodology for the development of educational materials for Centres for Adult Education in Greece. *International Journal of Learning, 11*.

Karantzola, E., Kondyli, M., Intzidis, E., & Lykou, C. (2004b). Literacy for active citizenship: Educational materials for social inclusion. Athens, Greece: General Secretariat for Adult Education, Hellenic Ministry of Education and Religious Affairs.

Kress, G. (1997). *Before writing: Rethinking the paths to literacy.* London, UK: Routledge.

Kress, G. (2000a). Design and transformation: New theories of meaning. In B. Cope & M. Kalantzis (Eds.), *Multiliteracies: Literacy learning and the design of social futures* (pp. 153–61). London, UK: Routledge.

Kress, G. (2000b). Multimodality. In B. Cope & M. Kalantzis (Eds.). *Multiliteracies: Literacy learning and the design of social futures* (pp. 182–202). Melbourne, Australia: Macmillan.

Kress, G. (2003). *Literacy in the new media age.* London, UK: Routledge.

Kress, G., & van Leeuwen, T. (1996). *Reading images: The grammar of visual design.* London, UK: Routledge.

Lanchester, J. (2006). The global Id. *London Review of Books, 28*(2), 3–6.

Luke, A., Cazden C., Lin, A., & Freebody, P. (2005). *A coding scheme for the analysis of classroom discourse in Singapore schools* (Tech. Rep.). National Institute of Education, Singapore, Center for Research on Pedagogy and Practice.

Newfield, D. (2005). "The most precious thing I have ever done in my life":Visual literacy in a Soweto language classroom. In R. Griffin, S. Chandler, & B. Cowden (Eds.), *Visual literacy and development: An African experience.* Madison, WI: Omnipress.

Newfield, D., & Stein, P. (2000).The Multiliteracies Project: South African teachers respond. In B. Cope & M. Kalantzis (Eds.), *Multiliteracies: Literacy learning and the design of social futures* (pp. 292–310). London, UK: Routledge.

Newfield, D., Stein, P., Rumboll, F., Meyer, L., Badenhorst, C., Drew, M., et al. (2001). Exploding the monolith: Multiliteracies in South Africa. In M. Kalantzis & B. Cope (Eds.), *Transformations in language and learning: Perspectives on multiliteracies* (pp. 121–152). Melbourne, Australia: Common Ground.

New London Group. (1996). A pedagogy of multiliteracies: Designing social futures. *Harvard Educational Review, 66*, 60–92.

Pandian, A. (Ed.). (1999). *Global literacy: Vision, revisions and vistas in education.* Serdang, Malaysia: Universiti Putra Malaysia Press.

Pandian, A. (2001). Technological literacies for English literacy in the Malaysian classroom. In A. Pandian (Ed.), *Technologies of learning: Learning through and about the new information technologies* (pp. 7–18). Melbourne, Australia: Common Ground.

Pandian, A. (2003). Linking literacy, lifelong learning and living in the New Times. In A. Pandian & G. Chakravarthy (Eds.), *New literacies, new practices and new times.* Serdang, Malaysia: Universiti Putra Press.

Pandian, A. (2004a). Literacy, information technology and language learning. *Journal of Communication Practices, 1* [July].

Pandian, A. (2004b). Multiliteracies, technology and teaching in the classroom: Perspectives from teachers taking distance learning programs in Malaysia. *Malaysian Journal of Distance Education, 6*(1), [June], 1–26.

Pandian, A., & Balraj, S. (2005). Approaching "Learning by Design" as an agenda for Malaysian schools. In M. Kalantzis & B. Cope (Eds.), *Learning by design* (pp. 285–313). Melbourne, Australia: Victorian Schools Innovation Commission.

Scollon, R. (2001). *Mediated discourse: The nexus of practice.* London, UK: Routledge.

Stein, P. (2003). The Olifantsvlei fresh stories project: Multimodality, creativity and fixing in the semiotic chain. In C. Jewitt & G. Kress (Eds.), *Multimodal literacy* (pp. 123–138). New York, NY: Peter Lang.

Stein, P., & Newfield, D. (2002a). Shifting the gaze in South African classrooms: New pedagogies, new publics, new democracies. *International Journal of Learning, 9*.

Stein, P., & Newfield, D. (2002b). Agency, creativity, access and activism: Literacy education in Post-Apartheid South Africa. In M. Kalantzis, G. Varnava-Skoura, & B. Cope (Eds.), *Learning for the future* (pp. 155–165). Melbourne, Australia: Common Ground.

Stein, P., & Newfield, D. (2003). Recovering the future: Multimodal pedagogies and the making of culture in South African classrooms. *International Journal of Learning, 10*.

Vygotsky, L. (1962). *Thought and language.* Cambridge, MA: MIT Press.

Yelland, N. (2006). *Shift to the future: Rethinking learning with new technologies in education.* New York, NY: Routledge.

7

REGROUNDING CRITICAL LITERACY

Representation, Facts and Reality

Allan Luke

Introduction

Since the turn towards language and discourse in the social sciences in the past three decades, it has became increasingly rare for writers to refer to 'reality' or 'facts' without using single or double quote marks. For the conventional wisdom is, indeed, that realities are socially constructed by human beings through discourse. This has been historically complicated by the degree to which new media and expressive forms managed to blur, simulate and disrupt Aristotelian distinctions between art and life, between image and object, between sign and signified, between discourse and representation. The concept of *mimesis*, after all, depended on the independent existence of the object to be artistically represented. The risk always has been that bloggers and journalists, teachers and students alike are left unmoored to social or material reality, to work in a relativist universe of competing significations with no fixed epistemological grounds—with education reduced to a hall of intertextual mirrors.

Reality still looms large in everyday life, despite all attempts to theoretically and pharmacologically eradicate it, technologically overwrite it, or, at the least, place a large philosophic asterix next to it. Consider the debate over climate change. However this might appear to be a competition between contending versions of scientific knowledge, contending media representations of the debate, and unsavory political ideologies at work—few human beings would doubt that there is a biosphere out there with some degree of actual facticity. We might argue about how to name it, about the relative calibrations of change, and about causes. All these would indeed be discourse representations of 'truth'. But the alteration of an ecosystem, the loss of a species, the emergence of a new biological pheno-menon are substantive and material, real and consequential. All things may be constructed or construed through discourse—but some phenomena kill you, others just do not matter much. So even if we acknowledge the discourse construction of possible worlds, we need to make a parallel acknowledgement that all discourses are not the things of which they speak, nor do they have equivalent or comparable consequences, effects and impacts.

Perhaps the key philosophical and political issue in this millennium is this relationship between cultural systems of representation—traditional print texts, writing, mass media, journalism, advertisements, web pages, texts, instant messages, digital communications—and social and economic reality. In regions with advanced urban information infrastructure, young people and adults live in a mediasphere that surrounds them with a seemingly endless and limitless flow of talk, broad and narrowcast media, visual images and texts of all modalities, instant and digitally enabled communication. This sits alongside a robust transnational industry in the provision of the printed word, whether through books, newspapers or screens. Governments, corporations, and educational institutions strive to mediate these flows—that is, to control and censor, tax, regulate and capitalize upon who gets access to flows of information, and which texts and discourses are translatable into cultural and economic value and status, power and functionality. In these milieux, critical literacy involves a normative analysis of the relationship between designs, shapes and features of texts *and* their consequences in material and social contexts.

The rapidity of technological development, of media shift and crossover, and the unruliness of users, designers and developers have generated a volatility without precedent. Digital media (Google, Facebook), hardware and software (Microsoft, Lenovo, Apple, Oracle), digital infotainment and media (Sony, Dreamworks), and more traditional mixed information corporations (e.g., Thomson/Reuters, Pearson, News Corp.) vie to manage and capitalize upon information, consolidate corporate control and ownership, regulate intellectual property, and overtly shape its ideological and cultural content and uses (Castells, 2011).

The control, ownership and ideological uses of these new flows are volatile and dynamic—yielding new forms of social agency, anarchist, libertarian and, depending on whose point of view you take, outright criminal action, while courts struggle to establish the parameters of legality and criminality in systems designed to govern print and face-to-face social relations, and to regulate commerce based on the exchange of material goods. Powerful underground and grassroots communities of hackers, bloggers and users work to establish their own procedural rules and protocols, with many destabilizing and attacking state and corporate governance over communications, intellectual property, proprietary access and pay-per-cost structures. If indeed the alchemy created by Gutenberg and Luther in 15th century Europe led to assaults on canonical knowledge and, ultimately, book burnings on all sides—this universe of hacking of corporate and state security servers, intellectual property and copyright lawsuits, and *Wikileaks* is the new battleground, as is the social and economic regulation of the value of textual representation.

There are worlds outside of this mediasphere, where issues of access to basic literacy still persist. Many autocratic states attempt to maintain strict ideological control—Burma and North Korea, for example. But the ongoing bids to censor the internet and instant messaging in, for example, China and the Middle East point to the difficulties that ubiquitous and instant information flows pose for governments and multinational corporations that rely upon the control of who knows what and what will count as factual, truthful, and of significance. In a country like Singapore, for example, the public gained uncensored access to CNN and other global media after the first Gulf War. While the government maintains indirect and direct regulatory influence and control over print and broadcast media, and monitors and partially filters Internet traffic, it relies strongly on self-censorship by users (Lee, 2010). There are parallel lessons to be learned from *Wikileaks* and recent high profile hackings of government and corporate (Sony, CIA) servers about the fragility of control that government institutions, corporations and individuals have over their proprietary information and texts.

There remain major populations, communities and cultures that are not part of global information flows—either by spatial/technological isolation (e.g., Indigenous peoples in the Amazon, West Java, Central Africa), by economic marginalization (e.g., parts of Africa, West Asia, North and Western China), or by deliberate cultural choice (e.g., Amish communities in Pennsylvania). As economies of scale shift, there are more cases of, for instance, the expanded use of mobile phone technology or satellite-based laptops amongst rural and remote populations to enhance trade and exchange, crop productivity or medical and community infrastructure. The effects of this spread remain mixed, often disrupting traditional knowledge, vernacular languages and ways of life. But at the same time the spread of communications media historically has and continues to provide tools for the shaping and reshaping of material, social and eco-biological relations (Innis, 1949).

While it is increasingly rare to refer to reality as a freestanding, non-problematic phenomenon, this new information and semiotic order is, in and for itself, a compelling social fact and reality. The theoretical and practical questions at the core of critical literacy programs is simple: Do changing media images, political statements, news reports, internet websites, the language of laws, workplaces and everyday face-to-face talk have material effects upon peoples, lives, their work, the quality of social relationships, civic and their access to and use of resources? Certainly, communications technologies have changed the way many people work and learn; they have reshaped consumption and leisure, politics and commerce. A curriculum focus on how they shape and can be used to reshape everyday lives, experience and knowledge is certainly something that—critical literacy educators have already demonstrated—is viable with 8-year-olds developmentally in early print acquisition (e.g., Comber & Simpson, 2001; Vasquez, 2004), with disengaged, minority youth who have turned away from traditional print literacy pathways (e.g., Morrell, 2007), and with adults who have been economically and politically marginalized (e.g., Kumishiro & Ngo, 2007).

Educational work in the field of critical literacy provides a key opportunity for the debating, unpacking and learning about this family of questions: How do language, text, discourse and information make a difference? For whom? In what *question* material, social and consequential ways? In whose interests? According to what patterns, rules, and in what institutional and cultural sites?

These, I want to argue, are not fringe or boutique concerns of an elite literary, cultural studies or political education. Nor should these be elective options in an education system that is locked into the production of its human subjects as competitive capital for these new economies. Critical literacy is now old news. We can document four decades of diverse approaches to critical literacy that have arisen in the contexts of schooling, university study, adult basic and vocational education, second language education and, indeed, informal community-based education. In education systems in the US and Commonwealth, and other English-speaking countries, critical literacy has taken different developmental paths in a range of curriculum areas: English, Second Language study, literature study, college composition and communication, language arts, arts and visual education, technology and design education, and indeed, crossovers to numeracy and mathematics, social studies and history, and science education. Unlike many other educational developments, critical literacy did not originate or initially flourish in the countries of the English-speaking North and West. It originated in what was then called the "third world", in regions undergoing decolonization, through languages other than English, with prototypical work in Portuguese and Spanish—and applications underway in Mandarin, Cantonese, Slovenian, Japanese, Arabic, Bahasa Indonesian, Farsi, and other languages.

This chapter has two purposes. It provides a brief introductory overview of the two major approaches to critical literacy: critical pedagogy and critical text analysis. This review is both theoretical and practical, covering the foundational assumptions of each approach, their historical genealogies and linking these to practical strategies for the teaching and learning of literacy. They are well established and documented (e.g., Morgan & Ramanathan, 2005). My purpose here is *not* to make a case for them as an original, innovative or 'radical' alternatives yet again.

Instead, my second task is to make the case that all approaches of critical literacy attempt to practically bring together two distinct philosophies of text and representation: historical materialist critique of the state and political economy, on the one hand, and poststructuralist and postmodern theories of discourse, on the other. Various pedagogic languages are used to bridge the two, including literary and cultural studies text analysis, functional and critical linguistics. But this theoretical tension is *the* central practical pivot for approaches to critical literacy: understanding how the representation of possible worlds through language and image, texts and discourses shapes and alters the material and social, bio-ecological and economic realities and facts of these worlds. What are the real and material consequences of texts and discourses? And how can we reshape them?

Literacy and the Production of the Subject

Literacies—in both traditional print and multimodal forms—are malleable social and cultural practices with communications technologies. While there may indeed be particular cognitive and social 'affordances' affiliated with particular technologies (Kress, 2003)—the specific practices, functions and uses of texts and discourses that are prescribed and transmitted in any particular literacy education model are not given by the linguistic or technical features of the medium per se. They are rather specific selections from a theoretically infinite array of possible practices. Consider, for example, what schools typically teach 6- and 7-year-olds to 'do' with print texts: that they are stories, that stories are for pleasure and fun, that we can think and talk about what they mean, individual effect and so forth. Far from being natural or intrinsic to the medium of print—we could as readily teach children that texts are for memorization and chanting, that they are never to be contested, etc., indeed as some communities do. That is, we could assign very different sociocultural functions, discourse contents and cognitive 'affordances' to the medium and text in question. Such are the normative choices that all schemes for literacy education must make, whether deliberately or by default.

When we refer to the social practices of reading, then, we refer to particular psychological skills, linguistic competences, cognitive strategies, etc., but we also refer to specific preferred text types and conventionally affiliated discourses, particular social ideologies, particular cultural scripts for what people should do with text, when, where and to what social, political, economic, cultural—intellectual and spiritual—purposes and ends. To reiterate: these are normative cultural decisions—not technical scientific ones. The curriculum decisions about how to shape literate practices are based on a longitudinal and developmental vision of a fully-fledged literate subject using texts and discourses for particular forms of social and cultural action.

That the range of possible human practices with text is virtually infinite does not mean that these are, in a Saussurean sense, altogether 'arbitrary'. The relationships between signs and signifiers, between words and objects, between grammar and action may indeed be theoretically arbitrary, and the institutional selection of one text, disposition or practice over another may, in a purely descriptive sense, be arbitrary vis-à-vis particular textual features or characteristics to be assigned cultural capital (cf. Bourdieu & Passeron, 1990). But they are not arbitrary in the sense that literate practices make up repertoires of conventional social functions with exchange value in specific institutional, disciplinary and social fields (e.g., in universities, particular workplaces, or specific disciplinary fields). Depending on the social and cultural fields of use, specific ways of doing things with text have exchange value.

My point, then, is that all models of literacy education are bids to intergenerationally reproduce particular forms of disciplined tool use with the technologies of print and other media. It is not surprising, then, that those who approach the definition and study of literacy from particular disciplinary and foundational per-spectives tend to normatively argue for the production of a literate subject who embodies that specific discipline. For example, literary poststructuralists advocate the production of specialized skills of deconstruction; cultural anthropologists argue for students to study language in use in the community; those who define literacy as a cognitive, scientific process define higher order literacy in terms of recall, taxonomic analysis and falsification; feminist poststructuralists argue for the deconstruct of gendered speaking positions and representations; functional lin-guists argue for students to acquire a detailed and explicit knowledge of lexico-grammatical system and choice—and, indeed, various religions define and align the reading of sacred texts tautologically as evidence of having mastered a particular spiritual discipline.

Models of critical literacy are not exempt. That is, they are not 'true' or 'untrue' but rather they are normative bids to construct a particular kind of cultural and political subject (Muspratt, Luke, & Freebody, 1998). They are tethered to parti-cular political bids to reconstruct what is done with the technology of writing in specific social class, cultural and political interests, under the auspices of broad principles of social and economic justice, freedom of expression and political self-determination, human rights and emancipation. Note that these are not necessar-ily locally generated cultural principles but may constitute, in themselves, forms of external cultural imposition. In consequence, models of critical literacy select and shape particular practices for students; and claims about, for example, "empower-ment" make broad assumptions about the political and cultural efficacy of specific textual practices. The most rudimentary models of functional literacy make the case that the acquisition of basic skills generates improved pathways to employ-ment. Similarly, models of critical literacy are predicated upon the assumption that particular approaches to reading (e.g., identifying social class ideologies underly-ing text messages; critiquing the economic or political motives of authors of particular texts) or writing (e.g., developing online digital art, digitally archiving community elders' stories), can generate both individual (e.g., identity, affiliation, agency) and collective effects (e.g., participation in larger social movements).

Critical Pedagogy

The term "critical" has a distinctive etymology in Western philosophy and science. It is derived from the Greek adjective *kriticos*, the ability to argue and judge. Paulo Freire's (1970) revolutionary educational philosophy defined *critical literacy* as the capacity to analyze, critique and transform social, cultural and politi-cal texts and contexts. Working in Indigenous and peasant communities in Brazil, Freire's approach to critical literacy was grounded in dialectical materialist and phenomenological philosophies. He argued that the literacy transmitted in con-ventional schooling was based on a "banking model" of education, where learners' lives, cultures, knowledge and aspirations were taken as irrelevant. He advocated a dialogical approach to literacy based on principles of reciprocal exchange. These would critique and transform binary relationships of oppressed and oppressor, teacher and learner. "Cultural circles" would begin with an analysis of participants' specific contexts, problems, struggles and aspirations.

The acquisition of literacy entails the naming and renaming, narrating and analyzing of lifeworlds as part of a problem-posing and problem-solving pedagogy. Accordingly, Freire's work focuses literacy educators on the transitivity and teleology of reading and writing: that they are always about substantive lives and material realities; and that they are always goal and problem-directed. "Reading the word", then, entails "reading the world" (Freire & Macedo, 1987), enlisting one's power to critique and supplant dominant ideologies and false consciousness. Technical mastery of written language and other codes, then, is a means to broader social and cultural agency, individual and collective transformation—not an end in itself.

There is an extensive literature that extends Freire's principles and approaches in a broad project of "critical pedagogy" (Lankshear & McLaren, 1993; Darder, Baltodano, & Torres, 2003). Freire's work draws from Marx the key concept that ruling class ideology defines school knowledge and ideology. By this view, approaches to literacy are expressions of dominant, ruling-class ideology that succeed in creating a *receptive* literacy, involving passive reproduction of systematically distorted views of the world. The alternative is to begin from learners' worldviews, in effect turning them into teachers and inventors of the curriculum. By this account, the process of critical literacy entails a renaming of the world. The focus then of critical literacy is on students' engaging in forms of ideology critique: exposing and reconstructing misleading ideological versions of the world provided in media, literature, textbooks and everyday texts (Shor & Freire, 1987).

Critical analyses of competing ideologies and economic conditions were central to literacy campaigns initiated by Freire and colleagues in Mozambique, and it is the focus of current efforts at explicitly political pedagogies in countries like Brazil, Venezuela, Peru and Mexico (Kukendall, 2010). In such curricula, students are involved in analysis of the effects of colonialism, imperialism, class division, and unequal economic relations. In Freirian terms, this entails working with learners to use language to name and 'problematicize' the world—that is to take everyday ideological constructions of class, race, gender relations, and to make them problematic through dialogic exchange. In such a setting, traditional authority and epistemic knowledge relations of teachers and student shift: learners become teachers of their understandings and experiences, and teachers become learners of these same contexts. This might entail setting open, dialogic conditions of exchange by establishing a cultural circle amongst adult learners. In school classrooms, it might entail establishing democratic conditions in classrooms where authentic exchange can occur around social, political and cultural issues (Lewison, Leland, & Harste, 2008). Note that these approaches are based on a key assumption from Marxist ideology critique: that once ruling class ideology is named and cleared out of the way, undistorted, accurate and factual versions of history, community formation, social and economic conditions can be brought to the table for analysis and action.

Current critical literacy practices also draw from British and American cultural studies. Landmark work by Richard Hoggart (1957) and Raymond Williams (1958) set the directions for approaches to critical literacy: (1) the expansion of textual and cultural objects beyond canonical and literary texts to include the everyday cultural forms and practices; (2) a focus on critical literacy as a counter-hegemonic form of critique that might, in turn, (3) enable a revoicing of marginalized class culture. Practical approaches to critical literacy advocated in US schools start from a focus on community relations or political events, moving towards agentive, alternative analyses (e.g., Vasquez, 2004). In schools and universities, these approaches also focus literacy on forms of community study, the analysis of social movements, and political activism (e.g., Kumishiro & Ngo, 2007). Drawing from cultural studies, they have also involved the development of a critical "media literacy", focusing on the analysis of popular cultural texts including advertising, news, broadcast media and the Internet (e.g., Alvermann & Hagood, 2000; Kellner & Share, 2005). Finally, there is a broad focus in these models on the development of alternative versions of history, altering dominant and hegemonic descriptions of national history, colonialism and political processes.

In this context, various marginalized groups have staked the grounds for approaches that require the aforementioned political ideology critique, but also set the grounds for a strong focus on the significance of culture, broadly construed as shared value systems, interactional patterns, and forms of affiliation. This was part of the major critique of critical pedagogy that emerged in the early 1990s, when feminist scholars began to argue that the model risked ideological imposition that was contrary to its ethos and did not adequately consider issues of gendered standpoint. In everyday practice, there was, and is, a parallel risk of pedagogic imposition given the complex forms of gendered and raced voice and power, identity, and subjectivity at work in the interactional contexts of classrooms and cultural circles (Luke & Gore, 1991). The critiques raised by poststructuralist feminists have had a major impact on critical pedagogy. Especially in Australia and Canada, approaches to school reading entail a critique of textual and media representations of women and girls as ideological and patriarchal, that is, as projecting dominant constructions of gender and sexuality and inequitable patterns of face-to-face interaction (Mellor, O'Neill, & Patterson, 2000). Relatedly, it led to a stronger focus on standpoint and agency in theory, including a critique of critical pedagogy itself as a potential form of patriarchal practice.

A parallel development draws upon postcolonial and critical race theory. American approaches to critical literacy have developed a strong focus on the "politics of voice" (Darder et al., 2003), on building interaction around the distinctive cultural histories, identities and contexts faced by groups marginalized on the basis of difference of gender, language, culture and race, and sexual orientation. A critical approach to language and literacy education requires the setting of culturally appropriate and generative contexts for enactment of identity and solidarity (Norton & Toohey, 2004; Kubota & Lin, 2009). It extends a focus of critique on the political economy to examine 'grand narratives' and the everyday practices of patriarchy, racism and sexism (Luke, 2004). There the enhancement of 'voice', 'speaking position' and 'standpoint' become central pedagogical foci, with the assumption that these can be translated into forms of self-determination, agency and social movement.

Discourse Analytic Approaches

The last three decades of ethnographic research on the social contexts and practices of literacy have established the cultural, social, cognitive and linguistic complexity of its development and acquisition. This raises two substantive educational challenges for critical pedagogy approaches. First, it is largely synchronic, advocating and practicing particular approaches to literacy pedagogy without a broader template for developmental acquisition and use. While Freirian models provide a pedagogical approach and a political stance, an orientation towards 'voice' and ideology, they lack specificity in terms of how teachers and students can engage with the detailed and complex structures of texts, both traditional and multimodal. The acquisition of language, text and discourse requires the developmental engagement with levels of linguistic and discourse complexity (e.g., Gee, 1992; Lemke, 1996). Later models of critical literacy, particularly those developed in Australia and the UK, attempt to come to grips with these key theoretical and practical issues.

An initial major critique of critical pedagogy approaches was that they overlooked the pressing need for students to master a range of textual genres, including those scientific forms that constitute powerful understandings of the physical and material world (Halliday & Martin, 1995). According to systemic functional linguists, the mastery of genre entails a grasp of the social functions of lexical and syntactic functions, and an understanding of the relationships of these with affiliated discourses and ideologies (Hasan & Williams, 1996). Equitable access to how texts work, they argue, is an essential component to redistributive social justice in literacy education, and cannot be achieved through a principal focus on 'voice' or ideology critique. The affiliated approach to critical literacy, then, argues for explicit instruction and direct access to "Secret English" and "genres of power" (Kalantzis & Cope, 1996). Yet there are unresolved issues about what balance of direct access to canonical and culturally significant text forms and critique might constitute an enfranchising and politically activist approach to critical literacy.

The alternative approach is based upon critical discourse analysis, an explicitly political derivative of systemic functional linguistics. Bringing together ideology critique with an explicit instructional focus on teaching how texts work,

Fairclough (1990) argues for the teaching of "critical language awareness". This entails teaching students the analysis of a range of texts—functional, academic, literary—attending to both their lexico-grammatical structure, their ideological contents and discourses, and their identifiable conditions of production and use. Drawing from Halliday, critical linguistics makes broad distinctions between ideological formations in texts, their social functions and their distinctive features. This enables teachers and students to focus on how words, grammar and discourse choices shape a representation or 'version' of material, natural and sociopolitical worlds (Janks, 2010). It also enables a focus on how words and grammar attempt to establish relations of power between authors and readers, speakers and addressees. Furthermore, it enables a critical engagement with the question of where texts are used, by whom, and in whose interests.

Critical literacy—by this account—entails the developmental engagement by learners with the major texts, discourses and modes of information. It attempts to attend to the ideological and hegemonic functions of texts, as in other critical pedagogy models. But it augments this by providing students with technical resources for analyzing how texts and discourses work. For example, this might entail the analysis of a textbook or media representation of political or economic life. But in addition to questions of how a text might reflect learners' life-worlds and experiences, it also teaches them how the structure of specific clauses and sentences attempts to define the world and situate the reader in relation to that definition (Wallace, 2003; Luke, 2001).

The Theoretical and Practical Problem: Representation and Reality

Critical literacy approaches view language, texts and discourses as principal means for representing and reshaping possible worlds. The aim is the development of human capacity to use texts to analyze and transform social relations and material conditions. As a cultural and linguistic practice, then, critical literacy entails an understanding of how increasingly sophisticated texts and discourses can be manipulated to represent and, indeed, alter the world. Critical literacy education, further, is premised on the imperative for freedom of dialogue and the need to critique all texts, discourses and ideologies.

Yet it is inevitably confronted with the problem of normativity: of whose reading of a text will count, of whose version of the world will count, and on what grounds. Freirian models begin from an explicit focus on authenticity of voice of participants in cultural circles, and in practice have moved to stress cultural standpoint and speaking rights. Critical discourse analysis models have tended to focus on the ideological contents and social relations coded in texts. The broad premise is that reality is constructed socially through discourse, that all texts are potentially ideological, and hence should be the subject of critical analysis and scrutiny. But both approaches raise a core practical question: How do we ascertain 'truth' and fact? This requires an acknowledgement of the existence of 'truth' and 'reality' outside of the particular texts in question and, indeed, realities outside the complex web of intertextual descriptions and relations formed by multiple available texts.

Consider this current example. With the support of the Tea Party, religious and conservative groups, the *Louisiana Science Education Act of 2008* set new grounds for curriculum debate. It argued that the discussion of intelligent design and "alternative" views of science was necessary to ensure academic freedom in schools. But are we to treat the texts of 'evolution', for example, as ideological representations or scientific truths? The move towards critical discourse analysis and text deconstruction may place discourse-based models of critical literacy at odds with traditional Marxist ideology critique. Does critical literacy mean, for example, that texts about the Holocaust or slavery, or about global warming constitute yet further or more textual representations of the world? To be critiqued and deconstructed in terms of their rhetorical positioning devices or hidden ideological assumptions? What about truths, facts about history, social and material reality that they purport to represent?

My point here is that models of critical literacy in and of themselves require a commitment to the existence and accessibility of 'truth', 'facts' and 'realities' outside of the texts in question and, potentially, as having an existence independent of their immediate discursive construction. Freirian approaches typically resolve this through the mobilization of reading and writing as part of a broader investigation of issues and facts, histories and cultures, as a means for "reading the world" (Freire & Macedo, 1987). Critical discourse analytic approaches focus on the "conditions of production" and "conditions of reception" of the text (Fairclough, 1990): that is, the historical, cultural and political conditions of authorship and audience interpretation. In practical terms, this suggests the epistemological and educational limits of an exclusive focus on text analysis without broader cross-curricular scientific, social scientific and aesthetic inquiry. Simply, while authentic 'voice' *and* close textual analysis may be necessary elements of critical literacy education, neither in itself provides sufficient empirical grounds for social and cultural action. Both must turn to explore other texts and the facts, the material and social realities they purport to represent.

Particularly in the new mediasphere, the relationship between discourse and material biosocial worlds, between representation and historical/empirical reality remains the focal issue in critical pedagogy and critical literacy education. Far from being a conceptual or theoretical flaw or contradiction—it provides teachers and learners, curriculum developers and educational researchers with a starting point and overall goal for teaching and learning. Unpacking the relationship between discourse representation and reality remains *the* core question of critical literacy as theory and practice.

References

Alvermann, D., & Hagood, M. (2000). Critical media literacy: Research, theory, and practice in "new times." *Journal of Educational Research, 93*(3), 193–205.

Bourdieu, P., & Passeron, J. C. (1990). *Reproduction* (2nd ed., R. Nice, Trans.). London, UK: Sage.

Castells, M. (2011). *Communication power.* Oxford, UK: Oxford University Press.

Comber, B., & Simpson, A. (Eds.). (2001). *Negotiating critical literacies in classrooms.* Mawah, NJ: Erlbaum.

Darder, A., Baltodano, M., & Torres, R. (Eds.). (2003). *The critical pedagogy reader.* New York, NY: Routledge.

Fairclough, N. (Ed.). (1990). *Critical language awareness.* London, UK: Longman.

Freire, P. (1970). *Pedagogy of the oppressed.* New York, NY: Continuum.

Freire, P., & Macedo, D. (1987). *Literacy: Reading the word and the world.* South Hadley, MA: Bergin & Garvey.

Gee, J. P. (1992). *Social linguistics and literacies.* London, UK: Taylor & Francis.

Halliday, M. A. K., & Martin, J. R. (1995). *Writing science.* London, UK: Taylor & Francis.

Hasan, R., & Williams, G. (Eds.). (1996). *Literacy in society.* London, UK: Longman.

Hoggart, R. (1957). *The uses of literacy.* Harmondsworth, UK: Penguin.

Innis, H. (1949). *The bias of communications.* Toronto, Canada: University of Toronto Press.

Janks, H. (2010). *Literacy and power.* London, UK: Routledge.

Kalantzis, M., & Cope, B. (Eds.). (1996). *The powers of literacy.* London, UK: Taylor & Francis.

Kellner, D., & Share, J. (2005). Toward critical media literacy: Core concepts, debates, organisation and policy. *Discourse, 3,* 369–386.

Kress, G. (2003). Literacy in the new media age. London, UK: Routledge.

Kubota, R., & Lin, A. (Eds.). (2009). *Race, culture and identities in second language learning.* New York, NY: Routledge.

Kukendall, A. J. (2010). *Paulo Freire and the cold war politics of literacy.* Chapel Hill: University of North Carolina Press.

Kumishiro, K., & Ngo, B. (Eds.). (2007). *Six lenses for anti-oppressive education.* New York, NY: Peter Lang.

Lankshear, C., & McLaren, P. (Eds.). (1993). *Critical literacy.* Albany, NY: State University of New York Press.

Lee, T. (2010). *The media, cultural control and government in Singapore.* London, UK: Routledge.

Lemke, J. (1996). *Textual politics.* London, UK: Taylor & Francis.

Lewison, M., Leland, C., & Harste, J. (2008). *Creating critical classrooms: K-8 reading and writing with an edge.* Mawah, NJ: Lawrence Erlbaum.

Luke, A. (2001). Critical literacy in Australia. *Journal of Adolescent & Adult Literacy, 43*(5), 448–461.

Luke, A. (2004). Two takes on the critical. In B. Norton & K. Toohey (Eds.), *Critical pedagogies and language learning* (pp. 21–31). Cambridge, UK: Cambridge University Press.

Luke, C., & Gore, J. (Eds.). (1991). *Feminisms and critical pedagogy.* London, UK: Routledge.

Mellor, B., O'Neill, M., & Patterson, A. (2000). *Reading stories.* Perth, Australia: Chalkface Press/National Council of Teachers of English.

Morgan, B., & Ramanathan, V. (2005). Critical literacies and language education: Global and local perspectives. *Annual Review of Applied Linguistics, 25,* 151–169.

Morrell, E. (2007). *Critical literacy and urban youth.* New York, NY: Routledge.

Muspratt, S., Luke, A., & Freebody, P. (1998). *Constructing critical literacies.* New York, NY: Hampton Press.

Norton, B., & Toohey, K. (Eds.). (2004). *Critical pedagogies and language learning.* Cambridge, UK: Cambridge University Press.

Shor, I., & Freire, P. (1987). *A pedagogy for liberation.* South Hadley, MA: Bergin & Garvey.

Vasquez, V. (2004). *Negotiating critical literacies with young children.* Mahwah, NJ: Lawrence Erlbaum.

Wallace, C. (2003). *Critical reading in language education.* London, UK: Palgrave Macmillan.

Williams, R. (1977). *Marxism and literature.* Oxford, UK: Oxford University Press.

8

BILITERACY CONTINUA

Nancy H. Hornberger

Biliteracy can be defined as "any and all instances in which communication occurs in two (or more) languages in or around writing" (Hornberger, 1990, p. 213), where these instances may be events, actors, interactions, practices, activities, classrooms, programs, situations, societies, sites, or worlds (Hornberger, 2000, p. 362; Hornberger & Skilton-Sylvester, 2000, p. 98). The continua model of biliteracy offers a framework in which to situate research, teaching, and language planning in bilingual and multilingual settings. The model's intersecting and nested continua demonstrate the multiple, complex, and fluid interrelationships between bilingualism and literacy and of the contexts, media, and content through which biliteracy develops. From the continua framework, we have argued that for multilingual learners, the *development* of biliteracy occurs:

> along intersecting first language–second language, receptive–productive, and oral–written language skills continua; through the *medium* of two (or more) languages and literacies whose linguistic structures vary from similar to dissimilar, whose scripts range from convergent to divergent, and to which the developing biliterate individual's exposure varies from simultaneous to successive; in *contexts* that encompass micro to macro levels and are characterized by varying mixes along the monolingual–bilingual and oral–literate continua; and . . . with *content* that ranges from majority to minority perspectives and experiences, literary to vernacular styles and genres, and decontextualized to contextualized language texts.
>
> *(Hornberger, 1989; Hornberger & Skilton-Sylvester, 2000, p. 96)*

Parts of this chapter appear also in Hornberger, N. H. (2012). Bilingual literacy. In C. A. Chapelle (Ed.), *The Encyclopedia of Applied Linguistics*. Reprinted here with permission from Wiley-Blackwell. Copyright © 1999–2013 by John Wiley and Sons, Inc. All Rights Reserved.

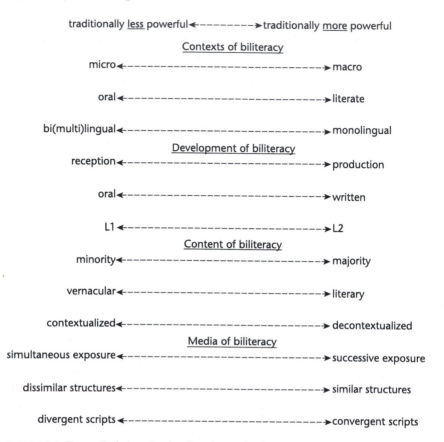

traditionally <u>less</u> powerful ◄------► traditionally <u>more</u> powerful

Contexts of biliteracy

micro ◄-------------------------------► macro

oral ◄-------------------------------► literate

bi(multi)lingual ◄-------------------------------► monolingual

Development of biliteracy

reception ◄-------------------------------► production

oral ◄-------------------------------► written

L1 ◄-------------------------------► L2

Content of biliteracy

minority ◄-------------------------------► majority

vernacular ◄-------------------------------► literary

contextualized ◄-------------------------------► decontextualized

Media of biliteracy

simultaneous exposure ◄-------------------------------► successive exposure

dissimilar structures ◄-------------------------------► similar structures

divergent scripts ◄-------------------------------► convergent scripts

FIGURE 8.1 Power Relations in the Continua of Biliteracy. Taken from 'Revisiting the Continua of Biliteracy: International and Critical Perspectives' by Nancy H. Hornberger & Ellen Skilton-Sylvester (2000). In *Language and Education*, *14*(2), pp. 96–122 (Taylor & Francis Ltd, www.tandfonline.com, reprinted by permission of the publisher).

Further, we suggest there is a need to contest traditional top-down power weightings in education toward compartmentalized, monolingual, written, decontextualized language and literacy practices, by intentionally opening up implementational and ideological spaces for fluid, multilingual, oral, contextualized practices and voices at the local level (Hornberger, 2002, 2005b, 2006; Hornberger & Skilton-Sylvester, 2000; see Figure 8.1).

The model has been exhaustively described and exemplified elsewhere (e.g., Hornberger, 1989, 1990, 2003, 2005a, 2008); here, I briefly review its origins and then take up each of the four sets of continua—contexts, development, content, and media—in relation to recent and enduring assumptions and perspectives in research in anthropological linguistics and sociolinguistics, literacy studies, and bilingualism and multilingualism.

The original impetus for the continua model of biliteracy was an ethnographic research project that I initiated in two multilingual communities of Philadelphia in 1987: the Literacy in Two Languages project, which continued for more than a decade with participation also from my students and colleagues. In search of a framework to underpin that research and finding very little scholarly work attending explicitly to biliteracy (the conjunction of bilingualism and literacy), I looked instead to its component parts, i.e., research on bilingualism and the teaching of second/foreign languages and on literacy and the teaching of reading/writing. An enduring perspective that emerges in common across these literatures is that although scholars, practitioners, and policymakers often characterize dimensions of bilingualism and literacy in terms of polar opposites such as first versus second languages (L1 vs. L2), monolingual versus bilingual individuals, or oral versus literate societies, in each case those opposites represent only theoretical endpoints on what is in reality a continuum of features (cf. Kelly, 1969, p. 5). Further, when we consider biliteracy as the conjunction of literacy and bilingualism, it becomes clear that these continua are interrelated dimensions of highly complex and fluid systems; and that it is in the dynamic, rapidly changing and sometimes contested spaces along and across the intersecting continua that most biliteracy use and learning occur.

These insights became the basis for the continua of biliteracy model that I proposed in 1989 and which has since informed my own and others' research in Philadelphia, nationally and internationally (e.g., Hornberger, 2003, 2008; Hult & King, 2011). This work includes research in Philadelphia on Korean heritage language education (Pak, 2003), identities, literacies and educational policies in the Cambodian community (Hornberger, 1990, 1992; Skilton-Sylvester, 1997, 2003), curricular adaptations and culturally contextualized teaching strategies in bilingual classrooms in the Puerto Rican community (Hornberger, 1990, 1992; Cahnmann, 2003; Schwinge, 2003), and language minority community bilingualism in Philadelphia (Freeman, 2004). Nationally, the continua of biliteracy framework has informed analysis and interpretation of language minority student voices in Arkansas (Lincoln, 2003), Chinese heritage language education (Wang, 2004), biliteracy development among Latino youth in New York City (Mercado, 2003), bilingual teacher preparation in the U.S. Southwest (Pérez, Flores, & Strecker, 2003), transnational practices and identities of the Dominican community in New York City (Utakis & Pita, 2005), Latino students' transactions with narrative texts in U.S. linguistic borderlands of the southwest (Martínez-Roldán & Sayer, 2006), Cherokee language revitalization and early childhood immersion (Peter & Hirata-Edds, 2008), and a comparative look at children's participation in family literacy events in Latino families in the U.S. southwest and in a Maya community in the Yucatán, Mexico (Reyes, 2009).

Internationally, scholars have found the continua of biliteracy useful in analyzing and understanding bilingual education in India (Basu, 2003; Vaish, 2008), multilingual classroom teaching in a formerly 'coloured' school in Cape Town, South Africa (Bloch & Alexander, 2003), language planning and the Welsh

National Curriculum in Wales (Baker, 2003), ideological principles and biases underlying language policies in France (Hélot, 2006), appropriation of academic biliteracy by French-speaking students at an English-medium university in Quebec (Gentil, 2005), Chinese heritage children's biliteracy acquisition in Scotland (Hancock, 2009), and curriculum planning and classroom pedagogy in an English-Sepedi dual-medium B.A. degree program in Limpopo, South Africa (Hornberger, 2010).

Along the way, the continua framework has evolved and adapted to accommodate both a changing world and a changing scholarly terrain. Recent scholarship in the field of bilingualism on languaging, translanguaging, and flexible bilingual pedagogy, and in anthropological linguistics, sociolinguistics and literacy studies on mobility, communicative repertoire and transnational literacies highlight threads woven into the continua, as I attempt to explore in the sections which follow.

Contexts of Biliteracy: Mobility and Sociolinguistic Scales

The continua model of biliteracy posits that contexts influence biliteracy development and use at every level from two-person interaction (micro) to societal and global relations of power (macro) and that they comprise a mix of oral-to-literate, monolingual-to-multilingual varieties of language and literacy (Hornberger, 1989). Recognition of context as an important factor in all aspects of language use dates back at least to the 1960s and the beginnings of sociolinguistics, linguistic anthropology, and the ethnography of communication (Fishman, 1970; Hymes, 1968; Pride & Holmes, 1972); and continues up to the present in work on sociolinguistic scales, indexicality, and polycentricity (Blommaert, 2010).

Sociolinguistics broke new ground in the 1960s by moving the analysis of language beyond a focus on structure to one on language use in social context. Rather than study homogeneous languages, sociolinguists (particularly those in the linguistic anthropological tradition) took up the study of speech communities and their verbal repertoires, described in terms of speech (or, more broadly, communicative) domains, situations, events, and acts. In his introduction to the 1964 special publication of the *American Anthropologist* on the ethnography of communication, Hymes proposed that:

> [The ethnography of communication] must take as context a community, investigating its communicative habits as a whole, so that any given use of channel and code takes its place as but part of the resources upon which the members of the community draw. . . . The starting point is the ethnographic analysis of the communicative habits of a community in their totality, determining what count as communicative events, and as their components . . . The communicative event thus is central.
>
> *(Hymes, 1964, pp. 3 & 13)*

Building from communicative theory and work by Roman Jakobson, he suggested an array of components that might serve as heuristic for the ethnographic study of communicative events, where such events refer to activities, or aspects of activities, that are directly governed by rules or norms for the use of language. This array of components he later formulated into the mnemonic SPEAKING (Setting, Participants, Ends, Act, Key, Instrumentalities, Norms, Genres; Hymes, 1974, pp. 53–62). Analysis of biliteracy events, from this perspective, then, involves describing the range of ways in which people "do" literacy in two (or more) language varieties and scripts, in terms of participants, settings, topics, purposes, norms, genres, and the like.

Gumperz, co-founder with Hymes of the ethnography of communication, built on work by sociologist Erving Goffman on face-to-face interaction in developing an approach which came to be known as interactional sociolinguistics.

> The key to Gumperz's sociolinguistics of verbal communication is a view of language as a socially and culturally constructed symbol system that is used in ways that reflect macrolevel social meanings (e.g., group identity, status differences) but also create microlevel social meanings (i.e., what one is saying and doing at a particular moment in time).
>
> *(Schiffrin, 1996, p. 315)*

This work investigates how contextualization cues, that is "signalling mechanisms such as intonation, speech rhythm, and choice among lexical, phonetic, and syntactic options" (Gumperz, 1982, p. 16), relate what is said to participants' background knowledge, enabling them to make situated inferences about their interlocutors' meaning. A biliteracy interaction, from this perspective, would be a face-to-face interaction involving a piece of writing and two or more language varieties and scripts—a notion closely related to biliteracy event in that the focus is on the "doing" of biliteracy, but with perhaps greater emphasis on the evolution of the interaction in real time and on *how* it creates and reflects micro and macrolevel social meanings.

More recently, Blommaert (2010) proposes and charts a further paradigmatic shift from a sociolinguistics of variation to a sociolinguistics of mobility. In keeping with an increasingly globalized world, he suggests, we need "a sociolinguistics of mobile resources, framed in terms of trans-contextual networks, flows, and movements" (2010, p. 1). Building on and citing a rich literature in linguistic anthropology and sociolinguistics over the past several decades, he offers three conceptual tools to help us think about language in this new sociolinguistics: sociolinguistic scales, orders of indexicality, and polycentricity—all sharing an emphasis on power and spatiotemporal sensitivity (2010, pp. 41–42).

Sociolinguistic scales are layered spatiotemporal scales at micro (e.g., local), macro (e.g., global) and intermediary (e.g., state) levels, distributed not only across horizontal space but also along vertical (hierarchical) dimensions (Blommaert, 2010, p. 34).

Indexicality refers to the jump from one scale to another. Blommaert notes that Gumperz' (1982) contextualization, Goffman's (1974) frames, Bakhtin's (cf. Fairclough, 1992) intertextuality, and Bourdieu's (1990) habitus all identify this jump—e.g., from token to type, from specific to general, from individual to collective. In all these cases, instances of communication at one scale point "socially and culturally ordered norms, genres, traditions, expectations" towards another (Blommaert, 2010, p. 33), either by presupposing/retrieving available meanings or entailing/producing new ones (Blommaert, 2010, p. 37; see also Silverstein, 2006). Indexicality is ordered in two senses: Silverstein's (2003) notion of *indexical order*, wherein "indexical meanings occur in patterns offering perceptions of similarity and stability that can be perceived as 'types' of semiotic practice with predictable (presupposable/entailing) directions" (p. 37)—e.g., registers that index specific personae and roles; but also *orders of indexicality*, as proposed by Blommaert following Foucault's (1984 [1971]) orders of discourse, in the sense of a "stratified general repertoire in which particular indexical orders relate to others in relations of mutual valuation—higher/lower, better/worse" (Blommaert 2010, p. 38), an ordering that indexes power and inequality.

Polycentricity refers to the multiple centers of authority to which people orient in communication. A center, or evaluating authority, is "what Bakhtin (1986) called a 'super-addressee': complexes of norms and appropriateness criteria" (Blommaert, 2010, p. 39), whether these reside in an individual, a collective, an abstract entity or ideal, etc. Every environment of human communication is almost by definition polycentric, even when it may look stable and monocentric. Polycentricity has parallels in sociolinguistic work on focal and non-focal activities (Goffman), polyphony, and multivocality, but Blommaert sees polycentricity as moving "from the descriptive to the interpretive level"—again to explicitly signal structures of power and inequality (2010, pp. 40–41).

Contexts of biliteracy, then, can be understood as scaled spatiotemporal complexes, indexically ordered and polycentric, in which multilingualism and literacies develop within mobile multilingual repertoires in local spaces, which are simultaneously translocal and global. In this light, the call for opening up implementational and ideological spaces for fluid, multilingual, oral, contextualized practices and voices in educational policy and practice becomes an even more powerful imperative for contesting the social inequalities of language.

Media of Biliteracy: Languaging and Communicative Repertoires

Biliteracy is about communication in two (or more) languages in or around writing; crucial in this are the languages and scripts—the media—through which biliteracy is learned and used. Media in the continua of biliteracy model refer to the actual communicative repertoires, i.e., the language varieties and scripts through which multilingual literacies are expressed, and the sequences or configurations in which they are acquired and used. The model defines these in terms of the linguistic structures of the languages involved (on a continuum from similar to dissimilar), their orthographic scripts (from convergent to divergent) and the sequence of exposure to or acquisition of the languages/literacies (ranging from simultaneous to successive) (Hornberger 1989). The media component in the continua model is roughly equivalent to Hymes' Instrumentalities in the SPEAKING heuristic (1974), including both code and channel, where Hymes' "code" refers to language varieties, dialects, styles, while "channel" includes written, as well as oral, telegraphic, and other communicative modes. Saville-Troike elaborates this into a grid of vocal/nonvocal channels and verbal/nonverbal codes; the instrumental alternatives or *media* of communication include such communicative modes as paralinguistic and prosodic features (vocal, nonverbal), silence, kinesics, and proxemics (nonvocal, nonverbal), and written and sign languages (nonvocal, verbal), as well as spoken language (vocal, verbal) (Saville-Troike, 1989, p. 145).

From the earliest formulations of the ethnography of communication on down to the present, linguistic anthropological research in sociolinguistics has emphasized a focus not on languages per se but on verbal or communicative repertoire. Gumperz (1964, 1965) introduced the term verbal repertoire in seeking to describe multilingualism in India. In addition to the broad concept of repertoire evident in Instrumentalities in the SPEAKING mnemonic noted above, Hymes referred to the verbal repertoire of the child as "the range of varieties of language, the circumstances, purposes, and meanings of their use" (Hymes, 1980, p. 106). More recently, Blommaert writes of repertoires as the complexes of linguistic, communicative, semiotic "resources people actually possess and deploy," such as "concrete accents, language varieties, registers, genres, modalities such as writing— ways of using language in particular communicative settings and spheres of life, including the ideas people have about such ways of using, their language ideologies" (2010, p. 102). Similarly, García (2007, 2009), in recognition of the mobility and fluidity of linguistic resources, the disinventing and reconstituting of languages (Makoni & Pennycook, 2007), calls for a focus not on language per se but on "the multiple discursive practices that constitute . . . languaging" (García, 2009, p. 40; see also Cortese & Hymes, 2001), wherein languages are seen not as fixed codes, but "fluid codes framed within social practices" (García, 2009, p. 32; cf. García, 2007, p. xiii).

Assumptions within the continua model about diversity of language varieties and scripts, multiple paths and varying degrees of expertise in the learning and use of communicative repertoire are consistent not only with the theoretical stance of the ethnography of communication and the sociolinguistics of mobility, but also with work on multimodal expression and multiliteracies. The New London Group (Cazden et al., 1996; Cope & Kalantzis, 2000) uses the term "multiliteracies" to refer to the multiple communications channels and media in our changing world (and to the increasing saliency of cultural and linguistic diversity in literacy learning and use). The concept of multiliteracies in this sense extends literacy beyond reading and writing to other domains, such as the visual, audio, spatial, and behavioral. Consideration of the media of biliteracy entails attention not just to different languages, but also to different dialects, styles, discourses, and different communicative modes including technological ones, as they are acquired and used not in a dichotomized sequence but more often in criss-crossed, hybrid mixes and languaging practices.

This is not to suggest that incorporating multiple varieties, scripts, communicative modes, and criss-crossed paths of acquisition and use proceeds unproblematically in schools or other biliteracy learning contexts. Indeed, given that biliteracy implies the scaled, polycentric, and indexical intersection of biliterate learners' multiple literacy worlds in particular literacy sites (cf. Hornberger, 2000, p. 362), some implicit conflict in norms, practices, and identities is inevitable. The new sociolinguistics of mobility brings with it a focus on locating linguistic and literacy practices as parts of larger systems of social inequality (Gal, 1989, p. 347), taking contexts of cross-cultural or intercultural communication as units of study:

> ... for instance, speakers in institutions who do not share interpretative rules; local populations of speakers viewed in relation to the policies or discourses of states; and contrasting groups of speakers differentially located within a political economic region.
>
> *(Gal, 1989, p. 349)*

It is precisely in these contexts of cross-cultural or intercultural communication, where "notions of group membership and community can no longer be accepted as fixed characteristics and well-defined totalities" (Rampton, 1992, p. 54), that relationships among differing language and literacy practices are most evident, in the same way that sociolinguistic norms of interaction are most salient when they are breached and the existence of speech situations and events is most observable at their boundaries (cf. Hymes, 1968, p. 123; Hymes, 1972, p. 56; Saville-Troike, 1989, pp. 135–136).

The shift in research focus to studying biliteracy practices as parts of systems of social inequality and to choosing sites of cross-cultural interaction as units of study bring notions of mediation and hybridity to the fore. The role of literacy mediator (Reder, 1987) is a recurring one as, for example, local people negotiate with 'outsiders,' government bureaucracies, or other national or globalizing agencies, and their languages and literacies. Hybridity, a notion derived from the work of Russian philosopher Bakhtin (1981, pp. 358–359), and captured succinctly as "the productive tension between official and unofficial discourse" (Cahnmann, 2001), is evidenced by children mixing, blending, and recasting literacy practices from home and school to unique new patterns and forms (as documented, for example, in East London by Gregory & Williams, 2000, p. 52), or by teachers' and students' acceptance and encouragement of multiple languages and registers, unauthorized side-talk, movement, spontaneous interaction and collaboration (as seen in the second–third grade two-way Spanish immersion classroom in Los Angeles studied by Gutiérrez, Baquedano-López, & Tejeda, 1999). In the latter case, Gutiérrez and co-authors use activity theory and Vygotsky's "zones of proximal development" as frames for closely analyzing one 6-week learning event, and show how the participants in this classroom reorganize the activity and incorporate local knowledge, thereby creating "third spaces in which alternative and competing discourses and positionings transform conflict and difference into rich zones of collaboration and learning" (Gutiérrez et al., 1999).

Work of the Santa Barbara Classroom Discourse Group (Floriani et al., 1995; Green & Dixon, 1993) provides similarly detailed insights into the situated, constructed, and consequential nature of learning in linguistically diverse classrooms (Green & Dixon, 1998). Drawing on a series of linked ethnographic studies focusing on inquiry-oriented teaching across content areas in third through sixth grade bilingual classrooms, this work offers rich documentation of bilingual literacy development realized through languaging in all its myriad, mediated, and hybrid forms. Mediation and hybridity are useful, indeed essential, constructs in understanding the role of multiple varieties, scripts, communicative modes, and criss-crossed paths of acquisition and use in biliteracy development.

Development of Biliteracy: Translanguaging and Flexible Bilingual Pedagogy

The continua model posits that the development of biliteracy may start at any point on any of three intersecting continua of first language-to-second language (L1–L2), oral-to-written, and receptive-to-productive language and literacy skills, uses, and practices; that biliteracy learning may proceed in any direction along those intersecting continua; and that it may do so by backtracking, spurting, or criss-crossing just as readily as by steadily progressing in linear fashion. There is in fact an infinite potential for transfer of skills across any of the three continua, but, by the same token, understanding or predicting transfer is elusive if not impossible, precisely because the three continua are interrelated and furthermore nested within all the other continua (Hornberger, 1989). The development of biliteracy in individuals occurs along the continua in direct response to contextual demands placed on these individuals.

> The environmental press that requires the successful interactant to use distinct subsets of linguistic and sociolinguistic knowledge can change from moment to moment in face-to-face interaction, and from one discourse

unit to another in a written text with which ego is confronted . . . Interaction with others in producing these diverse verbal and written texts constitutes practice in language use.

(Erickson, 1991, p. 342)

Research in bilingualism has consistently suggested an integrated, holistic, context-sensitive view of bilingual development, a view wherein the bilingual is much more than the sum of two monolinguals. Cummins' (1979) groundbreaking proposal of the developmental interdependence and thresholds hypotheses laid the theoretical ground for what remains a central tenet in scholarship on bilingualism (if not, sadly, in educational practice): namely, "that a child's first language skills must become well developed to ensure that their academic and linguistic performance in the second language is maximized" (Baker & Hornberger, 2001, p. 18). Close on the heels of this work, bilingualism scholars like Zentella (1981), Grosjean (1985), and Valdés (1982) provided empirical evidence for bilinguals' fluid codeswitching as highly context-sensitive, competent but specific language practice. Decades of research continue to corroborate, deepen and extend this understanding.

Just as Grosjean (1985) suggested that a bilingual is not the sum of two monolinguals any more than a hurdler is simply the sum of a sprinter and a high jumper, García (2009), in her recent tour-de-force on bilingual education in the 21st century, argues that bilingualism is "not monolingualism times two" (2009, p. 71), "not like a bicycle with two balanced wheels," but "more like an all-terrain vehicle," whose wheels "extend and contract, flex and stretch, making possible, over highly uneven ground, movement forward that is bumpy and irregular but also sustained and effective" (2009, p. 45). García captures this view of bilingualism with the term *translanguaging,* referring to the "multiple discursive practices in which bilinguals engage in order to make sense of their bilingual worlds" (2009, p. 45). "Rather than focusing on the language itself and how one or the other might relate to the way in which a monolingual standard is used and has been described, the concept of translanguaging makes obvious that there are no clear-cut borders between the languages of bilinguals" (García, 2009, p. 47).

García borrows and extends the term translanguaging, originally *trawysiethu* in Welsh, as proposed by Cen Williams in his Welsh-medium thesis (1994) and taken up by Baker as translanguaging (2001) and also transliteracy (2003) in reference to pedagogical practices where students hear or read a lesson, a passage in a book or a section of work in one language and develop their work in another (e.g., by discussion, writing a passage, completing a work sheet, conducting an experiment); input and output are deliberately in a different language and are systematically varied (Baker, 2001, p. 281; 2003, p. 82). Baker argues that the continua of biliteracy anticipate and extend the notion of translanguaging and transliteracy, providing a reminder of the tensions that will typically be present and the need to tip the balance toward the minority language to adjust for the greater prestige associated with the majority language, as well as the strategic need "to consider all the dimensions of the continua to create full biliteracy in students" (Baker, 2003, p. 84).

Translanguaging practices in the classroom, in the extended sense in which Baker and García envision them, have the potential to explicitly valorize all points along the continua of biliterate context, media, content, and development. Multilingual classroom practices, recently and eloquently theorized and documented also as hybrid classroom discourse practices (Gutiérrez et al., 1999), multilingual classroom ecologies (Creese & Martin, 2003), a four-quadrant pedagogic framework for developing academic excellence in a bilingual B.A. degree program (Joseph & Ramani, 2004; Ramani & Joseph, 2010; see also Hornberger, 2010), bilingual supportive scaffolding practices (Saxena, 2010), and flexible bilingual pedagogy (Blackledge & Creese, 2010), offer the possibility for teachers and learners to access academic content through the linguistic resources and communicative repertoires they bring to the classroom while simultaneously acquiring new ones.

In particular, Creese and Blackledge, in a series of articles and their recent book (Blackledge & Creese, 2010) document the flexible bilingual, translanguaging pedagogies uncovered through ethnographic team research in UK complementary schools—four interlocking case studies in four cities focusing on complementary schools in Gujarati, Turkish, Bengali, and Chinese heritage communities. They offer ethnographic illustration of specific translanguaging knowledge and skills at play in the schools, such as: use of bilingual label quests, repetition, and translation across languages; ability to engage audiences through translanguaging and heteroglossia; students' use of translanguaging to establish identity positions both oppositional to and encompassing of institutional values; and teachers' endorsement of simultaneous literacies and languages to keep pedagogic tasks moving. Importantly, they offer a clearly articulated argument for a release from monolingual instructional approaches and easing of the burden of guilt associated with translanguaging in multilingual educational contexts. This goes beyond acceptance or tolerance of children's languages to developing and cultivating them for teaching and learning. The research builds on and significantly extends work on the pedagogic validity of codeswitching practices. These practices accrue increased student inclusion and understanding, less formal relationships between teachers and students, and more meaningful communication of ideas and lessons. The study provides recognition and demonstration of complementary schools as alternative, safe, and multilingual spaces for institutional bilingualism; and equally as sites where young people creatively use varieties of language including standard, regional, class, and youth-oriented varieties as well as parodic language to take up, resist, and negotiate multiple academic and heritage identity positionings.

Content of Biliteracy: Transnational Literacy Practices and Identities

The continua model posits that *what* (content) biliterate learners and users read and write is as important as *how* (development), *where* (context) or *when and by what means* (media) they do so. Whereas schooling traditionally privileges majority, literary, and decontextualized contents, the continua model argues for greater curricular attention to minority, vernacular and contextualized whole language texts. Minority texts include those by minority authors, written from minority perspectives. Vernacular ways of reading and writing include notes, poems, plays, and stories written at home or in other everyday non-school contexts. Contextualized whole language texts are those read and written in the context of biliteracy events, interactions, practices, and activities of biliterate learners' everyday lives (Hornberger & Skilton-Sylvester, 2000). Note that the term minority here connotes not numerical size, but "observable differences among language varieties in relation to power, status, and entitlement" (May, 2003, p. 118; cf. Hornberger, 1998, p. 453; May, 1996, p. 165). In today's usage, we might more likely use the term minoritized to "more accurately convey . . . the power relations and processes by which certain groups are socially, economically, and politically marginalized within the larger society. This term also connotes human agency to effect change" (McCarty, 2005, p. 48).

Assumptions within the continua model about the importance of incorporating minoritized identities and perspectives, vernacular genres and styles, and contextualized texts in biliteracy learning contexts parallel other developments in research on bilingualism and multilingualism including the 'funds of knowledge' project and work on multilingual and transnational literacies. Moll and colleagues have argued that "community funds of knowledge" (sometimes called household funds of knowledge or local funds of knowledge), defined as "historically accumulated and culturally developed bodies of knowledge and skills essential for household or individual functioning and well-being" (Moll & González, 1994, p. 443), are a resource which can and should be drawn on in schooling for language minority populations. The centerpiece of their work is collaboration with teachers in conducting household research, because, as they put it, "it is one thing to identify resources but quite another to use them fruitfully in classrooms" (Moll & González, 1994, p. 441). In the words of one teacher collaborator:

> the teacher mediates by creating curricula that reflect both the standard curriculum and the themes, languages, and culture of students' lives . . . when teachers incorporate household funds of knowledge into the curriculum and use dialogic teaching methods, students are liberated to direct their own learning.
>
> *(Floyd-Tenery, 1995, p. 12)*

Research in multilingual literacies—literacy practices of multilingual individuals and groups (Martin-Jones & Jones, 2000)—resonates also with the biliteracy continua (Hornberger, 2000); both formulations take the view that multiple languages and literacies, and the cultural practices and views of the world in which they are embedded, are resources on which individuals and groups may draw as they "take on different identities in different domains of their lives" (Martin-Jones & Jones, 2000, p. 1). Authors in Martin-Jones and Jones' (2000) volume provide richly detailed accounts and analyses of, for example, a minority group member who, as an act of resistance, refuses to become literate because acquisition of majority-culture literacy requires the adoption of some of the cultural behaviors and values of the majority group (Blackledge, 2000); or how the interactions between a young Welsh farmer and a delegate of the Ministry of Agriculture Fisheries and Food (as they fill out an Animal Movement form) reflect a hybrid combination of elements of bureaucratic and farmworld discourses in Welsh and English (Jones, 2000). Martin-Jones and Jones tell us that one of the reasons they chose the term multilingual for the title of their book is to focus attention on the multiple ways people draw on and combine the codes in their communicative repertoires to make meaning as they negotiate and display cultural identities and social relationships; in the same way, the continua of biliteracy focuses attention on the use of codes as meaning-making and identity-constructing resources for the expression of majority-to-minority identities and perspectives, literary-to-vernacular genres and styles, and decontextualized-to-contextualized texts and discourses.

Similarly, authors in Warriner (2007) take up multilingual and multimodal literacies and the identities and social relations maintained and transformed through those literacies. Here, the focus is on transnational youth and adults—New Yorkers of Dominican, Colombian, Bengali, and Chabad Jewish-American heritage, Mexican immigrants from Guanajuato and Jalisco in Iowa and California respectively, and adult women refugees from Bosnia, Iran, and Sudan now residing in the intermountain west. In every case, these are transmigrants who have moved bodily across national borders while maintaining and cultivating practices that are tied—in varying degrees—to their home countries. The authors make clear that the cross-border movements of bodies, as of goods and information, are the direct result of globalization and specifically the internationalization of systems of production (Richardson Bruna, 2007), processes which "tend to de-territorialize important economic, social and cultural practices from their traditional boundaries in nation-states" (McGinnis, Goodstein-Stolzenberg, & Saliani, 2007, p. 284, citing Suárez-Orozco & Qin-Hillard, 2004, p. 14).

Drawing from innovative, long-term, in-depth ethnographies, the accounts tell about the multilingual and multimodal literacies and literacy practices the transmigrants bring with them and those they develop in their new contexts, and about the identities and social relations maintained and transformed through those literacy practices. The local practices and identities are profoundly rooted in processes of globalization, and constantly shift and develop across time and space. Bartlett (2007) demonstrates Dominican student María's success in positioning herself and being positioned over time as a 'good' student at Luperón bilingual high school in New York, by drawing on resources provided by the school's local model of success, including high status for Spanish language and literacy, and their valuation of task-based literacy practices. In a collaborative book writing-and-illustrating project, Sánchez (2007) and three young Latinas draw on transnational funds of knowledge and social relations in developing their retelling of the 'return to Mexico' narrative, a retelling in which "the young women author themselves .. and construct a meta-narrative of their heretofore 'unofficial' (Dyson 1994) transnational lives" (Sánchez, 2007, p. 259), producing a counterstory to the deficit portrayals of Mexican immigrant families pervasive in popular media discourse. Richardson Bruna (2007) argues that newcomer Mexican students' informal literacy practices of tagging, branding, and shouting out at Captainville High can be understood as "literacies of display" (Hamilton, 2000, p. 20) of their transnational identities (Richardson Bruna, 2007, p. 233), in which they "take elements of the immediate U.S. context and, onto those, inscribe [their] membership in the imagined transnational community of Mexicans living outside of Mexico," a repositioning that marks them against the norm of "American," but also as "other" to their context of origin in Mexico (Richardson Bruna, 2007, p. 244).

McGinnis et al. (2007) document three youths' online multilingual, multimodal creative exploration and negotiation of complex multiple identities across race, ethnic, gender, socioeconomic, and nationalist lines. On a more sombre note, Warriner's (2007) ethnography of women refugee ESL learners demonstrates how a pedagogy of literacy practices that prioritizes reading, copying, responding to known-answer questions, filling in the blanks, and memorizing, at the expense of drawing on the first-language literacies and multilingual competencies that crossed the border with the women refugees, is actually not preparing the women for the world beyond the classroom; but rather, to the extent they are able to negotiate successful new work identities for themselves, it is in spite of, rather than because of, the ESL program.

Beyond illuminating identities constructed and negotiated through transnational literacy practices, these cases also highlight the transnational spaces, multimodal literacy practices, and trajectories across time and space that these transmigrants take up. These instances fit the continua of biliteracy remarkably well. Transnational spaces are after all contexts of biliteracy, multimodal communicative practices are biliterate media, trajectories across time and space are pathways of biliterate development, and identities constructed and negotiated through transnational literacy practices are expressions of biliterate content. The biliterate instances depicted—the Guanajuato students' traveling tags (Richardson Bruna, 2007), the Jalisco Latinas' retelling of the return-to-Mexico narrative in their book-making project (Sánchez, 2007), the NYC youths' multimodal blogs and webspaces (McGinnis et al., 2007), María's academic success within Luperón

High School's alternative local model of success (Bartlett, 2007), and the refugee women's negotiation of their individual pathways from ESL classes to employment (Warriner, 2007)—provide richly complex accounts of the contexts, content, and media through which multilinguals creatively develop biliteracy and voice.

These analyses and instances, and others I have mentioned in the preceding sections, broaden and deepen the continua of biliteracy in ways that could not have been foreseen twenty years ago—neither in the real world nor in the research world. I am struck simultaneously by how different and how much the same our world—and our ways of describing our world—are today, as compared to a quarter century ago when I started to research these issues. Globalization and mobility, multimodality and languaging, transnationalism and translanguaging were much less visible then, and the conceptual tools with which to study them much less developed, and yet the underlying realities of complexly multilingual contexts, richly diverse repertoires of communicative media, socially constructed meanings in textual content, and multiple potential trajectories of multilingual language and literacy development remain as enduringly and endearingly human now as then. Equally, or more so, multilingual learners deserve our continual re-imagining and opening up of educational spaces that foster their ongoing development and creative transformation of their mobile—and biliterate—lives and literacies.

References

Baker, C. (2001). *Foundations of bilingual education and bilingualism* (3rd ed.). Clevedon, UK: Multilingual Matters.

Baker, C. (2003). Biliteracy and transliteracy in Wales: Language planning and the Welsh National Curriculum. In N. H. Hornberger (Ed.), *Continua of biliteracy: An ecological framework for educational policy, research, and practice in multilingual settings* (pp. 71–90). Clevedon, UK: Multilingual Matters.

Baker, C., & Hornberger, N. H. (Eds.). (2001). *An introductory reader to the writings of Jim Cummins*. Clevedon, UK: Multilingual Matters.

Bakhtin, M. (1981). *The dialogic imagination*. Austin: University of Texas Press.

Bakhtin, M. (1986). *Speech genres and other late essays*. Austin: University of Texas Press.

Bartlett, L. (2007). Bilingual literacies, social identification, and educational trajectories. *Linguistics and Education, 18*(3–4), 215–231.

Basu, V. (2003). 'Be quick of eye and slow of tongue': An analysis of two bilingual schools in New Delhi. In N. H. Hornberger (Ed.), *Continua of biliteracy: An ecological framework for educational policy, research, and practice in multilingual settings* (pp. 291–311). Clevedon, UK: Multilingual Matters.

Blackledge, A. (2000). Power relations and the social construction of 'literacy' and 'illiteracy': The experience of Bangladeshi women in Birmingham. In M. Martin-Jones & K. Jones (Eds.), *Multilingual literacies: Reading and writing different worlds* (pp. 55–69). Philadelphia. PA: John Benjamins.

Blackledge, A., & Creese, A. (2010). *Multilingualism: A critical perspective*. London, UK: Continuum.

Bloch, C., & Alexander, N. (2003). A luta continua!: The relevance of the continua of biliteracy to South African multilingual schools. In N. H. Hornberger (Ed.), *Continua of biliteracy: An ecological framework for educational policy, research, and practice in multilingual settings* (pp. 91–121). Clevedon, UK: Multilingual Matters.

Blommaert, J. (2010). *The sociolinguistics of globalization*. New York, NY: Cambridge University Press.

Bourdieu, P. (1990). *The logic of practice*. Stanford, CA: Stanford University Press.

Cahnmann, M. (2001). *Shifting metaphors: Of war and reimagination in the bilingual classroom*. Unpublished doctoral thesis, University of Pennsylvania, Philadelphia.

Cahnmann, M. (2003). To correct or not to correct bilingual students' errors is a question of continua-ing reimagination. In N. H. Hornberger (Ed.), *Continua of biliteracy: An ecological framework for educational policy, research, and practice in multilingual settings* (pp. 187–204). Clevedon, UK: Multilingual Matters.

Cazden, C., Cope, B., Fairclough, N., Gee, J., Kalantzis, M., Kress, G., et al. (1996). A pedagogy of multiliteracies: Designing social futures. *Harvard Educational Review, 66*(1), 60–92.

Cope, B., & Kalantzis, M. (Eds.). (2000). *Multiliteracies: Literacy learning and the design of social futures*. London, UK: Routledge.

Cortese, G., & Hymes, D. (Eds.). (2001). *"Languaging" in and across human groups: Perspectives on difference and asymmetry*. Genova, Italy: Tilgher.

Creese, A., & Martin, P. (Eds.). (2003). *Multilingual classroom ecologies: Inter-relationships, interactions and ideologies*. Clevedon, UK: Multilingual Matters.

Cummins, J. (1979). Linguistic interdependence and the educational development of bilingual children. *Educational Research, 49*(2), 222–251.

Dyson, A. H. (1994). "I'm gonna express myself": The politics of story in children's worlds. In A. H. Dyson & C. Genishi (Eds.), *The need for story: Cultural diversity in classroom and community* (pp. 155–171). Urbana, IL: National Council of Teachers of English.

Erickson, F. (1991). Advantages and disadvantages of qualitative research design on foreign language research. In B. F. Freed (Ed.), *Foreign language acquisition research and the classroom* (pp. 338–353). Lexington, MA: D. C. Heath.

Fairclough, N. (1992). Intertextuality in critical discourse analysis. *Linguistics and Education, 4*, 269–293.

Fishman, J. (1970). *Sociolinguistics: A brief introduction*. Rowley, MA: Newbury House.

Floriani, A., Heras, A. I., Franquiz, M., Yeager, B., Jennings, L. B., Green, J. L., et al. (1995). Two languages, one community: An examination of educational opportunities. In R. F. Macías & R. G. G. Ramos (Eds.), *Changing schools for changing students: An anthology of research on language minorities, schools, & society* (pp. 63–106). Santa Barbara, CA: Linguistic Minority Research Institute.

Floyd-Tenery, M. (1995). Teacher as mediator. *Practicing Anthropology, 17*(3), 10–12.

Foucault, M. (1984 [1971]). The order of discourse. In M. Shapiro (Ed.), *Language and politics* (pp. 108–138). London, UK: Basil Blackwell.

Freeman, R. D. (2004). *Building on community bilingualism*. Philadelphia, PA: Caslon Publishing.

Gal, S. (1989). Language and political economy. *Annual Review of Anthropology, 18*, 345–367.

García, O. (2007). Foreword. In S. Makoni & A. Pennycook (Eds.), *Disinventing and reconstituting languages* (pp. xi–xv). Clevedon, UK: Multilingual Matters.

García, O. (2009). *Bilingual education in the 21st century: A global perspective*. Malden, MA: Wiley-Blackwell.

Gentil, G. (2005). Commitments to academic biliteracy: Case studies of Francophone university writers. *Written Communication, 22*(4), 421–471.

Goffman, E. (1974). *Frame analysis.* New York, NY: Harper and Row.

Green, J. L., & Dixon, C. N. (1993). "Talking knowledge into being": Discursive and social practices in classrooms. *Linguistics and Education, 5*(3–4), 231–239.

Green, J. L., & Dixon, C. N. (1998). *Ethnographics and sociolinguistics: Mutually informing theories.* Unpublished manuscript.

Gregory, E., & Williams, A. (2000). Work or play? 'Unofficial' literacies in the lives of two East London communities. In M. Martin-Jones & K. Jones (Eds.), *Multilingual literacies: Reading and writing different worlds* (pp. 37–54). Amsterdam, The Netherlands: John Benjamins.

Grosjean, F. (1985). The bilingual as a competent but specific speaker-hearer. *Journal of Multilingual and Multicultural Development, 6*(6), 467–477.

Gumperz, J. J. (1964). Linguistic and social interaction in two communities. *American Anthropologist, 66*(6, Part 2), 137–153.

Gumperz, J. J. (1965). Language. *Biennial Review of Anthropology, 4,* 84–120.

Gumperz, J. J. (1982). *Discourse strategies.* Cambridge, UK: Cambridge University Press.

Gutiérrez, K. D., Baquedano-López, P., & Tejeda, C. (1999). Rethinking diversity: Hybridity and hybrid language practices in the third space. *Mind, Culture, and Activity: An International Journal, 6*(4), 286–303.

Hamilton, M. (2000). Expanding the new literacy studies: Using photographs to explore literacy as social practice. In D. Barton, M. Hamilton, & R. Ivanic (Eds.), *Situated literacies: Reading and writing in context* (pp. 16–34). London, UK: Routledge.

Hancock, A. (2009). *Biliteracy development among Chinese children in central Scotland.* Unpublished doctoral thesis, University of Edinburgh, UK.

Hélot, C. (2006). Bridging the gap between prestigious bilingualism and the bilingualism of minorities: Towards an integrated perspective of multilingualism in the French education context. In M. O'Laoire (Ed.), *Multilingualism in educational settings* (pp. 49–72). Tübingen, Germany: Stauffenburg Verlag.

Hornberger, N. H. (1989). Continua of biliteracy. *Review of Educational Research, 59*(3), 271–296.

Hornberger, N. H. (1990). Creating successful learning contexts for bilingual literacy. *Teachers College Record, 92*(2), 212–229.

Hornberger, N. H. (1992). Biliteracy contexts, continua, and contrasts: Policy and curriculum for Cambodian and Puerto Rican students in Philadelphia. *Education and Urban Society, 24*(2), 196–211.

Hornberger, N. H. (1998). Language policy, language education, language rights: Indigenous, immigrant, and international perspectives. *Language in Society, 27*(4), 439–458.

Hornberger, N. H. (2000). Afterword: Multilingual literacies, literacy practices, and the continua of biliteracy. In M. Martin-Jones & K. Jones (Eds.), *Multilingual literacies: Reading and writing different worlds* (pp. 353–367). Philadelphia, PA: John Benjamins.

Hornberger, N. H. (2002). Multilingual language policies and the continua of biliteracy: An ecological approach. *Language Policy, 1*(1), 27–51.

Hornberger, N. H. (Ed.) (2003). *The continua of biliteracy: An ecological framework for educational policy, research and practice in multilingual settings.* Clevedon, UK: Multilingual Matters.

Hornberger, N. H. (2005a). Biliteracy. In R. Beach, J. Green, M. Kamil, & T. Shanahan (Eds.), *Multidisciplinary perspectives on literacy research* (2nd ed., pp. 319–347). Cresskill, NJ: Hampton Press.

Hornberger, N. H. (2005b). Nichols to NCLB: Local and global perspectives on U.S. language education policy. *Working Papers in Educational Linguistics, 20*(2), 1–17.

Hornberger, N. H. (2006). Voice and biliteracy in indigenous language revitalization: Contentious educational practices in Quechua, Guarani, and Maori contexts. *Journal of Language, Identity, and Education, 5*(4), 277–292.

Hornberger, N. H. (2008). Continua of biliteracy. In A. Creese, P. Martin & N. H. Hornberger (Eds.), *Encyclopedia of language and education: Vol. 9. Ecology of language* (pp. 275–290). New York, NY: Springer.

Hornberger, N. H. (2010). Language and education: A Limpopo lens. In N. H. Hornberger & S. L. McKay (Eds.), *Sociolinguistics and language education* (pp. 549–564). Bristol, UK: Multilingual Matters.

Hornberger, N. H. (2013). Bilingual literacy. In C. A. Chapelle (Ed.), *The encyclopedia of applied linguistics*. Oxford, UK: Wiley-Blackwell.

Hornberger, N. H., & Skilton-Sylvester, E. (2000). Revisiting the continua of biliteracy: International and critical perspectives. *Language and Education, 14*(2), 96–122.

Hult, F. M., & King, K. A. (Eds.). (2011). *Educational linguistics in practice: Applying the local globally and the global locally*. Bristol, UK: Multilingual Matters.

Hymes, D. H. (1964). Introduction: Toward ethnographies of communication. *American Anthropologist, 66*(6), 1–34.

Hymes, D. H. (1968). The ethnography of speaking. In J. A. Fishman (Ed.), *Readings in the sociology of language* (pp. 99–138). The Hague, The Netherlands: Mouton.

Hymes, D. H. (1972). Models of the interaction of language and social life. In J. Gumperz & D. H. Hymes (Eds.), *Directions in sociolinguistics: The ethnography of communication* (pp. 35–71). New York, NY: Holt, Rinehart, and Winston.

Hymes, D. H. (1974). *Foundations in sociolinguistics: An ethnographic approach*. Philadelphia: University of Pennsylvania Press.

Hymes, D. H. (1980). *Language in education: Ethnolinguistic essays*. Washington, DC: Center for Applied Linguistics.

Jones, K. (2000). Texts, mediation and social relations in a bureaucratised world. In M. Martin-Jones & K. Jones (Eds.), *Multilingual literacies: Reading and writing different worlds* (pp. 209–228). Philadelphia, PA: John Benjamins.

Joseph, M., & Ramani, E. (2004). *Cummins' four quadrants: A pedagogic framework for developing academic excellence in the new bilingual degree at the University of the North*. Paper presented at the International Conference of the Southern African Applied Linguistics Association (SAALA), University of Limpopo.

Kelly, L. G. (Ed.). (1969). *The description and measurement of bilingualism: An international seminar*. Toronto, Canada: University of Toronto Press.

Lincoln, F. (2003). Language education planning and policy in Middle America: Students' voices. In N. H. Hornberger (Ed.), *Continua of biliteracy: An ecological framework for educational policy, research, and practice in multilingual settings* (pp. 147–165). Clevedon, UK: Multilingual Matters.

McCarty, T. L. (Ed.). (2005). *Language, literacy, and power in schooling*. Mahwah, NJ: Lawrence Erlbaum.

McGinnis, T., Goodstein-Stolzenberg, A., & Saliani, E. C. (2007). "indnpride": Online spaces of transnational youth as sites of creative and sophisticated literacy and identity work. *Linguistics and Education, 18*(3–4), 283–304.

Makoni, S., & Pennycook, A. (Eds.). (2007). *Disinventing and reconstituting language*. Clevedon, UK: Multilingual Matters.

Martin-Jones, M., & Jones, K. (Eds.). (2000). *Multilingual literacies: Reading and writing different worlds*. Philadelphia, PA: John Benjamins.

Martínez-Roldán, C. M., & Sayer, P. (2006). Reading through linguistic borderlands: Latino students' transactions with narrative texts. *Journal of Early Childhood Literacy, 6*, 293–322.

May, S. (1996). Indigenous language rights and education. In J. Lynch, C. Modgil, & S. Modgil (Eds.), *Education and development: Tradition and innovation* (Vol. 1, pp. 149–171). London, UK: Cassell.

May, S. (2003). Rearticulating the case for minority language rights. *Current Issues in Language Planning, 4*(2), 95–125.

Mercado, C. (2003). Biliteracy development among Latino youth in New York City communities: An unexploited potential. In N. H. Hornberger (Ed.), *Continua of biliteracy: An ecological framework for educational policy, research, and practice in multilingual settings* (pp. 166–186). Clevedon, UK: Multilingual Matters.

Moll, L., & González, N. (1994). Lessons from research with language-minority children. *Journal of Reading Behavior, 26*(4), 439–456.

Pak, H. R. (2003). When MT is L2: The Korean church school as a context for cultural identity. In N. H. Hornberger (Ed.), *Continua of biliteracy: An ecological framework for educational policy, research, and practice in multilingual settings* (pp. 269–290). Clevedon, UK: Multilingual Matters.

Pérez, B., Flores, B., & Strecker, S. (2003). Biliteracy teacher education in the U.S. Southwest. In N. H. Hornberger (Ed.), *Continua of biliteracy: An ecological framework for educational policy, research, and practice in multilingual settings* (pp. 207–231). Clevedon, UK: Multilingual Matters.

Peter, L., & Hirata-Edds, T. (2008). *Learning to read and write Cherokee: Toward a theory of literacy revitalization*. Unpublished manuscript.

Pride, J. B., & Holmes, J. (1972). *Sociolinguistics: Selected readings*. Harmondsworth, UK: Penguin Books.

Ramani, E., & Joseph, M. (2010). *Developing academic biliteracy: A case study of a bilingual BA degree (in English and Sesotho sa Leboa) at the University of Limpopo*. Unpublished manuscript.

Rampton, M. B. H. (1992). Scope for empowerment in sociolinguistics? In D. Cameron, E. Frazer, P. Harvey, M. B. H. Rampton, & K. Richardson (Eds.), *Researching language: Issues of power and method* (pp. 29–64). London, UK: Routledge.

Reder, S. M. (1987). Comparative aspects of functional literacy development: Three ethnic American communities. In D. Wagner (Ed.), *Future of literacy in a changing world* (pp. 250–270). New York, NY: Pergamon Press.

Reyes, I. (2009). An ecological perspective on minority and majority language and literacy communities in the Americas. *Colombian Applied Linguistics, 11*, 106–114.

Richardson Bruna, K. (2007). Traveling tags: The informal literacies of Mexican newcomers in and out of the classroom. *Linguistics and Education, 18*(3–4), 232–257.

Sánchez, P. (2007). Cultural authenticity and transnational Latina youth: Constructing a meta-narrative across borders. *Linguistics and Education, 18*(3–4), 258–282.

Saville-Troike, M. (1989). *The ethnography of communication: An introduction* (2nd ed.). New York, NY: Basil Blackwell.

Saxena, M. (2010). Reconceptualising teachers' directive and supportive scaffolding in bilingual classrooms within the neo-Vygotskyan approach. *Journal of Applied Linguistics & Professional Practice, 7*(2).

Schiffrin, D. (1996). Interactional sociolinguistics. In S. L. McKay & N. H. Hornberger (Eds.), *Sociolinguistics and language teaching* (pp. 307–328). New York, NY: Cambridge University Press.

Schwinge, D. (2003). Enabling biliteracy: Using the continua of biliteracy to analyze curricular adaptations and elaborations. In N. H. Hornberger (Ed.), *Continua of biliteracy: An ecological framework for educational policy, research, and practice in multilingual settings* (pp. 248–265). Clevedon, UK: Multilingual Matters.

Silverstein, M. (2003). Indexical order and the dialectics of sociolinguistic life. *Language and Communication, 23*, 193–229.

Silverstein, M. (2006). Pragmatic indexing. In K. Brown (Ed.), *Encyclopedia of language and linguistics* (Vol. 6, pp. 14–17). Amsterdam, The Netherlands: Elsevier.

Skilton-Sylvester, E. (1997). *Inside, outside, and in-between: Identities, literacies, and educational policies in the lives of Cambodian women and girls in Philadelphia.* Unpublished doctoral thesis, University of Pennsylvania, Philadelphia.

Skilton-Sylvester, E. (2003). Legal discourse and decisions, teacher policymaking and the multilingual classroom: Constraining and supporting Khmer/English biliteracy in the United States. *International Journal of Bilingual Education and Bilingualism, 6*(3–4), 168–184.

Suárez-Orozco, M., & Qin-Hillard, D. (Eds.). (2004). *Globalization, culture, and education in the new millennium.* Berkeley, CA: University of California Press.

Utakis, S., & Pita, M. D. (2005). An educational policy for negotiating transnationalism: The Dominican community in New York City. In A. S. Canagarajah (Ed.), *Reclaiming the local in language policy and practice* (pp. 147–164). Mahwah, NJ: Lawrence Erlbaum.

Vaish, V. (2008). *Biliteracy and globalization: English language education in India.* Clevedon, UK: Multilingual Matters.

Valdés, G. (1982). Social interaction and code-switching patterns: A case study of Spanish/English alternation. In J. Amastae & L. Elías-Olivares (Eds.), *Spanish in the United States* (pp. 209–229). New York, NY: Cambridge University Press.

Wang, S. C. (2004). *Biliteracy resource eco-system of intergenerational language and culture transmission: An ethnographic study of a Chinese-American community.* Unpublished doctoral thesis, University of Pennsylvania, Philadelphia.

Warriner, D. S. (2007). "It's just the nature of the beast": Re-imagining the literacies of schooling in adult ESL education. *Linguistics and Education, 18*(3–4), 305–324.

Williams, C. (1994). *Arfarniad o ddulliau dysgu ac addysgu yng nghyd-destun addysg uwchradd ddwyieithog.* Doctoral thesis, University of Wales, Bangor, Wales. Available from http://ethos.bl.uk/OrderDetails.do?uin=uk.bl.ethos.385775

Zentella, A. C. (1981). Tá bien, you could answer me en cualquier idioma: Puerto Rican codeswitching in bilingual classrooms. In R. Durán (Ed.), *Latino language and communicative behavior* (pp. 109–131). Norwood, NJ: Ablex.

9

INDIGENOUS LITERACIES

Continuum or Divide?

Teresa L. McCarty

> My first English literacy experiences were with the "Dick and Jane" basal
> readers. I remember looking at the books and wondering where this fantasy
> place was. "Will I ever get to see this place?" I wondered. . . . [Later, as]
> I worked on my degree and in my classroom, I began to learn to read and
> write my language along with my students. I had to pick up where I stopped
> when I entered . . . school, because my language and culture had been taken
> away from me.
>
> *(Dick, 1998, pp. 24–25)*

Introduction

For the past 30 years I have had the opportunity to work closely with Native
American communities on their language education projects and to collaborate
on similar efforts with Indigenous communities throughout the world. Literacy
has always had multiple and contested meanings in Indigenous communities. In
recent decades, however, questions surrounding the role of literacy have intensified
as pressures have mounted for families to abandon their mother tongues in favor
of dominant or "alpha" languages. For example, although 175 Native American
languages are still spoken in the United States, only 20 are being transmitted to
children as first languages in the home, and nearly all Native American languages
are in danger of falling silent within the next generation (Krauss, 1998). The
situation in Native North America is one instance of the threats to Indigenous
linguistic and cultural survival worldwide.

Why are Indigenous languages endangered? The fate of a language is directly
tied to the social positioning of its speakers and therefore to power relations
among groups (Fishman, 1991). Language loss reflects the transformation of group

identities through the domination of politically weaker peoples by those with greater power. The educational linguist Tove Skutnabb-Kangas refers to this as linguistic genocide or linguicide (2000, p. 312; see also Skutnabb-Kangas & Dunbar, 2010). As suggested in the opening epigraph, colonial schooling and the imposition of dominant print literacies have been conjoined weapons of linguistic genocide. Yet, as we will see, these alpha literacies are being appropriated for the anti-hegemonic project of Indigenous bilingual-bicultural education and language recovery. As López and Sichra write with respect to Indigenous bilingual-intercultural education in Latin America, it "is difficult to separate education and literacy from the struggle for rights and self-determination" (2008, p. 295).

This chapter has three primary goals. First, I examine Indigenous perspectives on literacy/ies historically and today, drawing on the work of Indigenous and non-Indigenous scholars in the fields of educational and linguistic anthropology, critical literacy studies, and language planning and policy. The approach to literacy taken here is based on a notion of literacy as a social and cultural practice (Gee, 2008; Rockwell, 2005; Street, 2008) and a pedagogy of multiliteracies, which recognizes "the increasing multiplicity and integration of significant modes of meaning-making, where the textual is also related to the visual, the audio, the spatial, [and] the behavioral" (New London Group, 1996, p. 64). This approach draws on Street's "alternative, ideological model of literacy [that] offers a more culturally sensitive view of literacy practices as they vary from one context to another" (Street, 2008, p. 4), but extends that model in important ways. Specifically, I argue that alphabetic or print literacy is only one facet of what "counts" as literacy; in Indigenous sociolinguistic ecologies, literacy is more broadly construed as "the ability to interpret the complex system of cultural symbols" that enable community members to participate actively and appropriately in communicative events (Benjamin, Pecos, & Romero, 1996, p. 116). I embrace a broader view of literacy that includes non-graphocentric texts and therefore carries with it new possibilities for Indigenous-community self-empowerment.

Second, I consider the role of these multimodal literacies in the increasingly important project of language revitalization. As we will see, while print literacy can assist language recovery, it is fraught with challenges and is sometimes met with resistance by members of Indigenous communities, who view oral tradition as the prime carrier of cultural knowledge (Benjamin et al., 1996; Romero-Little, 2010; Sims, 2005). Further, to the extent that print literacy is associated with schooling, it introduces into the revitalization situation a host of additional considerations, including the role of schools as agents of linguistic and cultural assimilation. On the other hand, in situations in which a language has fallen silent but has written documentation and a living heritage community, print literacy appropriated from colonial sources has been an indispensable resource for language revival. Moreover, new digital literacies present opportunities for elevating the status of Indigenous languages by expanding traditional language forms and uses. Thus, the relationship between literacy and language revitalization is complex, calling into question the forms of literacy present in a given community, the perceived status and utility of those literacies, the role of schools and medium-of-instruction policies as language planning agents, issues of dialect differences, and the community's self-determined language planning goals. The second section of the paper explores these issues through an analysis of comparative language revitalization cases in the Americas, the Pacific, and Scandinavia.

Finally, I take up the notion of the literacy continuum introduced by Tohono O'odham linguist Ofelia Zepeda (1992, 1995) and developed in our work together and with others (McCarty & Dick, 2003; McCarty & Watahomigie, 2004; McCarty & Zepeda, 2010). Applied to education practice, the literacy continuum moves beyond the binaries of oralcy versus written language and Indigenous versus Western education. Privileging family and community relationships as foundations for learning (Brayboy & Maughan, 2009), and valuing non-alphabetic literacies and discourse forms equally with graphocentric ones (Menezes de Souza, 2002), the continuum metaphor illuminates the potential for harmonizing alphabetic and non-alphabetic literacies and Indigenous and non-Indigenous knowledge systems. In so doing, this theoretical perspective opens up new "ideological and implementational spaces" (Hornberger, 2006) for liberatory pedagogies that empower young learners and promote the reclamation of heritage mother tongues.

It is important to point out that a single chapter cannot begin to do justice to these issues for all the world's 370 million Indigenous peoples and 5,000 (+/−) Indigenous languages. The contexts for Indigenous literacies are heterogeneous across and within Indigenous communities. Moreover, I write as a non-Indigenous academic and educator—an "allied other" (Kaomea, 2004) whose work has focused on certain sociolinguistic contexts and issues. The analysis here is necessarily partial and perspectival, based on my reading of these experiences as well as the research literature. Within these limitations my aim is to provide readers with both breadth and depth of coverage, examining crosscutting themes and periscoping select cases to tease out themes in greater detail. I begin by situating what "counts" as literacy in Indigenous settings across time and space.

Indigenous Literacies in Their Sociocultural and Sociohistorical Contexts[1]

In an analysis of multilingualism in Africa, Heugh (2009, p. 103) critiques the colonialist "loss of memory regarding the use of [Indigenous] languages in written form and as the primary mediums of education in pre-colonial times." Indigenous writing systems have a long history, thriving "independently of and prior to European writing systems" (King & Benson, 2008, p. 342). Mayan scripts consisting of glyphs (pictures) and phonetic systems date from the second century BCE and produced "an enormous literature," much of which the Spanish subsequently destroyed (England, 1998, p. 101). Zapotec writing from present-day Mexico dates to the seventh century CE; other pre-Columbian Mesoamerican glyphic systems include Aztec (Nahuatl) and Mixtec (Campbell, 1997; King & Benson, 2008). Sichra (2008) describes early Spanish chronicles of the Inca empire's "system of knots in multi-coloured wool . . . read in the manner of a poetic text"; the readers of these texts, recognized by titled social positions, "narrated historical facts and mythical stories that legitimized Inca power" (p. 284). Along the Niger River in Timbuktu, the recent uncovering of educational documents from 12th century mosques "provides extensive evidence of literacy and formal education across a wide range of fields in several [Indigenous African] languages" (Heugh, 2009, p. 103).

In what is now Liberia and Sierra Leone, the Vai script developed in 1820 by Memelu Duwalu Bukele is an early example of autochthonous syllabic writing. At the same time in North America, the Cherokee silversmith Sequoyah (whose Anglo name is said to be George Guess) created the Cherokee syllabary. The syllabary enabled the creation of other literacy forms and practices, including the *Cherokee Phoenix*, one of the first Native American-language newspapers, which rolled off the presses on February 28, 1829, and is still published today. The paper garnered international attention but has had as its primary audience diasporic Cherokee peoples in what is now the southeastern and south-central United States. In 1834, the first Hawaiian-language newspaper was published (*Ka Lama Hawai'i*), and by 1900 over 100 Hawaiian-language newspapers were in circulation (Wilson, 1998). In Latin America, the Popul Vuh, a corpus of 16th century historical narratives and creation stories written in K'iché (a Mayan language), used the Spanish alphabet. The historical record is replete with examples of Indigenous print literacies developed autochthonously and appropriated from colonial writing systems.

At the same time, it is widely recognized that oral tradition—"the stories, songs, prayers, and other oral media that carry a people's repository of knowledge" (McCarty & Nicholas, 2012, p. 5)—has been (and is) a primary carrier of Indigenous knowledges. The neglect and distortion of this form of knowledge as "pre-literate" or "non-literate" is a product of a false dichotomy that pits "formal" learning and Western schooling against "informal" out-of-school learning. For example, in his description of Arakmbut education in the Peruvian Amazon, Sueyo (2003) shows how he was taught to read the environment, with survival being the "ultimate test" (Lomawaima & McCarty, 2006, p. 30). During a trip with his father on a balsa raft down the Manu River, Sueyo's father taught him "about the forest and . . . its mysteries, how to respect it and care for it . . . how to face life in the forest and on the river. This was education in the indigenous world," Sueyo points out (2003, p. 194). Native Alaskan intellectual A. Oscar Kawagley (1995) describes environmental readings in the Alaska Native world:

> The Yupiaq people survived by learning to ask the right questions, use extensive observation . . ., experiment, memorize useful data, apply data for

explanation of natural phenomena, and use available resources to develop their technology.

(Kawagley, 1995, p. 84)

In a parallel vein, Sarangapani (2003) describes medicinal literacies among the Baiga of central India, where, by age five or six, children "can identify several of the more common medicinal properties, and many more . . . that could be eaten or were useful" (p. 203). Throughout the literature, the values of relationships, responsibility, and reciprocity recur as integral to these literacies and the knowledge systems they represent (Brayboy & McCarty, 2010).

My work with Navajo (Diné) communities in the southwestern U.S. has similarly shown that literacy is not the sole domain of the written word. The Navajo Blessingway ceremony, for instance—a core cultural practice that epitomizes Diné epistemology and worldview—involves intricate, finely detailed literary performances by ritual specialists who spend years, even a lifetime, in apprenticeship to acquire this knowledge. Part of the ritual involves the creation by the specialist of a sand painting—an elaborate visual representation made of multicolored sand on the floor of the ceremonial *hooghan* (a traditional Navajo dwelling)—which is a critical part of the patient's healing. This detailed visual text invokes shared understandings of the relationship of humans to the spiritual and physical world. Reciprocally, those who are the beneficiaries of the specialists' services—the patients, their families, and communities—spend lifetimes learning the nuanced meanings the ritual performances embody and enact (Frisbie & McAllester, 1967). Such oral performances and accompanying visual texts, as well as culturally regulated storytellings, song texts, prayers, and didactic teachings, represent both "formal" and "informal" literacy practices and events.

All of this is part of Indigenous multimodal literacies that interact with and depend upon a collective oral tradition. Mi'kmaq scholar Marie Battiste notes that these literacies include ideographic symbols such as winter counts, calendar sticks, textiles, petroglyphs, and pictographs to "record and store valuable knowledge, information, and records on available natural materials" (Battiste, 1986, p. 25). An example of this, Menezes de Souza (2002) describes Brazilian Kashinawá visual texts that consist of "highly codified multicolored or monochromatic geometric patterns" called *kene*—the word in the Kashinawá language for writing—that metonymically represent local knowledge and worldview. Indeed, for the Kashinawá, a purely alphabetic text "cannot be considered a text per se" because there is "no 'message' present" (Menezes de Souza, 2002, p. 273). Summarizing these literacies for Quechua communities in the Peruvian Andes, de la Piedra states, "in other words, drawings, songs, and rituals together become a unity where people construct meaning" (2009, p. 111).

These accounts suggest the ways in which Indigenous mother tongues have for millennia conveyed highly complex concepts through multiple modalities and fields of inquiry, including agronomy, art, history, law, religion, philosophy, music, science, medicine, mathematics, and commerce (Heugh, 2009, p. 106). With the coming of Europeans, these literacies came under assault, even as new print literacies were imposed, resisted, appropriated, and transformed. In the Americas, missionary-influenced alphabetic literacy in Nahuatl, the official language of the Aztec empire (Heath, 1972), produced "a generation of Nahuatl writers ... [and] native language literacy as a social practice spread swiftly through the Spanish colonies" (Hamel, 2008, pp. 313–314). During the same period, missionary-produced grammars were developed for P'urepecha, Zapotec, and Mixtec in what was then called New Spain. In the U.S. and Canada, writing systems for Massachusett-Wampanoag, Mahican, and Micmac date to the 1600s, including the first Native American bible translation by the Puritan missionary John Eliot in 1663. Northern Iroquoian languages were written from the time of Jacques Cartier's 1534 expedition into what is now the northeastern U.S. and southeastern Canada, and centuries-old syllabaries exist for Great Lakes Algonquian, Winnebago, Cree-Montagnais, Ojibwe, Athapaskan, and West Greenlandic languages (Walker, 1996). Today, virtually all Native American languages have writing systems, although the forms they take are highly varied.

The European invasion irrevocably altered Indigenous societies and linguistic ecologies, as Western-introduced diseases and colonization brought about massive displacement and demographic collapse. Throughout the world, physical and linguistic genocide, de-culturation, and de-territorialization have been the combined goals of colonial regimes. In sub-Saharan Africa, this occurred as European missionaries constructed an artificial multilingualism whereby closely related African varieties—akin to British and American English—were recorded as distinct tongues. These artificial linguistic boundaries became the templates for dividing African peoples territorially and for "de-Africanisation through the exclusive use of colonial languages in high-prestige domains" (Makalela, 2005, p. 153; see also Prah, 2008, for an overview of these issues with regard to literacy and knowledge production in Africa). In North America, from the 17th through much of the 20th century, Native children were forcibly removed from their families and compelled to attend distant residential schools where "*No Indian Talk*" was the cardinal rule (Spack, 2002, p. 24; Reyhner and Eder, 2004). During this same period, Australia's British colonial government implemented an infamous "White Australia" policy designed to "produce a homogeneous English-speaking Anglo-Saxon culture" (Romaine, 1991, p. 3). As part of this policy, a "stolen generation" of Aboriginal and Torres Strait Islander children were forcibly taken from their homes, "sometimes even by taking the child from the mother's arms," to distant schools where they were prevented from learning their heritage language and suffered physical and emotional abuse (Commonwealth of Australia, 1997, p. 4). In the Nordic countries, beginning in the mid-19th century, Sámi children "were punished for using their language on school premises [and] teachers were ... paid extra to keep a close eye on parents' language use" (McCarty, Skutnabb-Kangas, & Magga, 2008, p. 300). In Latin America, "a clear and often publicly conceded intention of eradicating Indigenous ethno-cultural differences" underlay centuries of policies designed to configure a uniform "national" society through segregated subtractive schooling (López, 2008, p. 43).

   In broad strokes, this is the sociocultural and sociohistorical context for understanding the role of literacy/ies among diverse Indigenous peoples today. Indigenous peoples constitute 4 percent of the world's population yet they speak 75 percent of the world's languages (UNESCO, 2005). As the previous discussion suggests, the contexts in which these languages are used are highly varied, from situations such as Quechua, spoken by eight to 12 million people in six South American countries; to the Sámi of Scandinavia, where five of 10 original Sámi languages are used as media of instruction in three Nordic states; to the Indian subcontinent, with 84.3 million scheduled tribes who speak 159 Indigenous languages; to sub-Saharan Africa, where a proliferation of Indigenous languages and language varieties compete with a handful of powerful colonial languages for a place in school curricula (Aikio-Puoskari, 2009; Mohanty, Mishra, Reddy, & Ramesh, 2009; Obondo, 2008). With some exceptions—Guaraní in Paraguay, for instance, where the Indigenous language is spoken by 90 percent of the population—the viability of Indigenous languages is threatened by legacies of linguistic oppression and the modern forces of globalization. Even "larger" languages such as Quechua face precarious futures (Hornberger & Coronel-Molina, 2004). Thus, for Indigenous peoples, language survival is a core language planning goal. I turn now to a discussion of these issues.

Literacy Planning and Language Revitalization

To revitalize a language is to create new domains for its acquisition and use among a heritage community associated with that language. The goal is to engender new vitality in a language that is in danger of falling silent because natural intergenerational language transmission mechanisms have broken down, causing the language to fall out of everyday use. Endangered languages have been described by linguists as "at risk" or "moribund," meaning their speakers are beyond childbearing age, or as "sleeping" or "dormant," meaning they have no native speakers but have written and/or audio-visual documentation and a living heritage community (Hinton, 2001; Leonard, 2008). Regeneration, renewal, recovery, reclamation, and reversal of shift are overarching terms to describe these language-planning processes.

   The role of literacy in language revitalization is inherently ideological, where ideology constitutes "the site of tension between authority and power on the one hand and resistance and creativity on the other" (Street, 2001, p. 34). We can see these tensions more clearly by examining specific cases. In the next sections, I provide miniature case studies from the Americas, the Pacific, and the Nordic region. I introduce each case with a brief sociolinguistic profile and then situate the role of literacy/ies historically within the case. I begin with Navajo, a case that offers a multifaceted lens into the ways that alphabetic literacy has been appropriated for Indigenous self-determined goals.

"We Came to Value Our Language When We Saw It in Print": The Case of Navajo

The Diné or Navajo people comprise the second largest Indigenous nation in the U.S., with more than 300,000 enrolled members. Geographically the Navajo Nation is the largest Indian reservation in the U.S., occupying a vast expanse of high desert, forested mountains, and plateau and canyon lands in the southwestern U.S. that is larger than many U.S. states and equivalent in size to the country of Ireland. Navajo is an Athabaskan language, a family of languages spoken from the circumpolar north to the U.S. border with Mexico. Consensus is lacking on the numbers of Navajo speakers, with estimates ranging from 80,000 to 150,000. Adding to the difficulties of enumeration is the fact that there is significant variability in language proficiencies and their definitions. As Benally and Viri described the status of Navajo in 2005, those over age 40 are likely to be "fluent" speakers and those younger "are likely to have less proficiency, with the majority of those 30 years and younger more likely to have no proficiency in Navajo" (Benally & Viri, 2005, p. 94).

The number of persons with proficiency in written Navajo is even less well known. Navajo print literacy dates at least to the mid-19th century, and the historical record is populated with a remarkable array of Navajo and non-Navajo linguists, anthropologists, missionaries, and military personnel. The first systematic attempts to develop written Navajo can be traced to 1852, when a U.S. army colonel stationed in the area translated 424 English words into Navajo for Schoolcraft's word lists of American Indian languages (Lockard, 1996, p. 40). Chee Dodge, a renowned Navajo interpreter and the first chairman of the Navajo Tribal Council, worked with the post surgeon at another military installation in the region to produce the first Navajo orthography, dictionary, and grammar (Holm, 1996; Lockard, 1995, 1996). Around the same time, Franciscan missionaries arrived in the area, later publishing a Navajo ethnologic dictionary and vocabulary. Meanwhile Protestant missionaries were also developing Navajo in written form. One of these missionaries subsequently worked with Navajo Marines in World War II to create what would become the unbreakable linguistic code used by Navajo Code Talkers to transmit military messages in the Pacific.

These efforts set the stage for the first government forays into Navajo print literacy, which began with the development of bilingual readers under John Collier, President Franklin D. Roosevelt's Commissioner of Indian Affairs. Enlisting the expertise of several well-known anthropologists, Collier commissioned a Navajo writing system that evolved into the standard-bearing orthography known today as the Young and Morgan alphabet, named for its creators, Robert Young, a non-Native linguist, and William Morgan, a linguist and native speaker. In 1943, Young and Morgan produced the first of three dictionaries, praised as "the best dictionary of a Native North American language at the time" (Hale, 2001, p. 83).

The Young and Morgan dictionary provided the essential tool "to enable people not just to read Navajo but also to write [it], for their own purposes" (Holm, 1996, pp. 8–9). Several studies have documented the ways in which this occurred. The ethnographer Daniel McLaughlin, for example, described how members of the pseudonymous community of Mesa Valley "read and write Navajo for indigenous purposes in home settings unconnected to church or school domains and identified as 'useful' [and] 'crucial to the survival of Navajo language and culture'" (McLaughlin, 1992, p. 12). In another ethnographic study Lockard (1995) showed how "new paper words" introduced by Anglo missionaries and schoolteachers were taken up by native speakers, inspiring them to become bilingual teachers in their home communities. Galena Sells Dick, whose epigraph begins this chapter, was one such bilingual educator. She writes that print literacy in Navajo enabled her natal community of Rough Rock, Arizona "to educate Navajo children in their native language ... [and] to teach youngsters their Navajo culture" (Dick & McCarty, 1996, p. 76) Moreover, she adds, "this was the first time Navajo parents had the opportunity to take ownership over their children's education" (Dick & McCarty, 1996, p. 76). Reflecting on her involvement with similar processes, Navajo linguist Irene Silentman states that, "We came to value our own language, particularly when we saw it in print ... our language was just as valuable and was on equal status with, if not above, the English language" (1995, pp. 16–17).

In this case, print literacy has been an integral element of a larger Indigenous self-determination movement organized around community-based bilingual-bicultural education (for a full discussion of these language planning processes, see Lomawaima & McCarty, 2006, Ch. 6; McCarty, 1993, 2002). Importantly, while Navajo print literacy has borrowed Western forms, the content and process for their use have drawn upon Navajo ways of knowing. McCarty and Dick (2003) illustrate this for the community of Rough Rock, where bilingual-bicultural education has involved children, parents, elders, and teachers "in storytelling, song, drama, art, and research and writing projects related to locally relevant themes" (2003, p. 114). These projects in turn became the basis for bilingual teachers' development of new print materials that grew out of:

> ... a collaborative social transaction between elders, parents, teachers, and youth. In the context of these socially meaningful interactions, children and adults co-construct knowledge from the cultural and linguistic capital ... within their community. In this process, they create new opportunities for the development of Indigenous literacies and reaffirm the value of Navajo language and culture in their lives.
>
> *(McCarty & Dick, 2003, p. 114)*

The K-5 Puente de Hózhǫ́ public magnet school in northern Arizona provides an example of these processes in an urban, off-reservation setting. The school's name comes from the Spanish words *puente de* (bridge of) and the Navajo *hózhǫ́*— beauty or harmony; this is "Bridge of Beauty" School. The school's co-founder, Michael Fillerup, explains the genesis of the school's name this way: In a district in which 25 percent of the students are American Indian (primarily Navajo) and 32 percent are Latino, "local educators were searching for innovative ways to bridge the seemingly unbridgeable gap between the academic achievement of language-minority and language-majority children" (Fillerup, 2005, p. 15).

To do this, Puente de Hózhǫ́ offers a conventional dual-language program in which native Spanish-speaking and native English-speaking children are taught jointly for a half-day in each language, and a Navajo immersion program in which English-dominant Navajo students are taught in Navajo. A major thrust of teachers' work has been the development of curriculum materials and pedagogies that embrace Diné ways of knowing while addressing requirements imposed by the state. To do this, teachers tapped into Diné oral tradition, organizing instruction around the macro-themes of earth and sky, health, living things, and family and community (Fillerup, 2011)—essential elements of a Diné theory of knowledge, *sa'ah naagháí bik'eh hózhóón*, the path of beauty, balance, and life-long happiness (Clark, 2009; House, 2002). The school has been highly successful in achieving its goals of promoting bilingualism, Diné language and culture revitalization, and academic achievement. Puente de Hózhǫ́ students consistently outperform comparable students in English-medium schools. Equally important, according to co-founder Fillerup, are the ways in which the school cultivates "ties that bind through the generations," as children learn the language and traditions of their cultural community (2005, p. 16).

"From This Renaissance Came a New Group of Speakers": The Cases of Māori and Hawaiian

We turn now to two cases that extend the lessons from Rough Rock and Puente de Hózhǫ́: Hawaiian and Māori, arguably the most successful Indigenous language revitalization movements in the world. Hawaiian and Māori are both Eastern Polynesian languages. From CE 1000 to 1778, Hawaiian was the only language used in the Hawaiian Islands, and for centuries it developed with little outside influence (Wilson, 1998). During the same period, Māori, the largest ethnic group in Aotearoa/New Zealand[2] prior to European contact, enjoyed a strong oral tradition that included "[c]arving, painting and various forms of weaving [that] all had messages for the initiated" (St. John, 2005, p. 2). Prior to and during the early periods of Anglo-European contact, both the Hawaiian and Māori people had organized education systems; in the Māori case, these schools "were sufficiently prestigious to take students from other regions" (St. John, 2005, p. 2).

Following the expeditions of Captain James Cook in the late 18th century, the Māori and Native Hawaiians were drawn into an international trade and political network. In Hawai'i, an internationally recognized Indigenous monarchy persisted until 1893, when the U.S. military staged an illegal coup, annexing Hawai'i as a U.S. territory. At the time, Hawaiians had the highest literacy rate of any ethnic group in the Hawaiian islands (Wilson & Kamanā, 2006). Meanwhile, Aotearoa/New Zealand was being colonized by the British, who imposed "an overtly assimilationist" policy agenda (May, 2004, p. 24). Although the Treaty of Waitangi, signed in 1840 between the British Crown and Māori leaders, "guaranteed" Māori people rights to their lands, homes, and treasured possessions, it was quickly violated by White settlers in pursuit of Māori lands. In both cases, the Indigenous languages were banned from the colonial education system, and people experienced "political disenfranchisement, misappropriation of land, population and health decline, educational disadvantage and socioeconomic marginalization" (May, 2005, p. 366). In New Zealand, whereas 90 percent of Māori school children spoke Māori in 1913, only 5 percent were identified as speakers of the language in 1975. In Hawai'i, by the mid-20th century, Hawaiian was spoken only by a few hundred inhabitants of the island of Nihau (Wilson, 1999).

This situation sparked coterminous ethnolinguistic revitalization movements. In 1978, a "Hawaiian Renaissance" led to a state constitutional change making Hawaiian co-official with English in Hawai'i (Warner, 1999, 2001; Wilson 1999). In 1987, the Māori Language Act made Māori co-official with English (and more recently, also with New Zealand Sign Language). Full-immersion Māori "language nest" preschools or *Te Kohānga Reo* began in 1982; the first Hawaiian immersion preschools (*'Aha Pūnana Leo*) were established in 1983 (May, 2005; Reedy, 2000; Warner, 1999; Wilson, 1999). These family-run preschools facilitate interaction between young children and fluent speakers entirely in the Indigenous language, with the goal of cultivating knowledge of the Indigenous language and culture as they were learned in the home and community in previous generations (Wilson & Kamanā, 2001, p. 151). The preschools, which operate from a Māori and Hawaiian epistemological framework, respectively, serve as the foundation for each group's language recovery and educational sovereignty efforts.

According to Māori educator Cath Rau, from the first days of European contact, Māori people "quickly adopted the print literacies of the West" (2005, p. 409). At the same time, literacy in Māori has not been universally accepted: While some language revitalization advocates "have rejected literacy in Māori as an unwanted intrusion of [European] technology into ... Māori culture, in general Māori educators have vigorously promoted the acquisition of literacy through Māori" (Benton & Benton, 2001, p. 433). This has been most effective where Māori language acquisition has been intertwined with Māori philosophy and ways of knowing, known as *kura kaupapa Māori* (Glynn, Berryman, Loader, & Cavanagh, 2005, p. 436).

Hill and May (2011) illustrate this approach with an ethnographic study of Māori–English biliteracy learning at Te Wharekura o Rakaumangamanga

(Rakaumanga) School, one of the largest and longest-running Māori-medium schools in Aotearoa/New Zealand. The school philosophy revolves around a Māori *tongi* (proverb), which emphasizes "seek[ing] solutions where problems earlier existed," building on students' strengths, and embracing their "culture as an essential factor in their achievement and success" (Hill & May, 2011, p. 167). As the school's principal, Barna Heremia, explained the philosophy in an interview with Hill:

> It [the proverb] is stating, don't leave his/her Māori world aside. These are the treasures of the Māori world ... The belief is that we should not be afraid to ask for help to whomever may be able to assist, if it means we are able to achieve our desires.
>
> *(Hill & May, 2011, p. 167)*

Thus bilingual, bicultural, biliteracy education is an instrument of Māori self-determination. Rakaumanga offers Māori-medium schooling for students from year 1 (age 5) to year 13 (age 18). Entering students must have attended *kōhanga reo* for at least two years, laying the foundation for four years of full Māori immersion, after which English is introduced for three to four hours per week. To ensure integrity of the Māori language environment, Māori and English instruction are separated by time, place, and teacher. The goal is for students to develop full bilingualism and biliteracy as a means of preparing them to be full participants in the Māori world and "citizens of the world" (Hill & May, 2011, p. 173).

To assess children's Māori reading abilities, Rakaumanga uses a Māori language framework in which each reading level (called a *kete,* a traditional woven flax bag named for a Māori plant) is arranged according to difficulty (Hill & May, 2011). Students' Māori writing is also evaluated using non-fiction Māori texts. These literacy assessments show that by year 8, students have reached or are approaching age-appropriate literacy development in both languages and are "well on their way to achieving the goal of bilingualism and biliteracy, a key aim of Māori-medium education" (2011, p. 178). Rau's (2005) research reinforces these findings for other Māori-medium schools. As in the Puente de Hózhǫ́ Navajo case, there is strong evidence that Māori-medium schooling—in particular, the sustained development of biliteracy—promotes both academic achievement and language and culture revitalization (Hill & May, 2011, p. 180).

Wilson and Kamanā (2001, 2006) describe similar outcomes at the Nāwahīokalani'ōpu'u (Nāwahī) Laboratory School in Hilo, Hawai'i, a full-immersion, early childhood through high school program affiliated with the University of Hawai'i -Hilo's College of Hawaiian Language and the 'Aha Pūnana Leo. The school offers a college preparatory curriculum, teaching all subjects through Hawaiian language and values; students also learn English and a third language such as Japanese. Like Rakaumanga, the goal is for learners to achieve Hawaiian dominance alongside high levels of English fluency and literacy, and to produce students who "psychologically identify Hawaiian as their dominant language and the one they will speak with peers and their own children when they have them" (Wilson & Kawaiʻaeʻa, 2007, p. 39). Nāwahī students not only surpass their non-immersion peers on English standardized tests, they outperform the state average for all ethnic groups on high school graduation, college attendance, and academic honors (Wilson, Kamanā, & Rawlins, 2006, p. 42). Meanwhile, the students have attained a high level of Indigenous-language fluency and literacy and the "psychological benefits to their identity" as Native Hawaiians (Wilson et al., 2006, p. 43).

Consistent with international research on second language acquisition, the academic outcomes in both the Hawaiian and the Māori case can be traced to these programs' overall additive language learning approach (adding, rather than subtracting, a second language from students' communicative repertoires), within a larger, culturally based system of support. The Hawaiians refer to this as *honua*: the "places, circumstances, structures where use of Hawaiian is dominant" and the Hawaiian *mauli,* culture or "life force," is supported and maintained (Wilson & Kawaiʻaeʻa, 2007, p. 38). Across a spectrum of processes and outcomes, Hawaiian and Māori can be viewed as Indigenous language and literacy revitalization "success stories" that have empowered learners while reuniting older and younger generations through literacy engagements in the Indigenous mother tongue.

Offering "Real Hope": The Case of New and Old Literacies in Language Revitalization

Increasingly, information technology plays a central role in these language planning processes. Hornberger and Coronel-Molina (2004) and Coronel-Molina and McCarty (2011) examine the role of digital literacies for Quechua in South America. With millions of speakers in six South American countries, Quechua (called Quichua in Ecuador) is nevertheless endangered as a result of more than five centuries of linguistic and cultural oppression and the continued social, economic, and political marginalization of its speakers. Over the past four decades, a region-wide Indigenous resurgence has led to national policies mandating bilingual-intercultural education and designating Quechua as co-official in Peru and Bolivia and Quichua as co-official in Ecuador (Godenzzi, 2008). Audiovisual and video resources now provide opportunities for language learning in authentic cultural contexts; multimedia DVD, Internet resources, and interactive textbooks complement hard-copy texts. Online Quechua dictionaries, glossaries, and Native-language interfaces with popular computer programs such as Windows have been developed, and Google has a search engine in Quechua (Coronel-Molina & McCarty 2011, p. 366). These new forms of literacy both reflect and construct new language learning opportunities while enabling "Indigenous languages to take their rightful place in the contemporary world" (Coronel-Molina & McCarty, 2011, p. 367).

At the same time, historic literacies have been instrumental in bringing "sleeping" languages back to life. In this regard the case of Wôpanâak is instructive. An Algonquian language spoken by peoples indigenous to what is now the northeastern U.S., the last native speakers of Wôpanâak (also called Massachusett or Wampanoag) passed away 150 years ago. Fortunately, Wôpanâak has a significant corpus of written texts, including lexicons, letters, diaries written by native speakers, and the 1663 Eliot Bible, the first bible to be translated into a Native American language. These resources have enabled the Wampanoag to formulate a dictionary and language curriculum to teach Wôpanâak to community members, including young children (Ash, Fermino, & Hale, 2001). Leonard (2008) describes similar revitalization processes for Miami, another Algonquian language, whose last native speaker died in the 1960s. Although Miami lacks audio documentation, its written documentation is "vast," including a 17th century dictionary discovered in 1999 (Leonard, 2008, p. 24; see also Baldwin, 2003). This and other historic texts have enabled the Myaamia Project, an initiative of the Miami Nation and Miami University of Ohio, to produce a host of contemporary language learning and teaching materials. The case of Miami, Leonard writes, offers "real hope to other communities whose language situations appear bleak" (2008, p. 26).

Challenges and Constraints

No revitalization effort is without problems. In the case of information technology, access is a major obstacle, a function of the geographic isolation of many Indigenous communities and of their continued economic, social, and political marginalization. Moreover, the development of Indigenous writing systems and teaching materials may be fraught with conflict. Such has been the case for Quechua and Quichua in Peru and Ecuador, where debates surrounding the number of vowel phonemes represented in the language's written form (three) versus those pronounced in speech (five) have hampered language revitalization. These debates veil larger issues of authority and control (Hornberger & King, 1998). In Ecuador, *Quichua Unificado* (Unified Quichua) was developed to encourage Quichua literacy and revitalization. As King (2001) explains for Saraguros in southern Ecuador, educated, economically successful Saraguros tend to speak the Unified Quichua learned as a second language in school, while older, less educated and more rural Saraguros speak the "authentic" variety as a first language. Paradoxically, *Quichua Auténtico* (Authentic Quichua) is viewed by users of Unified Quichua as "impure" because it includes Spanish loan words. Warner (1999) and Wong (1999, 2011) analyze similar issues for Hawaiian, arguing that the responsibility (*kuleana*) for Indigenous language revitalization and its representation in written form (what language planners call corpus planning) must lie with members of the Indigenous-language community themselves.

The fact that these language reclamation initiatives are carried out in the contentious space of schools creates additional challenges. The Sámi case provides valuable lessons in this regard. The Sámi are the Indigenous people of the Nordic countries who live in what is now Norway, Sweden, Finland, and western Russia—an Indigenous "nation divided by four states" (Todal, 2003, p. 185)—with about 40,000 living in Norway (Magga and Skutnabb-Kangas, 2003). Sámi is a Finno-Ugric language with three major branches and 11 subgroups. Well into the 20th century, the Sámi were subjected to harsh school-based assimilation policies. In the mid-20th century, this began to change as the Sámi pressed for education and language rights. In 1997, the Norwegian government introduced a separate Sámi curriculum with equal status as the national curriculum (Todal, 2003, pp. 185–186). This reform not only ensures that Sámi children living in high-density Sámi residential areas (the Sámi core) have access to instruction in their language and culture, but provides for teaching the Sámi language outside the Sámi core area as well (Hirvonen, 2008).

In the core Sámi area these goals are being achieved, but in mixed Sámi-Norwegian speaking communities, Sámi children are likely to be taught through Norwegian, with only "pull-out" Sámi language and culture instruction. According to Sámi scholar Vuokko Hirvonen (2008), this disables the goals of bilingualism, biculturalism, and biliteracy. Hirvonen therefore urges "special support and positive discrimination" for endangered Indigenous languages, noting that the "extent to which the school integrates the minority language and culture in its work has an impact on how effectively the language and culture are strengthened" (2008, pp. 38–39).

The Literacy Continuum: From Practice to Theory and Back

Most language planning scholars and practitioners agree that schools and alphabetic literacy alone cannot "save" a threatened language (see, e.g., the cases in Hornberger, 1996, 2008). As Joshua Fishman emphasizes in his classic treatise, *Reversing Language Shift*, oralcy cultivated in the context of family and community is the *sine qua non* of intergenerational language continuity (Fishman, 1991, p. 95). Under optimal circumstances this would no doubt be the goal of every language revitalizer. The difficulty is that revitalizing a language means confronting the very power structures that caused the breakdown in intergenerational continuity in the first place. Endangered languages require "special support," as Hirvonen points out for Sámi and as we have seen in practice for the cases of Diné, Māori, and Hawaiian. Alphabetic literacy and bilingual-bicultural schooling can provide some of that support. Otomí linguist and language activist Jesus Salinas Pedraza puts it this way: Writing an Indigenous language can help "recapture and nurture the cultural, scientific, and technical traditions" of the people associated with it (1996, p. 184).

The cases examined here suggest that this is most powerful when alphabetic literacy is engaged as one facet of a multifaceted literacy continuum that includes as an integral component Indigenous knowledge systems. According to Zepeda

(1995), the literacy continuum includes what "teachers cannot teach"—the "traditional knowledge of storytelling, the rhythm of traditional narratives, the oral structures of those narratives and the importance of this type of literature" in Indigenous communities (p. 14).[3] Examining the English-language texts of young O'odham writers with varying degrees of ability in their heritage language, Zepeda argues that these students bring to their writing the genres, styles, and orientations of O'odham oral tradition:

> They may write about a specific topic as assigned [by the teacher], but at the same time they gather insights from their own experience, their community, home and family to write what they feel makes a good story. . . . [A]s with the oral tradition, the writer is playing and . . . experimenting with the power of words. . . . [Young O'odham writers] tantalize the reader in the same way the storyteller holds the audience in an oral performance.
>
> *(Zepeda, 1995, p. 10)*

Similarly, in his study of Kashinawá local knowledge and multimodal texts in Brazil, Menezes de Souza shows the ways in which young Kashinawá writers draw upon Indigenous forms of knowledge in localizing and appropriating grapho-centric texts, infusing them with symbolism embodied in the Kashinawá language. The resulting syncretic or "transcultural" texts incorporate elements of both externally imposed and autochthonous literacies; "neither the local knowledge present in literacy and writing on the one hand nor in the Kashinawá community on the other hand leave the [writing] context unscathed" (Menezes de Souza, 2002, p. 274).

This is the essence of the literacy continuum—the harmonizing of oral and written language practices and forms. We see this instantiated in the Rough Rock example in the storytelling, drama, and song used to draw academic content from the culture of the community, and in the Puente de Hózhǫ́ example in the four Diné themes used to organize instruction and assessment. In the Rakaumanga case, the teachers of Māori students activate the continuum by grounding Māori-medium education in *kura kaupapa* Māori philosophy. Rooting instruction in Hawaiian *mauli* or life force, Hawaiian educators create the "places, circumstances, [and] structures where use of Hawaiian is dominant" (Wilson & Kawai'ae'a, 2007, p. 38).

Together, these examples illustrate the literacy continuum in practice, showing that there is no single, uniform literacy but rather multiple and hybrid ways of using language to construct and represent community knowledges and world-views. Literacy can widen the possibilities for revitalizing a language, but, when narrowly construed or lacking in necessary institutional support, literacy can constrain those possibilities as well. Literacy's emancipatory potential as an agent of Indigenous language and culture reclamation lies in its activation by the

Indigenous-language community itself. Evidence from research and practice shows that this can best be realized by the cultivation of multi-literacies for multi-purposes across multi-domains.

Notes

1   Parts of this section are adapted from McCarty and Nicholas (2012).
2   Aotearoa is the Māori word for the Māori peoples' traditional territory, known in English as New Zealand.
3   The notion of a literacy continuum incorporates elements of Hornberger's (2003, 2004) well-known "continuum of biliteracy," but broadens it to include oralcy, Indigenous knowledge systems, and the unique qualities of Indigenous oral traditions.

References

Aikio-Puoskari, U. (2009). The ethnic revival, language and education of the Sámi, an Indigenous people, in three Nordic countries (Finland, Norway and Sweden). In T. Skutnabb-Kangas, R. Phillipson, A. K. Mohanty, & M. Panda (Eds.), *Social justice through multilingual education* (pp. 238–262). Clevedon, UK: Multilingual Matters.

Ash, A., Fermino, J. L. D., & Hale, K. (2001). Diversity in local language maintenance and restoration: A reason for optimism. In L. Hinton & K. Hale (Eds.), *The green book of language revitalization in practice* (pp. 19–35). San Diego, CA: Academic Press.

Baldwin, D. (2003). *Miami language reclamation: From ground zero.* Lecture presented at the Center for Writing and the Interdisciplinary Minor in Literacy and Rhetorical Studies [Speaker Series 24]. Minneapolis: University of Minnesota.

Battiste, M. (1986). Cognitive assimilation and Micmac literacy. In J. Barman, Y. Hébert, & D. McCaskill (Eds.), *Indian nations in Canada: The legacy* (Vol. 1, pp. 23–41). Vancouver, Canada: University of British Columbia Press.

Benally, A., & Viri, D. (2005). *Diné bizaad* (Navajo language) at a crossroads: Extinction or renewal? *Bilingual Research Journal, 29*(1), 85–108.

Benjamin, R., Pecos, R., & Romero, M. E. (1996). Language revitalization efforts in the Pueblo de Cochiti: Becoming "literate" in an oral society. In N. H. Hornberger (Ed.), *Indigenous literacies in the Americas: Language planning from the bottom up* (pp. 115–136). Berlin, Germany: Mouton de Gruyter.

Benton, R., & Benton, N. (2001). *RLS in Aotearoa/New Zealand: 1989–1999.* In J. Fishman (Ed.), *Can threatened languages be saved? Reversing language shift, revisited: A 21st century perspective* (pp. 423–450). Clevedon, UK: Multilingual Matters.

Brayboy, B. M. J., & Maughan, E. (2009). Indigenous knowledges and the story of the bean. *Harvard Educational Review, 79*(1), 1–21.

Brayboy, B. M. J., & McCarty, T. L. (2010). Indigenous knowledges and social justice pedagogy. In T. Chapman & N. Hobbel (Eds.), *Social justice pedagogy across the curriculum: The practice of freedom* (pp. 184–200). New York, NY: Teachers College Press.

Campbell, L. (1997). *American Indian languages: The historical linguistics of Native America.* Oxford, UK: Oxford University Press.

Clark, F. (2009). *Becoming sa'ąh naaghai bik'eh hozhoon: The historical challenges and triumphs of Diné College.* Unpublished Ph.D. dissertation, University of Arizona, American Indian Studies Program.

Commonwealth of Australia (1997). *Bringing them home: Report of the national inquiry into the separation of Aboriginal and Torres Strait Islander children from their families.* Sydney, Australia: Human Rights and Equal Opportunity Commission.

Coronel-Molina, S. M., & McCarty, T. L. (2011). Language curriculum design and evaluation for endangered languages. In P. K. Austin & J. Sallabank (Eds.), *The Cambridge handbook of endangered languages* (pp. 354–370). Cambridge, UK: Cambridge University Press.

de la Piedra, M. T. (2009). Hybrid literacies: The case of a Quechua community in the Andes. *Anthropology and Education Quarterly, 40*(2), 110–128.

Dick, G. S. (1998). I maintained a strong belief in my language and culture: A Navajo language autobiography. *International Journal of the Sociology of Language, 132,* 23–25.

Dick, G. S., & McCarty, T. L. (1996). Reclaiming Navajo: Language renewal in a Navajo community school. In N. H. Hornberger (Ed.), *Indigenous literacies in the Americas: Language planning from the bottom up* (pp. 69–94). Berlin, Germany: Mouton de Gruyter.

England, N. (1998). Mayan efforts toward language preservation. In L. A. Grenoble & L. J. Whaley (Eds.), *Endangered languages: Language loss and community response* (pp. 99–116). Cambridge, UK: Cambridge University Press.

Fillerup, M. (2005). Keeping up with the Yazzies: The impact of high stakes testing on Indigenous language programs. *Language Learner*, September/October, 14–16.

Fillerup, M. (2011). Building a "bridge of beauty": A preliminary report on promising practices in Native language and culture teaching at Puente de Hózhǫ Trilingual Magnet School. In M. E. Romero-Little, S. J. Ortiz, & T. L. McCarty (Eds.), *Indigenous languages across the generations: Strengthening families and communities* (pp. 145–164). Tempe: Arizona State University Center for Indian Education.

Fishman, J. A. (1991). *Reversing language shift: Theoretical and empirical foundations of assistance to threatened languages.* Clevedon, UK: Multilingual Matters.

Frisbie, C. J., & McAllester, D. P. (Eds.). (1967). *Navajo Blessingway singer: The autobiography of Frank Mitchell 1881–1967.* Tucson: University of Arizona Press.

Gee, J. P. (2008). *Social linguistics and literacies: Ideology in discourses* (3rd ed.). New York, NY: Routledge.

Glynn, T., Berryman, M., Loader, K., & Cavanagh, T. (2005). From literacy in Māori to biliteracy in Māori and English: A community and school transition programme. *International Journal of Bilingual Education and Bilingualism, 8*(5), 433–454.

Godenzzi, J. C. (2008). Language policy and education in the Andes. In S. May & N. H. Hornberger (Eds.), *Encyclopedia of language and education: Vol. 1. Language policy and political issues in education* (2nd ed., pp. 315–329). New York, NY: Springer.

Hale, K. (2001). The Navajo language: I. In L. Hinton & K. Hale (Eds.), *The green book of language revitalization in practice* (pp. 83–85). San Diego, CA: Academic Press.

Hamel, E. (2008). Bilingual education for Indigenous communities in Mexico. In J. Cummins & N. H. Hornberger (Eds.), *Encyclopedia of language and education: Vol. V. Bilingual education* (2nd ed., pp. 295–309). New York, NY: Springer.

Heath, S. B. (1972). *Telling tongues: Language policy in Mexico—Colony to nation.* New York, NY: Teachers College Press.

Heugh, K. (2009). Literacy and bi/multilingual education in Africa: Recovering collective memory and expertise. In T. Skutnabb-Kangas, R. Phillipson, A. K. Mohanty, & M. Panda (Eds.), *Social justice through multilingual education* (pp. 103–124). Bristol, UK: Multilingual Matters.

Hill, R., & May, S. (2011). Exploring biliteracy in Māori-medium education: An ethnographic perspective. In T. L. McCarty (Ed.), *Ethnography and language policy* (pp. 163–183). New York, NY: Routledge.

Hinton, L. (2001). Sleeping languages: Can they be awakened? In L. Hinton & K. Hale (Eds.), *The green book of language revitalization in practice* (pp. 413–417). San Diego, CA: Academic Press.

Hirvonen, V. (2008). "Out on the fells, I feel like a Sámi": Is there linguistic and cultural equality in the Sámi school? In N. H. Hornberger (Ed.), *Can schools save Indigenous languages? Policy and practice on four continents* (pp. 15–41). New York, NY: Palgrave Macmillan.

Holm, W. (1996). On the role of "YounganMorgan" in the development of Navajo literacy. *Journal of Navajo Education, 8*(2), 4–11.

Hornberger, N. H. (Ed.). (1996). *Indigenous literacies in the Americas: Language planning from the bottom up.* Berlin, Germany: Mouton de Gruyter.

Hornberger, N. H. (Ed.). (2003). *Continua of biliteracy: An ecological framework for educational policy, research, and practice in multilingual settings.* Clevedon, UK: Multilingual Matters.

Hornberger, N. H. (2004). The continua of biliteracy and the bilingual educator: Educational linguistics in practice. *International Journal of Bilingual Education and Bilingualism, 7*(2&3), 155–171.

Hornberger, N. H. (2006). *Nichols* to *NCLB*: Local and global perspectives on U.S. language education policy. In O. García, T. Skutnabb-Kangas, & M. E. Torres-Guzmán (Eds.), *Imagining multilingual schools: Languages in education and glocalization* (pp. 223–237). Clevedon, UK: Multilingual Matters.

Hornberger, N. H. (Ed.). (2008). *Can schools save Indigenous languages? Policy and practice on four continents.* New York, NY: Palgrave Macmillan.

Hornberger, N. H., & Coronel-Molina, S. (2004). Quechua language shift, maintenance, and revitalization in the Andes: The case for language planning. *International Journal of the Sociology of Language, 167*, 9–67.

Hornberger, N. H., & King, K. A. (1998). Authenticity and unification in Quechua language planning. *Language, Culture and Curriculum, 11*(3), 390–410.

House, D. (2002). *Language shift among the Navajos: Identity politics and cultural continuity.* Tucson: University of Arizona Press.

Kaomea, J. (2004). Dilemmas of an Indigenous academic: A Native Hawaiian story. In K. Mutua & B. B. Swadener (Eds.), *Decolonizing research in cross-cultural contexts: Critical personal narratives* (pp. 27–44). Albany: State University of New York Press.

Kawagley, A. O. (1995). *A Yupiaq worldview: A pathway to ecology and spirit.* Prospect Heights, IL: Waveland Press.

King, K. A. (2001). *Language revitalization processes and prospects: Quichua in the Ecuadorian Andes.* Clevedon, UK: Multilingual Matters.

King, K. A., & Benson, C. (2008). Vernacular and Indigenous literacies. In B. Spolsky & F. M. Hult (Eds.), *The handbook of educational linguistics* (pp. 340–354). Malden, MA: Blackwell.

Krauss, M. (1998). The condition of Native North American languages: The need for realistic assessment and action. *International Journal of the Sociology of Language, 132*, 9–21.

Leonard, W. (2008). When is an "extinct language" not extinct? Miami, a formerly sleeping language. In K. A. King, N. Schilling-Estes, L. Fogle, J. J. Lou, & B. Soukup (Eds.), *Sustaining linguistic diversity: Endangered and minority languages and language varieties* (pp. 23–33). Washington, DC: Georgetown University Press.

Lockard, L. (1995). New paper words: Historical images of Navajo language literacy. *American Indian Quarterly, 19*(1), 17–30.

Lockard, L. (1996). New paper words: Historical images of Navajo literacy. *Journal of Navajo Education, 8*(2), 40–48.

Lomawaima, K. T., & McCarty, T. L. (2006). *"To remain an Indian": Lessons in democracy from a century of Native American education.* New York, NY: Teachers College Press.

López, L. E. (2008). Top-down and bottom-up: Counterpoised visions of bilingual intercultural education in Latin America. In N. H. Hornberger (Ed.), *Can schools save Indigenous languages? Policy and practice on four continents* (pp. 42–65). New York, NY: Palgrave Macmillan.

López, L. E., & Sichra, I. (2008). Intercultural bilingual education among Indigenous peoples in Latin America. In J. Cummins & N. H. Hornberger (Eds.), *Encyclopedia of language and education: Vol. 5. Bilingual education* (2nd ed., pp. 295–309). New York, NY: Springer.

McCarty, T. L. (1993). Federal language policy and American Indian education. *Bilingual Research Journal, 17*(1 & 2), 13–34.

McCarty, T. L. (2002). *A place to be Navajo: Rough Rock and the struggle for self-determination in Indigenous schooling.* Mahwah, NJ: Lawrence Erlbaum.

McCarty, T. L., & Dick, G. S. (2003). Telling The People's stories: Literacy practices and processes in a Navajo community school. In A. I. Willis, G. E. García, R. B. Barrera, & V. J. Harris (Eds.), *Multicultural issues in literacy research and practice* (pp. 101–122). Mahwah, NJ: Lawrence Erlbaum.

McCarty, T. L., & Nicholas, S. E. (2012). Indigenous education: Local and global perspectives. In M. Martin-Jones, A. Blackledge, & A. Creese (Eds.), *Routledge handbook on multilingualism.* London, UK: Routledge.

McCarty, T. L., Skutnabb-Kangas, T., & Magga, O. H. (2008). Education for speakers of endangered languages. In B. Spolsky & F. M. Hult (Eds.), *The handbook of educational linguistics* (pp. 297–312). Malden, MA: Blackwell.

McCarty, T. L., & Watahomigie, L. J. (2004). Language and literacy in American Indian and Alaska Native communities. In B. Pérez (Ed.), *Sociocultural contexts of language and literacy* (pp. 79–110). Mahwah, NJ: Lawrence Erlbaum.

McCarty, T. L., & Zepeda, O. (2010). Native Americans. In J. A. Fishman & O. García (Eds.), *Handbook of language and ethnic identity* (2nd ed., pp. 323–352). Oxford, UK: Oxford University Press.

McLaughlin, D. (1992). *When literacy empowers: Navajo language in print.* Albuquerque: University of New Mexico Press.

Magga, O. H., & Skutnabb-Kangas, T. (2003). Life or death for languages and human beings: Experiences from Saamiland. In L. Huss, A. Camilleri Grima, & K. King (Eds.), *Transcending monolingualism: Linguistic revitalisation in education* (pp. 35–52). Lisse, The Netherlands: Swets & Zeitlinger.

Makalela, L. (2005). "We speak eleven tongues": Reconstructing multilingualism in South Africa. In B. Brock-Utne & R. K. Hopson (Eds.), *Languages of instruction for African emancipation: Focus on postcolonial contexts and considerations* (pp. 147–173). Cape Town, South Africa and Dar es Salaam, Tanzania: Centre for Advanced Studies of African Society (CASAS) and Mkuki n Nyota Publishers.

May, S. (2004). Māori-medium education in Aotearoa/New Zealand. In J. W. Tollefson & A. B. M. Tsui (Eds.), *Medium of instruction policies: Which agenda? Whose agenda?* (pp. 21–41). Mahwah, NJ: Lawrence Erlbaum.

May, S. (Guest Ed.) (2005). *Bilingual/immersion education in Aotearoa/New Zealand.* Special issue, *International Journal of Bilingual Education and Bilingualism, 8*(5), 365–376.

Menezes de Souza, L. M. T. (2002). A case among cases, a world among worlds: The ecology of writing among the Kashinawá in Brazil. *Journal of Language, Identity, and Education, 1*(4), 261–278.

Mohanty, A., Mishra, M. K., Reddy, N. U., & Ramesh, G. (2009). Overcoming the language barrier for tribal children: Multilingual education in Andhra Pradesh and Orissa, India. In T. Skutnabb-Kangas, R. Phillipson, A. K. Mohanty, & M. Panda (Eds.), *Social justice through multilingual education* (pp. 283–297). Bristol, UK: Multilingual Matters.

New London Group. (1996). A pedagogy of multiliteracies: Designing social futures. *Harvard Educational Review, 66*(1), 60–92.

Obondo, M. A. (2008). Bilingual education in Africa: An overview. In J. Cummins & N. H. Hornberger (Eds.), *Encyclopedia of language and education: Vol. 5. Bilingual education* (2nd ed., pp. 151–161). New York, NY: Springer.

Prah, K. K. (2008). Language, literacy, and knowledge production in Africa. In B. V. Street & N. H. Hornberger (Eds.), *Encyclopedia of language and education: Vol. 2. Literacy* (pp. 29–39). New York, NY: Springer.

Rau, C. (2005). Literacy acquisition, assessment and achievement of Year 2 students in total immersion in Māori programmes. *International Journal of Bilingual Education and Bilingualism, 8*(5), 404–432.

Reedy, T. (2000). Te reo Māori: The past 20 years and looking forward. *Oceanic Linguistics, 39*(1), 157–168.

Reyhner, J., & Eder, J. (2004). *American Indian education: A history.* Norman: University of Oklahoma Press.

Rockwell, E. (2005). Indigenous accounts of dealing with writing. In T. L. McCarty (Ed.), *Language, literacy, and power in schooling* (pp. 5–27). Mahwah, NJ: Lawrence Erlbaum.

Romaine, S. (1991). Introduction. In S. Romaine (Ed.), *Language in Australia* (pp. 1–24). Cambridge, UK: Cambridge University Press.

Romero-Little, M. E. (2010). How should young Indigenous children be prepared for learning? A vision of early childhood education for Indigenous children. *Journal of American Indian Education, 49*(1 & 2), 7–27.

St. John, V. (2005) *Maori literacy in New Zealand, 1810–1855.* Retrieved March 5, 2011, from http://journals.culture-communication.unimelb.edu/au/the-pub/pdfs/Victoria StJohn.pdf/

Salinas Pedraza, J. (1996). Saving and strengthening indigenous Mexican languages: The CELIAC experience. In N. H. Hornberger (Ed.), *Indigenous literacies in the Americas: Language planning from the bottom up* (pp. 171–187). Berlin, Germany: Mouton de Gruyter.

Sarangapani, P. M. (2003). Indigenising curriculum: Questions posed by Baiga Vidya. *Comparative Education, 39*(2), 199–209.

Sichra, I. (2008). Language diversity and Indigenous literacy in the Andes. In B. V. Street & N. H. Hornberger (Eds.), *Encyclopedia of language and education: Vol. 2. Literacy* (pp. 283–297). New York, NY: Springer.

Silentman, I. (1995). *Navajo bilingual education in the 1970s: A personal perspective.* Unpublished manuscript.

Sims, C. (2005). Tribal languages and the challenges of revitalization. *Anthropology and Education Quarterly, 36*(1), 104–106.

Skutnabb-Kangas, T. (2000). *Linguistic genocide in education: Or worldwide diversity and human rights?* Mahwah, NJ: Lawrence Erlbaum.

Skutnabb-Kangas, T., & Dunbar, R. (2010). *Indigenous children's education as linguistic genocide and a crime against humanity? A global view.* Guovdageaidnu/Kautokeino Gáldu, Resource Centre for the Rights of Indigenous Peoples. Retrieved July 5, 2010, from http://www.e-pages.dk/grusweb/55/

Spack, R. (2002). *America's second tongue: American Indian education and the ownership of English, 1860–1900.* Lincoln: University of Nebraska Press.

Street, B. (2001). *Literacy and development: Ethnographic perspectives.* London, UK: Routledge.

Street, B. (2008). New literacies, new times: Developments in literacy studies. In B.V. Street & N. H. Hornberger (Eds.), *Encyclopedia of language and education: Vol. 2. Literacy* (2nd ed., pp. 3–14). New York, NY: Springer.

Sueyo, H. (2003). Educational biography of an Arakmbut. *Comparative Education, 39*(2), 193–197.

Todal, J. (2003). The Sámi school system in Norway and international cooperation. *Comparative Education, 39*(2), 185–192.

UNESCO. (2005). *Education for all global monitoring report 2006. Literacy for life.* Paris, France: UNESCO. Retrieved December 28, 2009, from http://www.unesco.org/en/efareport/reports/2006-literacy/

Walker, W. B. (1996). Native writing systems. In I. Goddard (Vol. Ed.) & W. C. Sturtevant (Series Ed.), *Handbook of North American Indians: Vol. 17. Languages* (pp. 158–184). Washington, DC: Smithsonian Institution.

Warner, S. L. N. (1999). *Kuleana*: The right, responsibility, and authority of Indigenous peoples to speak and make decisions for themselves in language and cultural revitalization. *Anthropology and Education Quarterly, 30*(1), 68–93.

Warner, S. L. N. (2001). The movement to revitalize Hawaiian language and culture. In L. Hinton & K. Hale (Eds.), *The green book of language revitalization in practice* (pp. 133–144). San Diego, CA: Academic Press.

Wilson, W. H. (1998). I ka ʻōlelo Hawaiʻi ke ola, "Life is found in the Hawaiian language." *International Journal of the Sociology of Language, 132*, 123–137.

Wilson, W. H. (1999). The sociopolitical context of establishing Hawaiian-medium education. In S. May (Ed.), *Indigenous community-based education* (pp. 95–108). Clevedon, UK: Multilingual Matters.

Wilson, W. H., & Kamanā, K. (2001). "*Mai loko mai o ka ʻiʻini*: Proceeding from a dream": The ʻAha Pūnana Leo connection in Hawaiian language revitalization. In L. Hinton & K. Hale (Eds.), *The green book of language revitalization in practice* (pp. 147–176). San Diego, CA: Academic Press.

Wilson, W. H., & Kamanā, K. (2006). "For the interest of the Hawaiians themselves": Reclaiming the benefits of Hawaiian-medium education. *Hūlili: Multidisciplinary Research on Hawaiian Well-Being, 3*(1), 153–181.

Wilson, W. H., Kamanā, K., & Rawlins, N. (2006). Nāwahī Hawaiian Laboratory School. *Journal of American Indian Education, 45*(2), 42–44.

Wilson, W. H., & Kawaiʻaeʻa, K. (2007). I *kūmū; I lala*: "Let there be sources; Let there be branches": Teacher education in the College of Hawaiian language. *Journal of American Indian Education, 46*(3), 37–53.

Wong, K. L. (1999). Authenticity and the revitalization of Hawaiian. *Anthropology and Education Quarterly, 30*(1), 94–115.

Wong, K. L. (2011). Language, fruits, and vegetables. In M. E. Romero-Little, S. J. Ortiz, & T. L. McCarty (Eds.), *Indigenous languages across the generations: Strengthening families and communities* (pp. 1–15). Tempe: Arizona State University Center for Indian Education.

Zepeda, O. (1992). Foreword. In Y. M. Goodman & S. Wilde (Eds.), *Literacy events in a community of young writers* (pp. ix–xi). New York, NY: Teachers College Press.

Zepeda, O. (1995). The continuum of literacy in American Indian communities. *Bilingual Research Journal, 19*(1), 5–1.

10
DIGITAL LITERACIES

Steven L. Thorne

Introduction

It is an obvious observation, but one worth repeating: there have always been multiple literacies. Historically, literacy practices span from a diverse array of inscription technologies to contemporary digitally enabled practices that are rooted in creative borrowing and semiotic assemblage processes. Even the pared down version of literacy, understood as a set of cognitive and technical skills used to read and write graphically rendered language, shows variation across time periods, communities and cultures, and contexts.

Digital literacies is a term used to describe semiotic activity mediated by electronic media. This chapter discusses various conceptions of literacy and digital literacies, describes the historical trajectory of the field, and then examines contexts and environments, including cases involving both first language and second and foreign language (L2) learning, and their significances. This is followed by a discussion of the affordances and challenges that digital literacies present to modern day schooling—and here it is argued, in alignment with other research, that new media communication practices, cultures, and forms of engagement have great potential to enhance existing, and perhaps more importantly, to radically transform, formal educational processes and outcomes. In conclusion, I will address how and why concepts associated with digital literacies matter for language learning in and out of formal instructional settings and for the ongoing project of lifelong language development.

The Practice of Literacies

Literacy, and particularly reading, is critical to success in schooling and full participation in contemporary societies. Because of the importance of literacy, a few prefatory remarks are in order to spell out the baseline issues and definitions that frame the remainder of the chapter.

As many literacy theorists have remarked, the learning and use of literacies are fundamentally interwoven with social, technological, economic, political, and cultural dynamics (Gee, 1992; Lankshear & Knobel, 2006; Street, 1995). An extension of this observation is that literacy is a *social practice* and not merely an individual or cognitive one, a view which complexifies and contests the notion of literacy as primarily a brain-local skill involving an individual engaged in deciphering and producing graphically rendered language.

The term *practice* is here used in a technical sense to describe socially structured, and socially structuring, patterns and resources that form the core of everyday life activity. These can include acts of classification, reasoning and logic, forms of rationality, and historically developed patterns of communication (e.g., Bourdieu, 1991; de Certeau, 1984; Ortner, 1984; Russell, 2009). In this sense, social practices are ways of understanding and doing things in the world.

Different systems of literacy can be seen to dynamically evolve in a wide variety of often interrelated semiotic modes, genres, and cultural contexts, as well as in relationship to the changing social and functional purposes they serve. There are many such examples in the digital age, but a brief discussion of a few historical cases offers useful illustrations of the development of diverse and dynamically evolving processes of written communication. Conklin (1949), for example, describes the development and use of the Mindoro script, or 'bamboo literacy,' among the Hanunóo in the Philippines, where authors use an Indic syllabary (individual marks comprise a consonant and vowel) to write on palm leaves (often with cuttlefish ink) or inscribe marks on shafts of bamboo. The Hanunóo literacy system is not taught in schools, but rather is passed down from individual to individual and is most often used for recording and then memorizing serenades and love songs for the purpose of courting a romantic partner. Rather astoundingly for anyone who has tried to read a text held up to a mirror, left-handed individuals, holding the knife in their dominant hand, reverse both the axis of the written characters and the direction of the sequential flow of their texts. Due to the syllabic nature of the Mindoro script, Conklin reports that left-handed "mirror scripts" can be deciphered almost as quickly as texts produced by right-handed individuals.

A second example, described by Scribner and Cole (1981), examined literacy practices and their varying developmental effects among the Vai people in Liberia, where three very diverse literacy practices co-exist. The first is an indigenous Vai script, which is learned outside of school and used for personal and commercial purposes. The second is Arabic, which is learned and used in religious settings for reading and reciting the Qur'an. English, learned in school, is the third literacy system, which is commonly used for public and official governmental functions. In the case of the Vai, each of these literacy practices are socially, situationally, and culturally specific in origin and function.

In a broader historical sense, early writing practices in Europe (as well as elsewhere in the world, India for example) were very different from those of today due to the fact that language was written as a continuous flow without demarcated word boundaries. White space between words was only developed in the seventh and eighth centuries as a way to facilitate comprehending complex technical texts. The introduction of white space between words greatly facilitated the diffusion of reading into broader society. It also transformed the public literacy practice of oral reading of texts to audiences by specialists to silent reading by individuals (e.g., Saenger, 1997). In each of the historical cases briefly described above, we can see that diverse forms of literacy evolved in ecological relation with distinctive social and community purposes. Also illustrated by these examples is the dialectical relationship between literacy practices and life activities. That is, language, and its graphical representation in literacy, is a human creation that in turn structures and transforms the cognitive and social conditions of human existence (see Bundsgaard & Steffensen, 2000, for a discussion). As Hanks (1996) has argued, language and the world of human experience interweave with one another, so even the "inner logic of a linguistic system bears the trace of the routine practices to which it is adapted" (p. 236).

In the contemporary age and throughout much of the world, language and literacy practices have become central to the cultural organization of all aspects of social life (Pennycook, 2010). While certain literacy practices are widespread, state sponsored (for example through public education), and hence highly standardized, actual persons become literate within a dynamic interplay of personal and social-collective experience. In this sense, and to a significant degree, literacy is polymorphous even among highly educated populations.

Literacy is a cultural technology that is social in both origin and function. Thus 'literacy' is more accurately described in the plural, as 'literacies' or as 'literacy practices'. Understood in this way, literacies are semiotic practices that develop over time and which become conventionalized as recognizable forms of expression (Gee, 1999, 2004; Lankshear & Knobel, 2006). At first glance, this may appear to be an over-broad characterization of 'literacy,' but developmental approaches that see learning as functionally emergent of particular temporal, spatial, and cultural contexts demonstrate the importance of concrete social and material conditions as they relate to specific developmental outcomes. In essence, becoming literate in a particular semiotic practice (or set of practices) involves the ability to interpret and generate meaningful signs within communities of practice (Lave & Wenger, 1991). It also involves developing identity dispositions that are appropriate to that practice, including the performance of recognizable social roles in interlocutor, context, and community-relevant ways (Gee, 1996, 2004).

Digital Literacies

Some of the first things we can say about digitally mediated informational and communicative activity are that it is abundant and diverse. There are currently more texts on the Internet, many of which are multimodal, than there are in all of the world's libraries combined. While Internet access remains unequally distributed across social classes and geopolitical regions (e.g., Van Dijk, 2005; Warschauer, 2003), in an increasing number of areas, technology-mediated life activity has become ubiquitous. Global numbers of Internet users continue to climb rapidly, with current estimates at approximately 2 billion people, nearly one-third of the world's population (www.internetworldstats.com/). In recent decades recreation and leisure, as well as business and academic activities, increasingly involve information exchange, communication, and self-representation in Internet-mediated spaces. This is especially the case for teens and young adults. According to a recent Pew Internet & American Life survey, 64 percent of online teens engage with interactive social media, create original content themselves, and share this content online (Lenhart, Madden, Macgill, & Smith, 2007). Such activities include creating and sharing stories, photos, and videos, contributing to social media sites, blogs, and online journals, and remixing existing material into their own creative works (Lenhart et al., 2007). For many youth, full participation in these activities involves not only traditional, print-based literacy, but also facility with newer literacies and communicative genres that are emerging in tandem with Internet-mediated social contexts (Herring, 1996; Knobel & Lankshear, 2007; Jenkins, 2006; Thorne & Black, 2007; Warschauer & Grimes, 2007).

The historical flow of literacy development into the modern era has been described in various ways. Kress (2003), for example, discusses the importance of two principle shifts, the first marked by a swing in dominance from writing, emphasizing the logic of time as one reads/writes, to image, which engages the logic of space. This second shift involves the change in media from the book and paper-based publications to that of the screen. The transition to image and screens, argues Kress, has been transformative in part because of the tremendous flexibility it affords for borrowing and appropriating pre-existing materials. Of course, language learning and use has always been a process of creative appropriation. As Bakhtin described it:

> We acquire language through a 'process of assimilation—more or less creative—of others' words (and not the words of a language). These words of others carry with them their own expressions, their own evaluative tone, which we assimilate, rework and re-accentuate.
>
> *(Bakhtin, 1986, p. 89)*

Acknowledging this dynamic, Kress argues that digital composing greatly facilitates textual borrowing and repurposing and that this has had a massive effect on the forms and processes of written and multimodal expression. Writing, Kress (2003) argues, "is becoming 'assembling according to designs' in ways which are overt, and much more far-reaching, than they were previously" (p. 6). Prior and Hengst (2010) describe a similar assemblage-based communicative process that they call 'semiotic remediation': "Remediation points to ways that activity is (re)mediated – not mediated anew in each act – through taking up the materials at hand, putting them to present use, and thereby producing altered conditions for future actions" (see also Prior, 2010). As will be discussed later, remix practices in many modes (writing, multimedia, video, music) pre-existed the advent of digital technologies, but recent information and communication technologies have made recombinatory expression more available, easier to do, and readily sharable to both intimate and specified as well as global audiences.

Beyond reading and writing per se, the rise in digitally mediated communication has also radically transformed the quality and quantity of semiosis in everyday life in the areas of relationship development and maintenance, information consumption and production, and the practices and modalities associated with identity performance. Addressing these more holistic and situated literacy dynamics, the New Literacy Studies (NLS) movement (e.g., Bazerman & Russell, 2003; Gee, 1992, 1996; Street, 1995) has been prolific and this diverse body of scholarship has in part defined current understandings of literacy and language learning as socially and culturally situated, shaped by context, and mediated by various technologies. This paradigm provides a theoretical and methodological alternative to individual and psycholinguistic approaches to literacy (Lankshear & Knobel, 2006) and is useful for understanding online contexts where identity and community are discursively constructed through a variety of text-based and multimodal interactions. As will be further discussed below, NLS scholars have also made an active contribution to the pedagogy of literacy education by proposing the concept of 'multiliteracies' and the principle of 'design' (e.g., New London Group, 1996; Cope & Kalantzis, 2000; see Kalantzis & Cope, 2008, for a retrospective history). The term multiliteracies is meant to encompass two important arguments, 1) the acknowledgement of growing cultural and linguistic diversity at the global level, and 2) the increasing importance of digital and multimodal forms of meaning and expression. As expressed by the New London Group (1996, p. 88), "multiliteracies describes the elements of design, not as rules, but as a heuristic that accounts for the infinite variability of different forms of meaning-making in relation to the cultures, the subcultures, or the layers of an individual's identity that these forms serve." Importantly, the NLS movement builds upon other scholarly orientations that have shown the validity of socially distributed and materially situated approaches to understanding all forms of cognitive development and communicative activity (e.g., Barsalou, 2008; Cole & Engeström, 1993; Cowley, 2007; Engeström, 1999; Prior, 1998; Salomon, 1993; Hutchins, 1995).

What's New About 'New Media'?

In a recent text, Baron acknowledges that "new forms [of language] arise, but more often than not the functions they serve remain surprisingly stable" (2008: x). Baron's claim about functional stability may be debatable, but it raises a critically important question: What, exactly, is 'new' about communication and literacy practices in 'new' media environments? In a recent book-length treatment, Lankshear and Knobel (2006) thoughtfully explore and parse the issue of what is qualitatively new in contemporary literacy practices and research by attempting to discriminate between *paradigmatic* and *ontological* novelty. As described by the authors, paradigmatic novelty refers to the advent of sociocultural conceptions of literacy that view literacy development and use as one aspect of learning to participate in socially significant practice (this is the perspective that, broadly speaking, informs this chapter and the NLS movement). Lankshear and Knobel use paradigmatic 'newness' to describe the perspective of researchers who are committed to a more expansive notion of situated literacy practices, one that evokes a progressive and cultural framework that includes, but expands beyond, individual cognition and psycholinguistic processes.

Ontological novelty refers to the new communicative genres and social practices associated with post-typographic forms of text and textually mediated social performances. Lankshear and Knobel argue that ontologically new literacies reflect how "changes have occurred in the character and substance of literacies that are associated with larger changes in technology, institutions, media, and the economy, and with the rapid movement toward global scale in manufacture, finance, communications, and so on" (2006, p. 24; see also Gebhard, 2004; Gee, Hull, & Lankshear, 1996). The concept of ontological novelty encompasses new literacies and communicative genres associated with technological mediation and it emphasizes how digital communication environments impact literacy-related social practices along several fronts, including but not limited to scale (e.g., communication with large numbers of people), space (e.g., conflation of geographic distance), aesthetic and communicative sensibility (e.g., emergence of collaborative and remixed forms of expression and knowledge construction), and frequency (e.g., staying in touch with more people more often using social media such as Facebook, Twitter, and the like).

Early Perspectives on Digital Literacies and Education

Back in the day of local area networks, Gopher (an early hypertext protocol that preceded modern web browsers), and bulletin board systems for email and synchronous chat, early pedagogical rationales for uses of computer-mediated communication (CMC) often involved bringing students' thinking and writing into the classroom as legitimate knowledge (Bruce, Peyton, & Batson, 1993). The "electronic writing space," as Bolter (1991) described it, was assessed by many writing researchers and instructors as a convention, process, and genre-transforming phenomenon that possessed an almost causal capacity to alter interactional dynamics in composition classrooms. As an example of the early enthusiasm for a computer-mediated paradigm for learning, Landow argued that "we must abandon the conceptual systems founded upon ideas of center, margin, hierarchy, and linearity and replace them with ones of multilinearity, nodes, links, and networks" (1992, p. 2). Voicing a similar vision, Lanham (1993, p. 1) predicted that "[s]ooner or later, ... electronic texts will redefine the writing, reading, and professing of literature ...", and later, further suggested that "electronic technology is full of promising avenues for language instruction; it will be lunacy if we do not construct a sophisticated comparative-literature pedagogy upon it" (1993, p. 23). Both Landow and Lanham were emphasizing the substantive material and aesthetic shifts that digital and networked technologies seemed capable of producing, such as the changing structure of 'texts' that are produced and consumed in digital and hypertext environments and a reduction in the time and space constraints that characterized pre-digital communication and information practices. Digital communication and literacy practices were widely acknowledged to catalyze a potential new age of community building through communication (e.g., Rheingold, 1993) and to support committed, radical reform to educational practice (Lankshear, Peters, & Knobel, 1996).

Throughout the 1990s, direct personal experience with digital technologies initiated a pedagogical shift that moved many language educators from cognitivist assumptions about knowledge and learning as individual and cognitive phenomena to collaborative and social-interactional approaches to literacy development and activity (e.g., Cummins & Sayers, 1995; Hawisher, 1994; Hilz & Turoff, 1993; Noblitt, 1995; Warschauer & Kern, 2000). Particularly in the context of synchronous CMC, or real-time "chat" style communication, the novelty and defamiliarization of communication within these spaces was provocative. To illustrate some of these themes with a personal anecdote, in the summer of 1993 I facilitated a workshop on the use of networked writing environments for foreign language and English composition instructors. All participants were new to real-time computer mediated communication. At the end of the workshop, the group was asked to use the chat tool one last time to reflect on the day's activities. An instructor from the English department wrote the following:

> I'm a bit fractured. Is this what those in the know call a post-modern moment? I'm situated on the margins of assorted discourse communities, not sure how to construct myself for (or how I'll be constructed by) each audience. Help me. . . .
>
> *(Reported in Thorne, 1999, p. 4)*

For this participant, the chat experience confounded conventional genres of educational communication, such as formal writing or face-to-face conversation.

To borrow from Faigley, a digital researcher of this era, the real-time conversation in writing evoked a disruption in expectations that involved a "reconfiguring of discursive relations" (1992, p. 180). Of relevance here is that even a few years later, in the mid- and late-1990s, a wide array of Internet-mediated practices were common to the point of complete transparency for habituated late modern communicators.

Extending the Event Horizon of Language and Literacy Use and Learning

A number of studies have indicated the capacity for a shift in communicative modality to correlate with changes in communicative dynamics as well as to present opportunities and resources for variable presentations of self (Jenkins, 2006; Merchant, 2006; Thurlow & McKay, 2003; Turkle, 1995; Walther, 1996). Relatively early studies, in particular those carried out in the 1990s, focused on the power of anonymity in digital, generally text-mediated environments, and the seemingly extraordinary capability of participants to construct relationships and identities and to produce with others distinctive social ontologies (Lea & Spears, 1995; Parks & Floyd, 1996; Rheingold, 1993). Turkle, for example, described digital communication, particularly in text-based virtual worlds, as "doing more than providing an evocative object for our self-reflection ... it is the basis for a new culture of simulation and a fundamental reconsideration of human identity" (1995, p. 321). One of Turkle's informants contrastively described his real life (RL) and digital "realities" as follows: "RL is just one more window and it's not usually my best one" (1995, p. 13). While relative anonymity is still common in many online settings, in contrast to reports from Turkle's informants in the early 1990s, the contemporary era of ubiquitous forms of mediated communication, social networking technologies, online gaming, and Internet interest communities illustrate a tendency toward interactional and social dynamics that more directly relate to, and amplify, offline selves (Merchant, 2006; Miller & Slater, 2000).

Research on Internet use in L2 education has increasingly found benefit from theoretical traditions that focus on mediation and activity system analysis (e.g., Thorne, 2000, 2004, 2005, 2008a; see also Engeström, 2001; Nardi, 1996; Prior, 1998; Russell, 1997). One of the early findings in this line of research was that students' discursive framing of Internet-mediated L2 activity was strongly influenced not by standard conventions of academic discourse, but by their prior and ongoing participation in school-exogenous online speech communities and environments (e.g., Thorne, 2000). The key to understanding why this should be the case came through a focus on artifact mediation, that Internet communication tools, like all human creations, are cultural artifacts (e.g., Cole, 1996; Nardi, 1996) that carry with them historical traces of usage, preferred and dispreferred uses, and expectations of genre-specific communicative activity. Correspondingly, mediated communicative practice is informed by distinctive "cultures-of-use," that is, in interaction with immediate contextual conditions, "the historically sedimented characteristics that accrue to a [computer-mediated-communication] tool from its everyday use" (Thorne, 2003, p. 40; see also Thorne & Black, 2007).

In application to instructed L2 contexts, the cultures-of-use notion emphasizes that technologies are historically structured forms of culture which can influence whether certain desired (from the instructor's point of view) interactions are even possible. A good illustration of this issue comes from an Internet-mediated intercultural exchange project between students studying French as an L2 in the U.S. and students studying English in France. Email was selected as the primary communication tool. Surprisingly (to the designers of the intervention), a significant number of the American students refused to engage in age-peer communication using email. For these students, email was used exclusively for vertical communication across generational and power lines (e.g., with teachers, parents, employers) but was not suitable for age-peer relationship building, which was the core pedagogical thrust of the project. A few dissatisfied students self-initiated a migration of their correspondence to instant messenger (IM) and the effect was enormous. A focal student reported, and provided transcripts to illustrate, daily IM conversations with her French key-pal, some of which extended to multiple hours of mixed French–English communication (Thorne, 2003). The obvious variable in this instance is selection of communication tool. It is important to underscore, however, that while Internet communication tools carry the historical residue of their use across time, patterns of past use inform, but do not determine, present and future activity. Rather, the cultures-of-use framework for addressing research and pedagogical innovation in Internet environments provides an axis along which to perceive and address issues of genre conflict, variation, and alignment (see also Kramsch & Thorne, 2002).

In a recent study examining foreign language learning in open Internet environments, Hanna and de Nooy (2003) reported on the interactional and identity related activity of four students of French who participated in public Internet discussion fora associated with the Parisian newspaper *Le Monde* (for a continuation of this research, see also Hanna & de Nooy, 2009). Hanna and de Nooy's rationale for opting to use a public discussion forum was to move students entirely outside of the relative safety of explicitly educational interactions where participants occupy the institutionally bounded subject position of student or learner. *Le Monde* discussion fora, by contrast, exist to support argumentation and debate about mostly contemporary political and cultural issues. Hanna and de Nooy followed four students, two of whom opened with stand-alone messages that requested help to improve their French. They received a few cordial as well as abrupt replies, each of which suggested the need to take a position in the ongoing discussion. Neither did and both disappeared from the forum. In contrast, the other two students opened with a response to an existing message, directly entering the ongoing debates. One student primarily used English in his posts but still engaged members of the forum and garnered numerous responses to his contributions. With coaching and support from other participants, he was able to fully participate in the discussions, suggesting that "neither politeness nor linguistic accuracy is the measure of intercultural competence here" (Hanna and de Nooy, 2003, p. 78). Rather, in the circumstances of this *Le Monde* discussion forum, participation in the genre of debate was the minimum threshold for continued participation. From an instructional perspective, encouraging students to participate in non-educationally oriented online communities would involve coaching them to recognize contingent and often localized cultures-of-use of Internet communication tools. This could include developing awareness of appropriate genres of language use and patterns and styles of participation with the goal of gaining the capacity to contribute to ongoing discussions in ways that do not ultimately privilege "the self . . . as the exotic little foreigner/the other" (Hanna & de Nooy, 2003, p. 73).

In a multi-site research project that resulted in the book *Electronic Literacies*, Warschauer (1999) examined technology use in linguistically and ethnically diverse college level ESL, Hawaiian language, and English writing courses. His emphasis was to assess the impact of technology-mediated learning activities across divergent contexts, with a focus on understanding the limits and possibilities of computer-mediation as a potentially transformative force in the development of computer literacy, L2 communicative competence, and L1 writing. To examine two of the cases, the undergraduate ESL course emphasized discrete point surface-level grammatical accuracy and subsequently, computer-mediated activities involved primarily grammar drills and attention to linguistic form. The Hawaiian language course, by contrast, was ideologically committed to writing as a form of collective empowerment, with computer-mediated activities involving linkages to the community and the production of applied research that could support Hawaiian language revitalization and maintenance. In terms of technology integration into formal educational contexts, Warschauer's (1999; see also 2005) work has suggested that socially and/or professionally relevant "strong purpose activities" are more productive, but equally, that the uses of various technologies should include modality specific and rhetorically appropriate opportunities for expression. Warschauer's analysis showed that the processes and outcomes of technology use differed greatly across the various contexts, suggesting constitutive ecological relationships (e.g., Bateson, 1972) between institutional mission and culture, teacher beliefs about the processes and expected outcomes associated with learning, and student-participants as subjects with agency and independent life goals.

In a conceptually related study, Thorne (2009) reports on American high school students enrolled in an advanced placement (or AP, a designation reflecting university-level instruction) Spanish foreign language course. Careful attention was given to the kinds of technologies that students were already using for social interaction outside of school. Based on this assessment, weekly blog assignments and out-of-class instant messaging (IM) were incorporated into the course activities. Students in the course were provided with blogs and were encouraged to use their personal IM accounts for Spanish language interaction with interlocutors of their choice. In addition to marked increases in volumes of communication, a number of students also reported cross-posting Spanish language entries to their English language personal blog spaces and conversely, translating into Spanish some of their writing that had initially been posted to their personal sites. Canagarajah (2006) describes such authorial choices with the term 'shuttling,' where individuals move between defined social-textual conventions and make strategic use of semiotic and narrative resources, sometimes across and sometimes within specific languages and genres, to achieve personally relevant intentions. To paraphrase Canagarajah, writing is not merely constitutive; it is also performative, context-transforming, and acts as an affordance for the ongoing negotiation of voice and presentation of self (2006, pp. 602–603). This is an especially pertinent point given the importance of blogging and related social media use to the social lives of many young adults. Also noteworthy is the evidence for centrifugal flows of textual practices that began in instructed settings but which also served additional purposes in domains that were relevant to the students' social lives. The use of IM was equally useful as students reported that rather than focusing purely on Spanish language grammar and formal accuracy, they focused on "finding a [communicative] style," "being clever and using words well," and "making up a personality" (Thorne, 2009: 88)—dynamics that suggest that IM use acted as a resource for solidarity building and production of the self as a multilingual and witty interlocutor. These blog and IM activities showed instances of use value for students emerging in tandem with instructed foreign language education; it also suggested the creation of an overarching semiotic ecology that was inclusive of both schooling and students' broader life contexts. This aligns with Engeström's (2001; Engeström & Sannino, 2010) framework of expansive learning, which is defined as a broadening of the object of activity (the overall goal or orientation of activity) through the collaborative creation and internalization of new mediational resources. For many of these students, the use of everyday communication tools such as blogs and IM seems to have helped to catalyze a new goal associated with Spanish language learning, that of figuring out how to become a viable, interesting person with Spanish as a resource for doing so.

Remix Literacies

Represented in venues such as Youtube.com and popular culture websites, best-selling novels that are produced, distributed, and read on cell phones in Japan (Onishi, 2008), and single- and multiply-authored blogs and wikis, a wide variety of participatory genre practices have emerged with linkages to texts as diverse as Japan-inspired anime and manga to the *Harry Potter* books and *Lord of the Rings*.

Lankshear and Knobel (2007) have described these remixing literacy practices and make the following observations:

> Even the concept of "text" as understood in conventional print terms becomes a hazy concept when considering the enormous array of expressive media now available to everyday folk. Diverse practices of "remixing"— where a range of original materials are copied, cut, spliced, edited, reworked, and mixed into a new creation—have become highly popular in part because of the quality of product it is possible for "ordinary people" to achieve.
>
> *(Lankshear & Knobel, 2007, p. 8)*

In a series of insightful papers and a book-length treatment describing 'fan fiction,' Black (2005, 2006, 2008) describes enthusiasts of various popular cultural media who build from existing literary tropes, settings, characters, and storylines to construct their own fictional narratives. Black's empirical investigation of an online fan fiction site centers on the multilingual composing practices of English language learner (ELL) youth. Drawing from a three-year ethnographic project, Black presents case studies of ELLs participating in a Japanese animation (anime) fan fiction writing community and highlights how the cosmopolitan nature of anime-based fan fiction enabled some ELL focal participants to act as cultural and linguistic "consultants" within the community by helping other fan fiction writers accurately incorporate elements of Asian cultures and languages into their story texts (Black, 2005).

In producing a fan fiction text, authors may remix media, combine or flout genre conventions, and use multiple languages and cultural themes. In application to language learning, fan fiction authors have the potential support, through artifacts and human mediators, to assemble complex texts based on personally interesting fictional worlds. And perhaps as importantly, they have a reason to do so—an attentive audience and peers providing feedback, and evidence that they are contributing to a greater creative enterprise through their participation. As has been argued in the second language development literature, the realization of nuanced levels of symbolic competence (in the sense of Kramsch, 2006) requires language production (Swain, 2000), which in fan fiction writing often involves the use of two or more linguistic varieties (see Thorne & Black, 2011, for examples). In a discussion of bilingual writing in fan fiction communities, Leppänen (2007) has explored the role and function of English in Finnish youths' online fan fiction texts. According to Leppänen, *alternational code switching*[1] serves as a stylistic as well as a symbolic resource for fan fiction authors, as they use both Finnish and English to creatively adapt U.S. popular cultural texts for a Finnish context and thus strategically position themselves, and in a way create a "shared social world" (Leppänen, 2007, p. 163) that is built from various media and linguistic resources.

Gaming and Language Use in Event-Driven Scenarios[2]

Online gaming is a massive force in contemporary media-based entertainment. Engagement in gaming environments is also being used in museums, management training, the military, and across a range of science and humanities subjects in formal educational settings. The integration of games as environments for exploration, simulation, and experiential learning is provoking a shift from models of learning based on information delivery and toward theories of human development rooted in problem-solving, direct participation, and complex forms of collaboration (Squire, 2008). Contrary to negatively valenced popular press accounts regarding teenage boys as the primary players of online gaming, many online games are not played by demographically narrow audiences, but rather have become rich digital environments within which individuals from diverse generations and social strata give expression to their identities, sometimes form new ones, and may engage in plurilingual and pluricultural mediated social activity (Thorne & Fischer, 2012). All of this has been accompanied by a rapid diversification of the types and genres of games being developed (see Sykes, Reinhardt, & Thorne, 2010).

The popularity of online gaming for recreational purposes has grown rapidly. In 2005, the communication researcher Edward Castronova noted that online virtual worlds (his term is *synthetic worlds*) were appearing at a rate of Moore's Law (doubling every two years) and minimally included an international population of 10 million people (Castronova, 2005, pp. 1–2). Only five years later, the single most popular online game at the time of this writing, *World of Warcraft*, has had an estimated peak population of approximately 12–13 million active players distributed among servers with interfaces supporting game play in a variety of languages and populated by players who communicate with one another in tens of additional languages.

Massively multiplayer online (MMO) games, the only genre of virtual world/gaming environment to be discussed here (in part because of the communication rich environment that they provide), are commercially designed and avatar-based persistent virtual worlds within which thousands of people simultaneously interact, collaborate, and compete. Popular commercial titles include *World of Warcraft*, *Warhammer Online*, *Everquest*, *Final Fantasy*, *Tabula Rasa,* and *Eve Online,* among others, with more becoming available all the time, especially for children and adolescents. MMOs are designed around goal-oriented tasks (usually called 'quests') that increase in difficulty as players progress. Players advance their characters and improve their skills and abilities by completing quests, collecting and making items and resources, and buying and selling goods and services in in-world economies (some of which are linked to global capital markets).

Participants engage in MMOs by controlling a digital avatar, defined as an on-screen representation that can be a three-dimensional figure, or in some cases, a two-dimensional icon or picture. Game play in spatialized 3-D MMOs requires navigation of challenging virtual cityscapes, intentionally convoluted built structures and underground labyrinths, and movement through a variety of landscapes. Game play involves hypothesis testing and strategy development, and research into the consequences of subtle choices regarding character development (Nardi, Ly, & Harris, 2007). As Gee (e.g., 2003, 2007) has suggested, MMOs, and video games more broadly, are engineered to enhance human experience in the realms of "control, agency, and meaningfulness" (2007, p. 10), which helps to explain why players invest such significant amounts of time in MMO play. For most individuals, it can require hundreds of hours of playtime to access advanced levels of game content. And while there is considerable repetition in the types of challenges presented, there is also a continual complexification of scenarios and a concomitant expansion of tools and strategies that support continued progress. As Gee (2007) has argued, these features catalyze developmentally productive processes that bring together pleasure and learning through a focus on difficult and engaging goal-directed activity. Other aspects of game world design are also relevant to rethinking educational cultures and environments, for instance the fact that players of different ability levels share a common space and frequently interact with one another. In most game worlds, knowledge is usually freely shared (because everyone benefits when there are better players to collaborate with), and over time, all players have ready opportunities to progress to higher levels of accomplishment. Gee (2005) has described such dynamics using the umbrella term "affinity spaces" and has argued that formal education could well be improved by adopting the pedagogical and developmental cultures that some games embody.

The default communication mode during online game play is synchronous text-based interactive written discourse of the sort common to other 'chat' style tools. Like the textual MUD and MOO environments that preceded them, MMOs typically provide multiple synchronous text channels (e.g., channels for general communication, trade and commerce-related activity, group- and guild-specific communication), as well as a channel for communication with co-present individuals, a "whisper" channel for one-to-one communication anywhere within the virtual world, a "mail" style tool for asynchronous communication, and increasingly, options for multi-party voice communication. MMOs also provide channels for ad hoc groups interacting together and for communication within structured social formations called guilds. Social banter, spontaneous collaborations of convenience, and organized play in small and large groups form the mainstay of online gaming activity, especially at more advanced levels of play. In terms of literacy use and learning, MMOs provide unique opportunities and good reasons for players to communicate, sometimes using scientific and technical genres of writing (see Steinkuhler & Duncan, 2008; Thorne, Fischer, & Lu, 2012). Examples include posting solutions to difficult in-game problems to strategy websites, cooperatively engaging in event-driven scenarios that involve situationally responsive language use, communication relating to planning and strategizing, and pragmatically sensitive talk in high stakes scenarios (e.g., communication that leads to success or failure in the situation at hand). In this sense, as was discussed earlier in the chapter, language is a resource for doing things and engaging in meaningful co-action—precisely the contexts that are difficult to create in L2 language classrooms.

There is considerable research examining the design of, and potential roles for, commercial MMOs and virtual environments in education (e.g., Gee, 2007; Lee & Hoadley, 2007; Squire, 2008; Steinkuehler, 2008a, 2008b). However, very little research exists that specifically addresses the issue of L2 learning (however, see Purushotma, Thorne, & Wheatley, 2008; Sykes, Oskoz, & Thorne, 2008). In one of the few empirical cases examining multilingual communication in a commercial MMO, Thorne (2008b) reported on a multilingual interaction in the game *World of Warcraft* that occurred between a speaker of English living in the U.S. and a speaker of Russian living in the Ukraine. The two were playing near to one another when the Ukrainian communicated the following text message: "ti russkij slychajno?" (*are you Russian by any chance?*) The American replied with a question mark and then asked, "what language was that?" This initiated 140 turns of dialogue that began with information exchange regarding spatial location and mutual interests in gaming and popular culture.

Early in the interaction, the American simultaneously began an instant messaging conversation with a hometown friend who had been raised in the Ukraine to ask for Russian language phrases he might use with his new-found Russian-speaking gaming partner. At various points in the roughly 30 minutes that the two played together, the American would post into the in-game chat channel Russian language utterances he'd received via instant messenger, some of which were humorously vulgar. The Russian speaker reacted with good-natured responses and, in turn, asked questions about the accuracy of the English he was using in his posts. Thorne (2008b) describes this encounter as a flow of semiosis, mediated by two Internet communication tools, which enabled just-in-time access to linguistic resources that helped the relationship move forward. The primary language used was English, but three languages (including one instance of a Latin aphorism) were used in total. The transcript illustrated a number of positive assets for language learning, such as natural and unscripted interaction, reciprocal alterations in expert status, explicit self- and other-correction at the level of linguistic form, extensive repair sequences, development of a positive affective bond, and exhibited motivation by both parties for learning the other's language. In a follow-up interview to this experience, the American gamer mentioned a strong interest in studying Russian, in part to improve his gaming experience with Russian speakers. The American, a student at a university in the U.S., also reported that another committed gamer he knew had enrolled in university Chinese courses in order to be able to more fully participate in game play with Chinese nationals (Thorne, 2008b).

These reports suggest that for some students, the motives for foreign language study reasonably may be speculated to include a desire to participate in

MMO-based or other digitally mediated plurilingual communities. In terms of additional language learning that has resulted from extensive MMO play, however, there remain many questions and few concrete studies. This said, there is research that demonstrates that novice and expert gamers produce measurably and qualitatively different message types, suggesting that movement from novice to expert involves a process of language socialization (e.g., Peña & Hancock, 2006). Additionally, anecdotal and testimonial evidence for language learning and intercultural engagement in MMOs is prevalent (e.g., Thorne, 2010). In MMOs, as in other recreational and professional contexts, the prevalence of goal-directed game play generates frequent opportunities for social discourse, from phatic communication and casual conversations with strangers to serious friendships and romantic bonds (e.g., Peña & Hancock, 2006; Taylor, 2006). As noted by Nardi et al. (2007) in regard to textual chat communication in MMOs, the high frequency genres of interaction—fact finding, learning game strategy, and acquiring a sense of the local ethos—were most typically enacted with emotional tenor such as drama, humor, and intimacy. For a language learner or educator wishing to find or establish a milieu conducive to participation, Nardi et al.'s assessment describes a generally supportive intercultural social space, and further, suggests a reason for wanting to communicate in the first place—in order to hang out with other folks who are passionate about gaming and who joke and establish friendships while they do it.

Education and Digital Literacy Practices: Affordances and Challenges

John Seely Brown (2008), among many others (e.g., Gee, 2007; Lankshear & Knobel, 2003; Kalantzis & Cope, 2008), has described a number of differences between predictable and historically stable literacies and the many emergent literacies that accompany social media and other digital environments, stating that:

> The world becomes more complex and interconnected at a lightning-fast pace, and almost every serious social issue requires an engaged public that is not only traditionally literate, but adept in a new, systemic literacy. This new literacy requires an understanding of different kinds of feedback systems, exponential processes, the unintended consequences inherent in evolving social systems ... the unrelenting velocity of change means that many of our skills have a shorter shelf life, suggesting that much of our learning will need to take place outside of traditional school and university environments.
> *(Brown, 2008, p. xi)*

The preceding discussion of social media, remix literacies, and online gaming communities has described instances of plurilingual communication, literacy development, and additional language learning that occur in these contexts.

Participants in these settings are doing things with and through the symbolic resources of sometimes multiple languages, such as negotiating transactions, making and maintaining relationships, and relationally positioning themselves as friend, antagonist, confidant, author, novice, expert, mentor, collaborator, and so on. For the participants themselves, success is measured by their growing ability to meaningfully contribute to ongoing collective activity. What is unclear, however, is how, and perhaps even if, language-based engagement in these digitally mediated intercultural settings have a useful place within institutionally located language education.

Part of the problem is that even very contemporary literacy curricula may include the use of emerging Internet communication tools and environments while largely ignoring, or worse, stigmatizing, the high-frequency new literacy practices that thrive in Facebook wall posts and Twitter feeds, locally specific and globally shared text messaging conventions, and as discussed in this chapter, communication via avatar in online games and composition and communication in Internet remix communities. Among economically advantaged populations where networked communication has come to mediate a great deal of everyday life, the question becomes how language educators should orient themselves to the changing qualities, purposes, and contexts of mediated language and literacy use, and specifically toward the challenge of deciding which emerging literacy practices to include in instructed educational curricula that extend beyond historically sanctioned formal registers (see Collins & Halverson, 2009, for a discussion).

Pedagogical choices in language and literacy education should be driven by an alignment between expected learning outcomes and opportunities for inspired language use. Of course explicit feedback, oriented toward the development of specific forms of linguistic and interactional expertise, is also critically important. The settings for online intercultural exchange described in this chapter differ radically in terms of the competencies that comprise them, in some instances converging with historically 'standard' literacy competencies while in other ways diverging from such norms. Convergent literacy outcomes are likely to occur in fan fiction authoring through peer feedback and an emphasis on formal accuracy in the context of fictional narratives. Reciprocally, learning outcomes that may notably diverge from conventional literacy competencies include some SMS (cell-phone-based Short Message Service), synchronous chat, commercial MMO and virtual world speech communities, where full participation may involve communicative repertoires such as l33tsp34k (or 'leet speak'—alphanumeric forms of writing that replace some letters with numbers), that would be less transferable to educational or other communicative settings. How might committed educators address this potential contradiction?

In response, there are a number of innovative approaches to literacy education that have been successfully applied in a variety of settings (see Reinhardt & Thorne, 2011, for a review). Addressing the increasingly important area of media literacy education, for example, Buckingham (2003) has proposed a critically framed comparative analysis of different media focusing on the four domains of production, language, representations, and audience, with encouragement to interrogate the motives that inform the design of different media products. Another major movement in digital literacies pedagogy, which I describe at greater length due to its prominence, is the aforementioned concept of Multiliteracies (for an application to L2 contexts, see Kern, 2000). Kalantzis and Cope describe the origins of this framework as follows:

> The changing social worlds of work, citizenship, and identities, require a new educational response. This was the core proposition underlying the Multiliteracies agenda from the start.
>
> *(Kalantzis & Cope, 2008, p. 198)*

Recognizing that educational disparities are a continuing problem, proponents of the multiliteracies approach argue for the benefit of overt instruction and the teaching of meta-language to enable conscious awareness and control of what is being learned in both formal schooling and informal life settings. Kalantzis and Cope (2008) define the key aspect of this approach, that of 'Design,' as a three-part process that highlights the transformative dynamics of meaning making:

> Design is a dynamic process, a process of subjective self-interest and transformation, consisting of (i) The Designed (the available meaning-making resources, and patterns and conventions of meaning in a particular cultural context); (ii) Designing (the process of shaping emergent meaning which involves re-presentation and recontextualisation—this never involves a simple repetition of The Designed because every moment of meaning involves the transformation of the Available Designs of meaning); and (iii) The Redesigned (the outcome of designing, something through which the meaning-maker has remade themselves and created a new meaning-making resource—it is in this sense that we are truly designers of our social futures).
>
> *(Kalantzis & Cope, 2008, pp. 203–204)*

Gunther Kress (2005), an original member of the New London Group, emphasizes the critical and agentive process of design in this way:

> Instead of competence in relation to stable social frames and stable resources ... we need the notion of design, which says: In this social and cultural environment, with these demands for communication ..., that audience, with these resources, and given these interests ..., what is the design that best meets these requirements? Design focuses forward; it assumes that resources are never entirely apt but will need to be transformed in relation to ... contingencies ... The focus on transformation rather than on acquisition makes the designer agentive.
>
> *(Kress, 2005, p. 20)*

The multiliteracies approach continues to expand in topical breadth and in its application among diverse educational institutions and practitioners.

The final pedagogical approach to be mentioned here, one that specifically addresses L2 education and which is informed by many of the ideas expressed above, is that of 'bridging activities' (Thorne & Reinhardt, 2008; Reinhardt & Thorne, 2011). Compelled by what they describe as a primary contradiction between the critical importance of high stakes power genres (i.e., formal registers of language taught in schools) and the emergent-contingent dynamics of digital vernaculars, bridging activities suggests that language educators should be targeting Internet-specific genres of language use as an explicit *goal* of formal instruction. This approach draws upon the concept of multiliteracies (e.g., New London Group, 1996) and principles of language awareness (e.g., McCarthy & Carter, 1994) and involves an iterative three-phase implementation cycle of:

1. Observation and collection of digital vernacular texts and contexts selected by students.
2. Guided exploration and analysis of these texts and contexts, involving possible contrastive analyses that pinpoint the ways in which the selected digital vernacular texts differ, or align with, conventional or other literacy and genre forms.
3. Creation of contributions to, and participation in, activity in the digital vernacular speech communities that are of keen interest to students.

In this way, bridging activities attempt to synergistically unite students' digital vernacular interests with instructor guidance to gain a better understanding of the structural, functional, and pragmatic dimensions of living language use. The immediate objective is to increase the relevance of L2 education by strengthening the relations between communicative abilities and identity dispositions developed within instructional settings with those comprising the plurilingual world that exists beyond the walls of formal education. Traditional literacies are an integral part of this model as the intended outcome is critical awareness of the features and functional organization of both digital and print literacy conventions. Further, in application to the lifelong learning we will all be required to pursue as new communication tools and speech communities arise, the ultimate aim "is not merely to gain the mastery necessary to reproduce language and culture practices, but also to be able to contribute to forging new ones in the crucible that forms everyday communicative interaction" (Thorne, 2009, p. 91).

Discussion

Some years ago, Tom Erickson (1997), a digital cultures researcher and designer, proposed the notion of participatory genre as a replacement for the analytic use of community in research on computer-mediated text-based social interaction. Erickson's suggestion is attractive for two reasons: first, for its attention to the systematic ways language functions in and co-produces social and cultural contexts (genre), and second, because it emphasizes participation within a framework that links historically developed activity systems with the grounded, discursive-material instantiation of communicative practice (see also Russell, 2009). Additionally, the notion of participatory genre emphasizes speaking subjects who shape and transform the genres in which they participate but who are also influenced by its regularities, selection biases, and performative conventions. Many of the digital literacy practices described here suggest that open participatory dynamics enable agentive language and literacy use, which in turn may afford significant developmental potentials to students who may otherwise feel dis-enfranchised from more historically, socially, and culturally distant literacy con-ventions. For this reason alone, a more inclusive curriculum that includes opportunities for meaningful literacy engagement warrants a place on the instructed educational agenda.

In a recent white paper commissioned by the MacArthur Foundation, Jenkins, Purushotma, Clinton, Weigel, and Robinson (2006, p. 4) strongly encourage changes in educational cultures and processes, with the goal that students should be able to "articulate their understanding of how media shapes perception," and further, that young people should be socialized into "emerging ethical standards" that would "shape their practices as media makers and participants in online com-munities." While the term literacy is not explicitly mentioned in this vision of educational outcomes, the notion that literacy education should be fundamentally concerned with the development of generative dispositions (to borrow a turn of phrase from Bourdieu, 1991) that would enable individuals and communities to shape and build their social worlds through participatory engagement is a powerful one.

A final research and pedagogical point is that forms of Internet-mediated activity are demonstrably embedded in, and functionally disassociable from, many off-line communicative contexts and social networks. The high frequency of interplay between on- and off-line activity has the potential to make develop-mentally and instructionally oriented uses of mediated communication more relevant and meaningful due to its articulation with students' broader amalgam of integrated on- and off-line lifeworlds. Extending this argument, digital information and communication tools and human cognitive and communicative activity can be seen to be fused into unified ecologies. Shaffer and Clinton (2006) describe the dialectical and co-constitutive relationship between tools and the cognitive-communicative activities they mediate, as follows:

> just as tools are externalizations of human designs, thoughts are internaliza-tions of our actions with tools. . . . In this view, tools are not distinct from thoughts; rather, the reciprocal relation between tool and thought exists in

both. Every tool contains thoughts, and every thought contains tools. Neither exists without the other.

(Shaffer & Clinton, 2006, p. 290)

In this sense, digital tools do more than simply mediate communication and uses of literacy; they *re-mediate* existing human activity to create new morphologies of action (see also Prior & Hengst, 2010). As Shaffer and Clinton (2006) have argued, drawing upon Latour (e.g., 1996), this position both builds upon Vygotskian principles of mediation while also challenging its dichotomization of tools as distinctive or separate from the humans who use them. In this stronger view of mediation, digital tools and environments are agentive participants in communicative settings, and as such, they influence human agents based on their material and ideal properties, histories of use, and contingent roles in ongoing activity. Extending this conceptual argument to the challenge of literacies development, literacy education would benefit from being more inclusive of the social and semiotic practices, digital and otherwise, that constitute everyday communicative action in the contemporary lifeworlds of students.

To conclude with a paraphrase from Thorne, Black, and Sykes (2009, p. 815), one of the marvels of communication is its endless potential for both reflecting and shaping human activity as it changes over time. Thus, as our quotidian linguistic and social practices shift through contrapuntal dialogue with new and emerging technologies, it seems only logical that educational practice also should shift to both reflect and provide learners with access to the communicative practices and social formations associated with these changes.

Notes

1   Leppänen (2007, p. 153) defines *alternational code switching* as "a situation in which Finnish and English alternate within the same discourse to the degree that it is difficult to establish which one of them is the dominant language (Auer, 1999, p. 317). It is alternational switching in that the discourse could be consistently conducted in either of the two languages—the producer and his/her recipients are sufficiently proficient in both."

2   Parts of the discussion of gaming and language learning in this chapter draw extensively from Thorne (2008b) and Thorne et al. (2009).

References

Bakhtin, M. M. (1986). *Speech genres and other late essays.* Austin, TX: University of Texas Press.

Baron, N. (2008). *Always on: Language in an online and mobile world.* Oxford, UK: Oxford University Press.

Barsalou, L. (2008). Grounded cognition. *Annual Review of Psychology, 59,* 617–645.

Bateson, G. (1972). *Steps toward an ecology of mind: Collected essays in anthropology, psychiatry, evolution, and epistemology.* Chicago, IL: University of Chicago Press.

Bazerman, C., & Russell, D. R. (2003). *Writing selves/writing societies: Research from activity perspectives*. Fort Collins, CO: The WAC Clearinghouse.

Black, R. W. (2005). Access and affiliation: The literacy and composition practices of English-language learners in an online fanfiction community. *Journal of Adolescent and Adult Literacy, 49*(2), 118–128.

Black, R. W. (2006). Language, culture, and identity in online fanfiction. *E-Learning, 3*(2), 170–184.

Black, R. W. (2008). *Adolescents and online fan fiction*. New York, NY: Peter Lang.

Bolter, J. D. (1991). *Writing space: The computer, hypertext, and the history of writing*. Hillsdale, NJ: Erlbaum.

Bourdieu, P. (1991). *Language and symbolic power*. Cambridge, MA: Harvard University Press.

Brown, J. S. (2008). Forward: Creating a culture of learning. In T. Iiyoshi & M. S.V. Kumar (Eds.), *Opening up education: The collective advancement of education through open technology, open content, and open knowledge* (pp. xi–xvii). Cambridge, MA: MIT Press.

Bruce, B., Peyton, J. K., & Batson, T. (Eds.). (1993). *Network-based classrooms*. New York, NY: Cambridge University Press.

Buckingham, D. (2003). *Media education: Literacy, learning, and contemporary culture*. London, UK: Blackwell.

Bundsgaard, J., & Steffensen, S. (2000). The dialectics of ecological morphology – or the morphology of dialectic. In A.V. Lindø & J. Bundsgaard (Eds.), *Dialectical ecolinguistics* (pp. 8–36). Odense, Denmark: University of Odense.

Canagarajah, S. (2006). Toward a writing pedagogy of shuttling between languages: Learning from multilingual writers. *College English, 68*(6), 589–604.

Castronova, E. (2005). *Synthetic worlds: The business and culture of online games*. Chicago, IL: University of Chicago Press.

Cole, M. (1996). *Cultural psychology: A once and future discipline*. Cambridge, MA: Belknapp Press.

Cole, M., & Engeström, Y. (1993). A cultural-historical approach to distributed cognition. In G. Salomon (Ed.), *Distributed cognitions: Psychological and educational considerations* (pp. 111–138). New York, NY: Cambridge University Press.

Collins, A., & Halverson, R. (2009). *Rethinking education in the age of technology*. New York, NY: Teachers College Columbia University.

Conklin, H. (1949). Bamboo literacy on Mindoro. *Pacific Discovery, 3*, 4–11.

Cope, B., & Kalantzis, M. (Eds.). (2000). *Multiliteracies: Literacy learning and the design of social futures*. New York, NY: Routledge.

Cowley, S. (2007). The cognitive dynamics of distributed language. *Language Sciences, 29*, 575–583.

Cummins, J., & Sayers, D. (1995). *Brave new schools: Challenging cultural literacy through global learning networks*. New York, NY: St. Martin's Press.

de Certeau, M. (1984). *The practice of everyday life*. Berkeley: University of California Press.

Engeström, Y. (1999). Activity theory and individual social transformation. In Y. Engeström, R. Miettinen, & R. L. Punamaki (Eds.), *Perspectives on activity theory* (pp. 19–38). New York, NY: Cambridge University Press.

Engeström, Y. (2001). Expansive learning at work: Toward an activity-theoretical conceptualization. *Journal of Education and Work, 14*(1), 133–156.

Engestrom, Y., & Sannino, A. (2010). Studies of expansive learning: Foundation, findings and future challenges. *Educational Research Review, 5*, 1–24.

Erickson, T. (1997). Social interaction on the net: Virtual community as participatory genre. *Proceedings of the Thirtieth Hawaii International Conference on Systems Science* (Vol. 6, pp. 23–30). Los Alamitos, CA: IEEE Computer Society Press.

Faigley, L. (1992). *Fragments of rationality: Postmodernity and the subject of composition.* Pittsburgh, PA: University of Pittsburgh Press.

Gebhard, M. (2004). Fast capitalism, school reform, and second language literacy practices. *Modern Language Journal, 88,* 245–265.

Gee, J. P. (1992). *The social mind: Language, ideology, and social practice.* New York, NY: Bergin & Garvey.

Gee, J. P. (1996). *Social linguistics and literacies: Ideology in discourses* (2nd ed.). London, UK: Taylor & Francis.

Gee, J. P. (1999). *Introduction to discourse analysis.* New York, NY: Routledge.

Gee, J. P. (2003). *What videogames have to teach us about learning and literacy.* New York, NY: Palgrave Macmillan.

Gee, J. P. (2004). *Situated language and learning: A critique of traditional schooling.* New York, NY: Routledge.

Gee, J. P. (2005). Semiotic social spaces and affinity spaces: From the age of mythology to today's schools. In D. Barton & K. Tusting (Eds.), *Beyond communities of practice: Language, power, and social context* (pp. 214–232). Cambridge, UK: Cambridge University Press.

Gee, J. P. (2007). *Good video games and good learning.* New York, NY: Peter Lang.

Gee, J. P., Hull, G., & Lankshear, C. (1996). *The new work order: Behind the language of new capitalism.* Boulder, CO: Westview Press.

Hanks, W. (1996) *Language and communicative practice.* Boulder, CO: Westview Press.

Hanna, B., & de Nooy, J. (2003). A funny thing happened on the way to the forum: Electronic discussion and foreign language learning. *Language Learning & Technology, 7*(1), 71–85.

Hanna, B. E., & de Nooy, J. (2009). *Learning language and culture via public Internet discussion forums.* New York, NY: Palgrave Macmillan.

Hawisher, G. (1994). Blinding insights: Classification schemes and software for literacy instruction. In C. Selfe & S. Hilligoss (Eds.), *Literacy and computers: The complications of teaching and learning with technology* (pp. 37–55). New York, NY: MLA.

Herring, S. (Ed.). (1996). *Computer-mediated communication: Linguistic, social and cross-cultural perspectives.* Philadelphia, IL: John Benjamins.

Hilz, S. R., & Turoff, M. (1993). *The networked nation* (2nd ed.). Cambridge, MA: MIT Press.

Hutchins, E. (1995). *Cognition in the wild.* Cambridge, MA: MIT Press.

Jenkins, H. (2006). *Convergence culture: Where old and new media collide.* New York, NY: New York University Press.

Jenkins, H., Purushotma, R., Clinton, K., Weigel, M., & Robinson, A. (2006). *Confronting the challenges of participatory culture: Media Education for the 21st century.* Chicago, IL: MacArthur Foundation. Retrieved February 22, 2011, from http://digitallearning.macfound.org/atf/cf/%7B7E45C7E0-A3E0-4B89-AC9C-E807E1B0AE4E%7D/JENKINS_WHITE_PAPER.PDF

Kalantzis, M., & Cope, B. (2008). Language education and multiliteracies. In S. May & N. H. Hornberger (Eds.), *Encyclopedia of language education: Vol. 1. Language policy and political issues in education* (2nd ed., pp. 195–211). New York, NY: Springer.

Kern, R. G. (2000). *Literacy and language teaching.* Oxford, UK: Oxford University Press.

Knobel, M., & Lankshear, C. (2007). *A new literacies sampler.* New York, NY: Peter Lang.

Kramsch, C. (2006). From communicative competence to symbolic competence. *Modern Language Journal, 90,* 249–252.

Kramsch, C., & Thorne, S. L. (2002). Foreign language learning as global communicative practice. In D. Block & D. Cameron (Eds.), *Globalization and language teaching* (pp. 83–100). London, UK: Routledge.

Kress, G. (2003). *Literacy in the new media age.* New York, NY: Routledge.

Kress, G. (2005). Gains and losses: New forms of texts, knowledge, and learning. *Computers and Composition, 22,* 5–22.

Landow, G. (1992). *Hypertext: The convergence of contemporary critical theory and technology.* Baltimore, MD: Johns Hopkins.

Lanham, R. (1993). *The electronic word: Democracy, technology, and the arts.* Chicago, IL: University of Chicago Press.

Lankshear, C., & Knobel, M. (2003). *New literacies.* Buckingham, UK: Open University Press.

Lankshear, C., & Knobel, M. (2006). *New literacies: Changing knowledge and classroom learning* (2nd ed.). Philadelphia, IL: Open University Press.

Lankshear, C., & Knobel, M. (2007). Sampling "the new" in new literacies. In M. Knobel & C. Lankshear (Eds.), *A new literacies sampler* (Vol. 29, pp. 1–24). New York, NY: Peter Lang.

Lankshear, C., Peters, M., & Knobel, M. (1996). Critical pedagogy and cyberspace. In H. Giroux, C. Lankshear, P. McLaren, & M. Peters (Eds.), *Counter narratives: Cultural studies and critical pedagogies in postmodern spaces.* New York, NY: Routledge.

Latour, B. (1996). On interobjectivity. *Mind, Culture, and Activity, 3*(4), 228–245.

Lave, J., & Wenger, E. (1991). *Situated learning: Legitimate peripheral participation.* New York, NY: Cambridge University Press.

Lea, M., & Spears, R. (1995). Love at first byte? Building personal relationships over computer networks. In J. T. Wood & S. Duck (Eds.), *Under-studied relationships: Off the beaten track* (pp. 197–233). Thousand Oaks, CA: Sage.

Lee, J., & Hoadley, C. (2007). Leveraging identity to make learning fun: Possible selves and experiential learning in massively multiplayer online games (MMOGs). *Innovate, 3*(6). Retrieved from http://www.innovateonline.info/index.php?view=article&id=348

Lenhart, A., Madden, M., Macgill, A. R., & Smith, A. (2007). Teens and social media. Pew Internet & American Life Project. Retrieved August 9, 2008, from http://www.pewinternet.org/pdfs/PIP_Teens_Social_Media_Final.pdf.

Leppänen, S. (2007). Youth language in media contexts: Insights into the functions of English in Finland. *World Englishes, 26,* 149–169.

McCarthy, M., & Carter, R. (1994). *Language as discourse.* London, UK: Longman.

Merchant, G. (2006). Identity, social networks and online communication. *E-Learning, 3*(2), 235–244.

Miller, D., & Slater, D. (2000). *The Internet: An ethnographic approach.* Oxford, UK: Berg.

Nardi, B. A. (1996). Activity theory and human–computer interaction. In B. A. Nardi (Ed.), *Context and consciousness: Activity theory and human–computer interaction* (pp. 7–16). Cambridge, MA: MIT Press.

Nardi, B., Ly, S., & Harris, J. (2007). Learning conversations in World of Warcraft. *The proceedings of the 2007 Hawaii International Conference on Systems Science.* New York, NY: IEEE Press. Retrieved February 20, 2007, from http://www.artifex.org/%7Ebonnie/pdf/Nardi-HICSS.pdf

New London Group. (1996). A pedagogy of multiliteracies. *Harvard Educational Review, 66*(1), 60–92.

Noblitt, J. (1995). The electronic language learning environment. In C. Kramsch (Ed.), *Redefining the boundaries of language study.* Boston, MA: Heinle & Heinle.

Onishi, N. (2008, January 20). Thumbs race as Japan's best sellers go cellular. *New York Times.*

Ortner, S. (1984). Theory in anthropology since the sixties. *Comparative Studies in Society and History, 26*(1), 126–166.

Parks, M. R., & Floyd, K. (1996). Making friends in cyberspace. *Journal of Communication, 46,* 80–97.

Peña, J., & Hancock, J. (2006). An analysis of socioemotional and task communication in online multiplayer video games. *Communication Research, 33*(1), 92–109.

Pennycook, A. (2010). *Language as a local practice.* New York, NY: Routledge.

Prior, P. (1998). *Writing/disciplinarity: A sociohistorical account of literate activity in the academy.* Mahwah, NJ: Erlbaum.

Prior, P. (2010). Remaking IO: Semiotic remediation in the design process. In P. Prior & J. Hengst (Eds.), *Exploring semiotic remediation as discourse practice* (pp. 206–234). London, UK: Palgrave Macmillan.

Prior, P., & Hengst, J. (2010). *Exploring semiotic remediation as discourse practice.* London, UK: Palgrave Macmillan.

Purushotma, R., Thorne, S. L., & Wheatley, J. (2008). *Language learning and video games.* Paper produced for the Open Language & Learning Games Project, Massachusetts Institute of Technology, funded by the William and Flora Hewlett Foundation. Retrieved April 11, 2011, from http://knol.google.com/k/ravi-purushotma/10-key-principles-for-designing-video/27mkxqba7b13d/2

Reinhardt, J., & Thorne, S. L. (2011). Beyond comparisons: Frameworks for developing digital L2 literacies. In N. Arnold & L. Ducate (Eds.), *Calling on CALL: From theory and research to new directions in foreign language teaching* (2nd ed.). San Marcos, TX: CALICO.

Rheingold, H. (1993). *The virtual community.* New York, NY: Addison-Wesley.

Russell, D. (1997). Rethinking genre in school and society: An activity theory analysis. *Written Communication, 14,* 504–554.

Russell, D. (2009). Uses of activity theory in written communication research. In A. Sannino, H. Daniels, & K. Gutiérez (Eds.), *Learning and expanding with activity theory.* Cambridge, UK: Cambridge University Press.

Saenger, P. (1997). *Space between words: The origins of silent reading.* Palo Alto, CA: Stanford University Press.

Salomon, G. (1993). *Situated cognitions: Psychological and educational considerations.* Cambridge, UK: Cambridge University Press.

Scribner, S., & Cole, M. (1981). *The psychology of literacy.* Cambridge, MA: Harvard University Press.

Shaffer, D., & Clinton, K. (2006). Toolforthoughts: Reexamining thinking in the digital age. *Mind, Culture, and Activity, 13*(4), 283–300.

Squire, K. (2008). Video-game literacy: A literacy of expertise. In J. Coiro, M. Knobel, C. Lankshear, & D. Leu (Eds.), *Handbook of research on new literacies* (pp. 639–673). Mahwah, NJ: Erlbaum.

Steinkuehler, C. (2008a). Cognition and literacy in massively multiplayer online games. In J. Coiro, M. Knobel, C. Lankshear, & D. Leu (Eds.), *Handbook of research on new literacies* (pp. 611–634). Mahwah, NJ: Erlbaum.

Steinkuehler, C. (2008b). Massively multiplayer online games as an educational technology: An outline for research. *Educational Technology, 48*(1), 10–21.

Steinkuehler, C., & Duncan, S. (2008). Scientific habits of mind in virtual worlds. *Journal of Science Education & Technology, 17,* 530–529.

Street, B. (1995). *Social literacies*. London, UK: Longman.

Swain, M. (2000). The output hypothesis and beyond: Mediating acquisition through collaborative dialogue. In J. Lantolf (Ed.), *Sociocultural theory and second language learning*. Oxford, UK: Oxford University Press.

Sykes, J., Oskoz, A., & Thorne, S. L. (2008). Web 2.0, synthetic immersive environments, and mobile resources for language education. *CALICO Journal, 25*(3), 528–546.

Sykes, J., Reinhardt, J., & Thorne, S. L. (2010). Multiplayer digital games as sites for research and practice. In F. Hult (Ed.), *Directions and prospects for educational linguistics* (pp. 117–136). New York, NY: Springer.

Taylor, T. L. (2006). *Play between worlds: Exploring online game culture*. Cambridge, MA: MIT Press.

Thorne, S. L. (1999). *An activity theoretical analysis of foreign language electronic discourse*. Unpublished doctoral dissertation, University of California, Berkeley.

Thorne, S. L. (2000). Beyond bounded activity systems: Heterogeneous cultures in instructional uses of persistent conversation. *Proceedings of the Thirty-Third Annual Hawaii International Conference on System Sciences (HICSS-33)*. Los Alamitos, CA: IEEE Press.

Thorne, S. L. (2003). Artifacts and cultures-of-use in intercultural communication. *Language Learning & Technology, 7*(2), 38–67.

Thorne, S. L. (2004). Cultural historical activity theory and the object of innovation. In O. St. John, K. van Esch, & E. Schalkwijk (Eds.), *New insights into foreign language learning and teaching* (pp. 51–70). Frankfurt, Germany: Peter Lang Verlag.

Thorne, S. L. (2005). Epistemology, politics, and ethics in sociocultural theory. *Modern Language Journal, 89*(3), 393–409.

Thorne, S. L. (2008a). Mediating technologies and second language learning. In D. Leu, J. Coiro, C. Lankshear, & M. Knobel (Eds.), *Handbook of research on new literacies* (p. 417–449). Mahwah, NJ: Erlbaum.

Thorne, S. L. (2008b). Transcultural communication in open Internet environments and massively multiplayer online games. In S. Magnan (Ed.), *Mediating discourse online*. Amsterdam, The Netherlands: John Benjamins.

Thorne, S. L. (2009). 'Community', semiotic flows, and mediated contribution to activity. *Language Teaching, 42*(1), 81–94.

Thorne, S. L. (2010). The "intercultural turn" and language learning in the crucible of new media. In F. Helm & S. Guth (Eds.), *Telecollaboration 2.0 for language and intercultural learning* (pp. 139–164). Bern, Switzerland: Peter Lang.

Thorne, S. L., & Black, R. (2007). Language and literacy development in computer-mediated contexts and communities. *Annual Review of Applied Linguistics, 27*, 133–160.

Thorne, S. L., & Black, R. W. (2011). Identity and interaction in internet-mediated contexts. In C. Higgins (Ed.), *Negotiating the self in a second language: Identity formation and cross-cultural adaptation in a globalizing world* (pp. 257–277). New York, NY: Mouton de Gruyter.

Thorne, S. L., Black, R. W., & Sykes, J. (2009). Second language use, socialization, and learning in Internet interest communities and online gaming. *Modern Language Journal, 93*, 802–821.

Thorne, S. L., & Fischer, I. (2012). Online gaming as sociable media. *ALSIC: Apprentissage des Langues et Systèmes d'Information et de Communication, 15*(1): 1–25. DOI: 10.4000/alsic. 2450 URL: http://alsic.revues.org/2450

Thorne, S. L., Fisher, I., & Lu, X. (2012). The semiotic ecology and linguistic complexity of an online game world. *ReCALL Journal, 24*(3): 279–301.

Thorne, S. L. & Reinhardt, J. (2008). "Bridging activities," New media literacies and advanced foreign language proficiency. *CALICO Journal, 25*(3), 558–572.

Thurlow, C., & McKay, S. (2003). Profiling 'new' communication technologies in adolescence. *Journal of Language and Social Psychology, 22*, 94–103.

Turkle, S. (1995). *Life on the screen. Identity in the age of the internet.* New York, NY: Simon and Schuster.

Van Dijk, J. (2005). *The deepening divide: Inequality in the information society.* London, UK: Sage.

Walther, J. B. (1996). Computer-mediated communication: Impersonal, interpersonal, and hyperpersonal interaction. *Communication Research, 23*(1), 3–43.

Warschauer, M. (1999). *Electronic literacies: Language, culture, and power in online education.* Mahwah, NJ: Lawrence Erlbaum.

Warschauer, M. (2003). *Technology and social inclusion: Rethinking the digital divide.* Cambridge, MA: MIT Press.

Warschauer, M. (2005). Sociocultural perspectives on CALL. In J. Egbert & G. M. Petrie (Eds.), *CALL research perspectives* (pp. 41–51). Mahwah, NJ: Lawrence Erlbaum Associates.

Warschauer, M., & Grimes, D. (2007). Audience, authorship, and artifact: The emergent semiotics of Web 2.0. *Annual Review of Applied Linguistics, 27*, 1–23.

Warschauer, M., & Kern, R. (2000). *Network-based language teaching: Concepts and practice.* Cambridge, UK: Cambridge University Press.

LIST OF CONTRIBUTORS

Bill Cope is a Research Professor in the Department of Educational Policy Studies at the University of Illinois. He is also Director of Common Ground Publishing, developing internet publishing software, *Scholar,* for schools and scholarly publications, located in the Research Park at the University of Illinois. Recent books include *The Future of the Academic Journal* (with Angus Phillips, ed), Chandos, Oxford, 2009 and *Towards a Semantic Web: Connecting Knowledge in Academic Research* (with Kalantzis and Magee), Woodhead, Cambridge, 2010. http://wwcope.com

Jim Cummins is a Canada Research Chair in the Department of Curriculum, Teaching and Learning of OISE/University of Toronto. His research focuses on literacy development in multilingual school contexts. His most recent book is *Identity Texts: The Collaborative Creation of Power in Multilingual Schools* (Trentham Books, 2011, with Margaret Early).

James Paul Gee is the Mary Lou Fulton Presidential Professor of Literacy Studies and the Chief Research Officer in the Center for Games and Impact at Arizona State University. His most recent book is *The Anti-Education Era: Creating Smarter Students Through Digital Learning* (Palgrave/Macmillan).

Margaret R. Hawkins is a Professor in the Department of Curriculum and Instruction at the University of Wisconsin-Madison. Her primary research interest is in languages and literacies in and out of school, including classroom, home, and community-based settings. Her published work examines classroom ecologies, families and schools, language teacher education, global digital partnerships for youth, education in Uganda, and responses of non-gateway communities to new immigrant and refugee populations.

Nancy H. Hornberger is Professor of Education and Chair of Educational Linguistics at the University of Pennsylvania in Philadelphia, USA. Her research interests include sociolinguistics in education, ethnography in education, language policy, bilingualism and biliteracy, Indigenous language revitalization and heritage language education. Her recent books and volumes include *Sociolinguistics and Language Education* (Multilingual Matters, 2010, co-edited with Sandra McKay), *Dell H. Hymes: His Scholarship and Legacy in Anthropology and Education* (Anthropology and Education Quarterly, 2011), and *Educational Linguistics: Critical Concepts in Linguistics* (Routledge, 2012).

Mary Kalantzis is Dean of the College of Education at the University of Illinois, Urbana-Champaign. She was formerly Dean of the Faculty of Education, Language and Community Services at RMIT University in Melbourne, Australia, and President of the Australian Council of Deans of Education. With Bill Cope, she is co-author or editor of: *Multiliteracies: Literacy Learning and the Design of Social Futures,* Routledge, 2000; *New Learning: Elements of a Science of Education,* Cambridge University Press, 2008/2nd edition 2012; *Ubiquitous Learning,* University of Illinois Press, 2009; and *Literacies,* Cambridge University Press, 2012. http://marykalantzis.com

Allan Luke teaches literacy education, sociology and policy at Queensland University of Technology. He is completing a major collaborative evaluation of large-scale school reform and leadership training for Aboriginal and Torres Strait Islander communities and students in Australia.

J. R. Martin is Professor of Linguistics at the University of Sydney and Visiting Chair Professor in the School of Foreign Languages at Shanghai Jiaotong University. His research interests include systemic theory, functional grammar, discourse semantics, register, genre, multimodality and critical discourse analysis, focusing on English and Tagálog – with special reference to the transdisciplinary fields of educational linguistics, forensic linguistics and social semiotics.

Teresa L. McCarty is the George F. Kneller Chair in Education and Anthropology in the Graduate School of Education and Information Studies at the University of California Los Angeles. Her books include *A Place To Be Navajo – Rough Rock and the Struggle for Self-determination in Indigenous Schooling* (2002); *Language, Literacy, and Power in Schooling* (2005); *"To Remain an Indian": Lessons in Democracy from a Century of Native American Schooling* (with K. Tsianina Lomawaima, 2006); *Ethnography and Language Policy* (2011); and *Language Planning and Policy in Native America: History, Theory, Praxis* (2013).

Vaidehi Ramanathan is a Professor of Applied Sociolinguistics in the Linguistics Department at the University of California, Davis. Her research interests include all aspects of literacy and learning as well issues relating to language, health and bodies. Her publications include *Alzheimer Discourse: Some Sociolinguistic Dimensions* (1997), *The Politics of TESOL Education: Writing, Knowledge, Critical Pedagogy* (2001), *The English-Vernacular Divide: Postcolonial Language Politics and Practice* (2005), and *Bodies and Language: Health, Ailments, Disabilities* (2010). She has also co-edited *Language, Body and Health* (2011) and special issues of *TESOL Quarterly* (with a focus on language policies) and *Language Policy* (with a focus on health).

Steven L. Thorne holds faculty appointments in the Department of World Languages & Literatures at Portland State University (USA) and the Department of Applied Linguistics at the University of Groningen (The Netherlands). His research interests include interpenetrations between historically differentiated systems of activity, the cultures-of-use of Internet communication tools, multiplayer online gaming, intercultural communication, indigenous language education, and work that draws upon cultural-historical activity theory, contextual traditions of language analysis, and usage-based and distributed approaches to language development.

INDEX

Italic page numbers indicate tables; **bold** indicate figures.